Information management in museums
Second edition

Second edition

Information management in museums

Elizabeth Orna and Charles Pettitt

Foreword by **Max Hebditch**

Gower

First edition published in 1980 as *Information
handling in museums* by Clive Bingley, a
member of the K G Saur International
Publishing Group.

This edition published by
Gower Publishing Company Limited
Gower House
Croft Road
Aldershot
Hampshire GU11 3HR
England,

Gower
Old Post Road
Broomfield
Vermont, 05036
USA

**British Library Cataloguing in Publication
Data**
Orna, Elizabeth
  Information management in museums.
  –2nd ed.
  1. Museums – Management 2. Information
  resource management
  1. Title 11. Pettitt, Charles, 1937 – 111.
  Information handling in museums
  069

ISBN 0–566–07776–0

**Library of Congress Cataloging-in-
Publication Data**
Orna, Elizabeth.
  Information management in museums /
  Elizabeth Orna and Charles Pettitt.
  --2nd ed.
    p. cm.
  Rev. ed. of: Information handling in
  museums. 1980.
  ISBN 0–566–07776–0
  1. Information storage and retrieval
  systems--Museums, 2. Museums--Great
  Britain--Documentation. 1. Pettitt, Charles.
  11. Orna, Elizabeth. Information handling
  in museums. 111. Title.
  AM125.007 1997
  069' .52--dc 21   97–1722
                                          CIP

Design, typesetting and drawings by Graham
Stevens. Printed in Great Britain by Biddles
Limited, Guildford and King's Lynn.

Contents

Foreword

Objects without information about them have little more than an aesthetic or curio value. For a group of objects to become a museum or gallery collection there has to be the intervention of the curator to generate and record knowledge about them. It is the systems that exist to maintain this knowledge and to transfer it to the future that give museums and galleries their ultimate value. In this respect they are unlike libraries and record offices where a book or manuscript, provided it is indexed, can largely stand on its own.

In the twenty-first century museums and galleries will find thenselves concerned not only with the traditional object – scientific specimen from the natural world or human artefact – but also with things that exist only in electronic form as sound, images or raw numerical data. The task of handling information about both object and electronic collections has to take place in the context of new approaches to the management of public museums and to disseminating information. Information is a tradable commodity, placing museums and galleries in a world marketplace in which investment can offer financial returns. At the same time sponsoring government authorities are asking museums to compete for resources from the public and private sectors. This is creating a tension between restricted purposes related to the museum or gallery's own agenda for interpretation, exhibition and income generation, and the open use of collections by people for purposes designed by themselves. In this environment it is important to hold on to the basic ethical values of the museum or gallery.

The pages which follow set out guiding principles and practices for the sound management of information in museums and galleries. They will enable those responsible for them to think clearly about what is needed by owners, guardians and users of information, and to allocate resources appropriately.

Max Hebditch
Director, Museum of London

Acknowledgements

One of the pleasantest aspects of writing a book like this is the opportunity of going 'backstage' and having good conversations with a lot of people who share the authors' interest in the subject.

Most of them in this instance are members of the staff of the 19 museums which have been kind enough to agree to be the subject of case studies. Their readiness to give time and thoughtful consideration to our questions goes beyond the mere call of duty, and we hope we have repaid their kindness and enthusiasm for their work by providing a just account of their institutions, and one which will be helpful to the readers of this book. We are grateful, too, to professional colleagues in various fields, who have been willing to share ideas and comment on drafts; they will recognize our indebtedness at many points throughout the book.

Individuals

ANN E BORDA, for information about her research (*A survey of museum information centres and libraries in the Greater London area*), undertaken in the School of Library, Archive and Information Studies, University College London.

DR DAVID BEARMAN, Archives and Museum Informatics, Pittsburgh, PA, USA, for reading and commenting on the text.

SUZIE DUKE, for thoughtful editorial support.

SUE MCNAUGHTON, for providing a good home for the book when its future was in the balance.

DR MICHAEL HOUNSOME, Keeper of Zoology, The Manchester Museum, for reading and commenting on the text.

SHAR JONES, Head of the Museum Studies Unit, University of Sydney, for the opportunity of sharing a preview of the book with Australian colleagues.

PROFESSOR SUSAN PEARCE, University of Leicester, for reading and commenting on the text.

ANDREW ROBERTS, Documentation Officer, Museum of London, for reading and commenting on the text.

PROFESSOR STEVE ROBERSTSON, Department of Information Science, City University, London, for reading and commenting on the text.

GRAHAM STEVENS, as always, for finding apt and ingenious typographic solutions that support the text, and enliven the duller bits.

Institutions

Institutions which form the subject of case studies are marked with an asterisk.✳ Others provided information and material which have been drawn on in various chapters of the book. Former members of staff are marked so:§

✳ BEAMISH, THE NORTH OF ENGLAND OPEN AIR MUSEUM. *Rosemary Allan,* Senior Keeper.

✳ BRADFORD ART GALLERIES AND MUSEUMS. *Anthea Bickley.*

✳ CALLENDAR HOUSE, FALKIRK. *Elspeth Reid,* Archivist. *Jack Sanderson,* Curator. *Carol Whittaker,* Collections Manager.

✳ CEREDIGION MUSEUM, ABERYSTWYTH. *Michael Freeman,* Curator.

✳ HAMPSHIRE MUSEUMS SERVICE. *Martin Norgate,* Registrar.

✳ LASSI PROJECT. *Alice Grant,* Head of Collections Information, and *Dr Suzanne Keene,* Head of Collections Management, the National Museum of Science and Industry.

✳ THE MUSEUM DOCUMENTATION ASSOCIATION. *Kevin Gosling,* Outreach Officer. *Matthew Stiff,* Terminology Projects Manager. *Louise Smith,* Assistant Director.

✳ THE NATIONAL MARITIME MUSEUM. *Rosa Botterill,* Information Manager, Information Division. *Terry Corbett,* Head of Collections Management Group, Collections and Museum Services Division. *Fiona Elliott,* Collections Development Manager, Collections Development Section, Collections and Museum Services Division.§

John Gordon, Collection Development Assistant, Collections Management Group, Collections and Museum Services Division.§ *Dr Margarette Lincoln,* Head of Research, Information Division. *Claire Nunns,* Registrar and Information Support Manager, Collections Management Group, Collections and Museum Services Division.

Mary Shephard, Manager, Maritime Information Centre, Information Division. *Rina Prentice,* Head of Collections Development, Collections Development Section, Collections and Museum Services Division. *Maria Rollo,* Collections Information Manager, Collections Information Section, Collections and Museum Services Division.§

✳ THE NATIONAL MUSEUM OF WALES. *Jennifer Stewart.*

THE NATURAL HISTORY MUSEUM. *Rex Banks,* Head of Library and Information Services.§ *David Cole,* IT Strategy Manager.§

✳ NORFOLK MUSEUMS SERVICE. *Brian Ayers,* Principal Field Archaeologist, Norfolk Archaeological Unit. *Myk Flitcroft,* Senior Project Manager, Norfolk Archaeological Unit.§ *Edwin Rose,* Records Officer, Norfolk Landscape Archaeology. *Martin Warren,* Documentation Officer, Cromer Museum.

✳ NORTH SOMERSET MUSEUM SERVICE, WESTON-SUPER-MARE. *Stuart Davison,* Museum Services Manager.

Institutions

* PORTSMOUTH CITY MUSEUMS AND RECORDS SERVICE.
  Rosalinda Hardiman.

* RAF MUSEUM. *Mike Budd,* Museum Registrar.§ *Andrew Cormack,* Curator,
  Aircraft and Exhibits. *Peter Elliott,* Keeper, Research and Information Services.
  Dr Michael Fopp, Director. *David Lawrence,* Keeper, Aircraft
  and Exhibits.

  Gordon Leitch, Curator, Library. *Tim Thorne,* Consultant, Collections
  Documentation and Data Management. *Ben Travers,* Curator, Document
  Archives.§ *Diana Wray,* Data Manager.§

* ROYAL COMMISSION FOR HISTORIC MONUMENTS OF ENGLAND
  Simon Grant.

* ST ALBANS MUSEUMS *David Thorald.*

* SCIENCEWORKS (MUSEUM OF VICTORIA, MELBOURNE, AUSTRALIA)
  Tim Bosher, Manager, IT Services. *Anne Diplock,* Curator, Multimedia.
  Ruth Leveson, Collection Manager (author of the case study). *Matthew Nickson,*
  Curator, Multimedia.

* THE TATE GALLERY. *Gillian Essam,* Documentation Officer. *Simon Grant,* Head
  of Information Systems. *Beth Houghton,* Head of Library and Archive. *Sandy
  Nairne,* Director of Public and Regional Services. *Graham Peters,* Information
  Projects Manager. *Peter Wilson,* Director of Buildings and Gallery Services.
  Simon Wilson, Curator of Interpretation.

* VICTORIA AND ALBERT MUSEUM. *David Anderson,* Head of Education
  Department. *Mary Butler,* Head of Publications,V&A Enterprises.
  Douglas Dodds, Head of Collection Management, National Art Library.
  Sarah Graham-Campbell, Management Services, Conservation Department.

  Frances Lloyd-Baynes, Documentation Manager, Records and Collections
  Services Section. *Serena Kelly,* Museum Archivist, National Art Library.
  Gwyn Miles, Head of Special Projects and Collections Management.

  Carl Nugent, Head of Computer Services.§ *Gill Saunders,* Head of
  Documentation, Prints, Drawings and Paintings Collection. *Alan Seal,* Head
  of Records and Collection Services Section. *James Stevenson,*
  Chief Photographer.

* THE THEATRE MUSEUM (A BRANCH MUSEUM OF THE V&A)
  Dr Jim Fowler, Deputy Head of the Museum. *Claire Hudson,* Head of Library and
  Information Service.

Preface

Prudent authors defer writing their preface until they see what they have written in the rest of the book. Now that we can stand back and consider the experiences of the past two years (which have not been entirely uneventful), there are one or two things that it seems worth telling our readers before they start their journey with us.

We began with ideas about what constituted 'information' in the context of museums, and about how it should be managed to help them survive and prosper. Those ideas had evolved in the years since our first collaboration on *Information handling in museums* under a variety of influences – from experience within the museum world, and in organizations outside it, and from recent developments in thinking about what 'information management' means in a variety of contexts. When we started developing them in relation to museums, and trying them out in the many discussions we had with colleagues in the course of our case studies, we found they stood up pretty well, and so we hope they will be acceptable to our readers.

We hope, too, that our choice of a practical orientation in dealing with the management of both information content and the supporting technology will meet their approval. This is not to say that there is no theoretical basis – those who offer practical tools for use have the obligation to construct them on the basis of sound principles, and this we have tried to do. The most significant area of theory concerns the questions of what is information and what constitutes its management in those organizations which are called museums. Readers who are interested will find pointers to some of the relevant sources that underlie our answers and the practical recommendations based on them, in particular in Chapter 2, but also in many of the case studies.

In the course of preparing the case studies, we found encouraging evidence of serious thinking and productive initiatives in museums both large and small about:

- Strategies for integrated management of the different kinds of information which museums need for survival and success
- Information technology to support the strategic use of information
- Meeting the real information needs of their users, both actual and potential. Some museums indeed seem to have a firmer hold on the problems of managing complex information than do many organizations that would claim to be more hard edged and closer to the 'real world'.

Just as we were completing the text, the Department of National Heritage published its 'review of museum policy'. If the Department is serious about what it says in *Treasures in Trust* on such matters as safeguarding collections information, making collections accessible through documentation, learning about visitors and target audiences by 'access audits', publicizing the scope of collections and facilities for access and study, and using information technology to improve access and collections management, the museums themselves will not be hanging back. They have a well-founded understanding that, in the words of the policy review, 'It will not be possible to exploit collections to the full until their contents are known and widely accessible'[1] But while so many of them show exemplary perseverance and refusal to be daunted by restricted resources, those excellent qualities cannot and should not be relied on to work miracles. And the less happy news that we bring back from writing this book is that too often this is what is happening.

[1] Accepted in June 1997 by the successor government elected in May 1997, but with no indication of extra government funding.

Reference

Department of National Heritage (1996), *Treasures in Trust; a Review of Museum Policy*, London: DNH.

Chapters 1 to 9

Introduction

This is a new edition of a book which was written 16 years ago. The museum world is in many ways a very different place today – though in some quite fundamental respects time has not wrought universal change. This introductory chapter sets out the differences between then and now, outlines the questions that we wish to help readers to answer, and defines the readership to whom we address ourselves.

Then and now

Table 1.1 shows the kind and degree of the differences between the early 1980s and the present, and indicates why it seemed necessary to return to the subject of information handling (or, in more contemporary terms, information management) in museums.

The most obvious and striking development is certainly the explosive growth of information technology; using information which is electronically managed and presented is part of everyday experience for most of us, and today there is hardly a museum without at least a personal computer. In preparing the first edition of this book it was sufficient to devote one chapter to 'Factors in the management of museum computer systems', because for most museums computer systems were a future prospect, rather than a present reality. Of the 18 institutions[1] which figured in the case studies, one was using a system based on a word processor; one a manual system supplemented by a micro-computer; two were the sites of Museum Documentation Advisory Unit pilot projects using the GOS package; one was making plans to implement GOS, and another was in the early stages of using GOS; one was using an early package

[1] Case studies in this book of institutions which
featured in the first edition:
Norfolk Museums Service;
BEAMISH, The North of England Open Air Museum;
St Albans Museum;
The Manchester Museum;
National Maritime Museum.

	Then	**Now**
❶	Wide difference between library and museum approach to handling information.	The gap between museum and library professions is narrowing; more interchange between museums and libraries; more recognition of common ground; clearer understanding of differences.
❷	'Lack of awareness of basic information storage and retrieval techniques' (Roberts, 1975).	More awareness, but it's still far from universal.
❸	'Insufficient resources' for analysing and recording (Roberts, 1978).	Still insufficient; and they can now be endangered by being regarded as secondary to those devoted to presentation and publicity.
❹	'Documentation … is often very uneven and rarely integrated into a complete system' (Homulos, 1978).	More museums are closer to integrated systems, but uneven documentation still prevails in many.
❺	Indexing was seen as a key topic for the first edition because it had received less attention than standards of recording.	Still probably true, though technology has helped to allow more 'ways in' to records. Access via subject and terminology control are still problem areas.
❻	Computer use in early phase: mainframes, batched processing. Limited to large institutions. Micros in their infancy; earliest days of text-retrieval software. A small 'elite' in the lead.	PCs almost universal. More special software available; much of it well designed. More people at home with computers; but still gaps in understanding between systems specialists and others. Distrust of the technology, and ignorant over-expectations of it, are still around.
❼	Idea of visitors using IT to find their own way into and around collections had not even been articulated as a future possibility.	Whole new area of interactive multi-media access; dangers of it overshadowing the information management powers of the technology, which has equal potential for giving access, and is the necessary basis for giving 'freedom and power' to users.
❽	Emphasis on preliminary thinking as essential for avoiding disasters in computer use; need for a strategy of information management.	Still essential; there is rather more of it about, but still not enough.
❾	'Computers can make chaos a great deal faster than can unaided human beings.'	They're still making chaos, thanks to human assistance! However the worst examples are not in the museum world.
❿	Public expenditure on the arts and on education was under pressure; museums needed to be able to show that they could exploit resources of information fully and economically.	Someone with foreknowledge of the future would have said: 'You ain't seen nothing yet.' Pressures on museums to act as business enterprises, selling themselves, seeking sponsorship, links with advertising industry. Some stimulating developments, but dangers of under-estimating value of knowledge resources.

designed for handling bibliographic records (FAMULUS); three were using specially written software (one on a local-authority mainframe, and another on a government department's mainframe). Batched handling of records was the norm; and only one of the museums was using an on-line system (this was a university museum, which was making use of the university's information-retrieval system). Some large and well-respected institutions among the case studies could still be described as having manual systems which were likely to remain so. See the case study of Norfolk Museums Service, p214, for an example of how far one such organization has travelled since then.

Essentially, the good news is this:

- The vast and mainly positive developments that have taken place in the use of technology, both for collections management and for public access
- Greater awareness of the importance of documentation, created by the Museums and Galleries Commission Registration Scheme, and supported by SPECTRUM (the Museum Documentation Association Documentation Standard, Grant/MDA 1994)
- More recognition of the common ground between museums and other organizations in information management, and a growing (though still small) number of information professionals working in museums
- More museums developing information and IT strategies (see the case studies of the National Maritime Museum, Scienceworks and the Victoria & Albert, for examples)
- Co-operative initiatives for information systems, especially LASSI. See the case study on p170.

The less good news (for an outline of some of the arguments on these points, see Orna, 1994):

- The wide spectrum of levels of development, of understanding of what information means in the museum context, of grasp of the basics of information management, and of resources for documentation that can be found in the UK's museums. (Holm, (1993) for example, found that a quarter of the museums in the West Midlands had no means of looking for items by anything other than accession number.)
- A tendency in some quarters for the interests of collections information management and public access to be seen as divergent and as rivals for resources, instead of complementary and mutually necessary
- Some indications of the under-valuing of curatorial knowledge as something that can at worst be substituted for by technology, and at best be embodied in the technology and then dispensed with.

The aims of this book

The comparison between then and now suggests that there is still a need, perhaps one that is greater than at the time of the first edition, for a text which:

1. Helps readers in the museum professions to think productively in the light of their own experience about such questions as:
- What is information in the museum context, and in the context of their own institutions?
- What is the museum's 'knowledge base'?
- Who are the users of museum information?
- What do they want/need to do with information?
- How do we organize the information to help them to do it?
- What's special about managing museum information?
- What features does managing museum information have in common with managing other collections of information?
- Technology – substitute or support for human knowledge and thought?
- Collections information management vs public access? Or are they really two sides of the same coin?

2. Presents basic principles and practical advice for productive information management, using appropriate human and technological resources, at various levels from the minimal upwards.

3. Spreads knowledge of successful practice in a range of museums by means of case studies exemplifying various approaches and specific strengths.

The first four chapters suggest some approaches to answering the questions, while the next two look at practical strategies for managing museum information, with particular emphasis on making productive use of human knowledge and experience in developing and implementing the strategies. The final three chapters deal with ideas and practical steps for making the best use of the technology.

The second part of the book consists of case studies which exemplify a range of current practice in the activities covered in the first part, which will, we hope, help readers to relate their own situation to that of other museums and to identify ideas and practices which are worth assimilating and adapting for their own purposes. In selecting case studies, we have tried to spread the net as widely as possible, so as to draw in institutions of many specialisms and varying sizes – including some that are not by strict definition museums, but whose activities are relevant to the topics of this book. Inevitably, readers will find that levels of detail in the treatment vary, and that different aspects are emphasized according to the character of the organizations considered. We have tried, however, to maintain some consistency in our approach, in particular in offering in each case an evaluation of the positive features that the organization's management of information exemplifies.

To our readers

We are writing for three main groups of readers:

1. Museum staff, especially those who have information responsibilities of various kinds:

- Curators, registrars, museum librarians and records managers, and specialists in documentation and information systems
- Those who interpret the collections through public programmes of various kinds, and those who interact with museum users.

We hope that these readers will find echoes of their own experience, and points at which they can apply their knowledge creatively to develop ideas about the tasks and challenges which face them.

2. Managers whose responsibility includes any aspect of the information activities of museums – whether inwardly or externally oriented.

We hope that this group of readers will find ideas which enrich the concept of information in the museum context, and which contribute to integrating those aspects of their remit which relate to information with their museums' overall strategies and key objectives.

3. Those who are studying in the disciplines of museum studies and information science. These are the readers who will influence the future of information management in museums. We hope that our book will contribute to mutual understanding between the disciplines – offering to those engaged in museum studies some approaches derived from what has until comparatively recently been a separate tradition of thinking; and to those studying information science, insight into the fascinating problems of managing unusually complex and unique information about objects infinitely more varied than 'documents'.

There is one group of museum readers to whom we particularly wish to offer help: those who work in small to medium-sized institutions, with limited resources. Talking with people from museums in this category, in the course of writing case studies, has reinforced our belief that small size and resources to match are not an insuperable barrier to intelligent and effective management of information, and indeed can sometimes be a help in sharpening ideas. We have tried throughout to make what we advocate applicable regardless of size of institution; in addition, where it seems relevant, we have added 'essentials for small museums' to the summaries at the end of chapters.

References

GRANT, A. (ed.)/MDA (1994), *SPECTRUM: The UK Museum Documentation Standard,* Cambridge: Museum Documentation Association[1]

HOLM, S. A. (1993), *Let's set the record straight: a report on the state of documentation in the museums of the West Midlands,* Bromsgrove: West Midlands Area Museum Service

HOMULOS, P. S. (1978), 'The Canadian National Inventory Programme', *Museum* xxx, (3|4) 153–69

ORNA, E. & PETTITT, C. (1980) *Information handling in museums,* London: K G Saur/Clive Bingley

ORNA, E. (1994), 'In the know', *Museums Journal,* November, 24–27

ROBERTS, D. A. (1975), 'Proposals for a survey of cataloguing practice in British museums', *Museums Journal,* 75 (2) 78–80

[1]A second edition was published in 1997:
COWTON, J. (ed) /MDA (1997) *SPECTRUM: The UK Museum Documentation Standard,* Cambridge: Museum Documentation Association

What is information in the museum context?

Any organization – including any museum – that is serious about using information to help it to achieve its aims has first to make its own definition of what information means for it, in the light of what those aims are. The idea that 'information' can mean different things for different organizations is perhaps an unfamiliar one, but it grows out of the general definition of information as the 'essential food of knowledge' which is adopted in this book. That definition relates information to knowledge in the minds of human beings, because it is only when information is transformed into knowledge and consciously applied to purposes defined by humans that it has value and power to bring about desired changes. In organizations like museums, different groups and individuals need to apply different kinds of knowledge to do their work, and so they have particular 'stakes' in different kinds of information. If a museum is to make productive and profitable use of information, it needs not only to define what information means for it, but also to understand itself as a community of users of information, to recognize the 'stakeholders' in information, and to provide them with the means of negotiating over the use of information.

Knowledge and information – some theory

While the avowed orientation of this book is a practical one, because this is our sense of what the readers we are addressing mainly wish to have, that is not to say that there is no theory underlying the ideas about information and its management which we propose. For those readers who are interested in knowing something about it, we shall say something here about its derivations; those who want to get on with the business can safely move on to the definitions on the next page.

We claim no originality for the theoretical basis. Its roots lie mainly in information science and the thinking of some of its founding fathers who went on contributing into the 1980s (in particular Brookes, 1980a and b, and Farradane, 1980) as well as such contemporary theorists as Ingwersen, 1992; Belkin, 1990; Ginman, 1988; and Saracevic, 1992. Their ideas underlie the emphasis we place on the transformations which human minds make of external information into internal knowledge, and of internal knowledge into information which can in turn be put into the outside world for others to transform to knowledge for their own purposes. The other contributing strand – which again is quite mainstream – comes from modern theories of organizations as what Eason (1988) calls 'socio-technical systems'. It draws on such concepts as the soft systems approach (see, for example, Checkland, 1969, 1985) and organizational learning (see, for example, Argyris & Schon, 1978; Fiol & Lyles, 1985; Senge, 1990; Garratt, 1994).

This strand underlies the attempt in this chapter to define what information means for a given organization. Organizations are seen essentially as consisting of human beings who are grouped together in socio-technical systems for explicit or implicit purposes. They interact both internally and with their 'outside world'; the interactions are of human beings with one another, and of human beings with technology. They create 'offerings' of products or services for their outside world; they have to seek 'sustenance' to keep in being; and they have a structure and a boundary. If these are the features singly necessary and jointly sufficient to make an organization, we can define the knowledge and the know-how they need in order to survive. They need to know what is happening inside their own boundaries, and in the 'outside world' on which they depend for sustenance; and they need to know how to recognize, interpret and act on significant changes within and without, how to create their 'offerings', and how to communicate. The actual content of the knowledge and know-how, and so the nature of the information they need to sustain it, will depend on their definition of their aims, of what they are in business for.

A general definition of knowledge and information

Knowledge is what we acquire from our interaction with the world; it is the results of experience organized and stored inside each individual's own mind in a way that is unique to each (though there are features common to how we all do it). It comes in two main kinds: knowledge *about* things, and *know-how*. We make it our own by *transforming* the experience that comes from outside into internal knowledge. Knowledge belongs to us more surely than most of our possessions, and is indeed the most precious and essential of all.

Information is what human beings transform their knowledge into when they want to communicate it to other people. It is knowledge made visible or audible, in written or printed words, or in speech, and put into external 'containers' like books, articles, conference papers, or databases. We can also usefully think of it as the *food of knowledge* because we need information and communication to nourish and maintain our knowledge and keep it in good shape for what we need to do in the world. Just as we have to transform food into energy before we can derive benefit from it, so we have to transform information into knowledge before we can put it to productive use. Figure 2.1. represents the process.

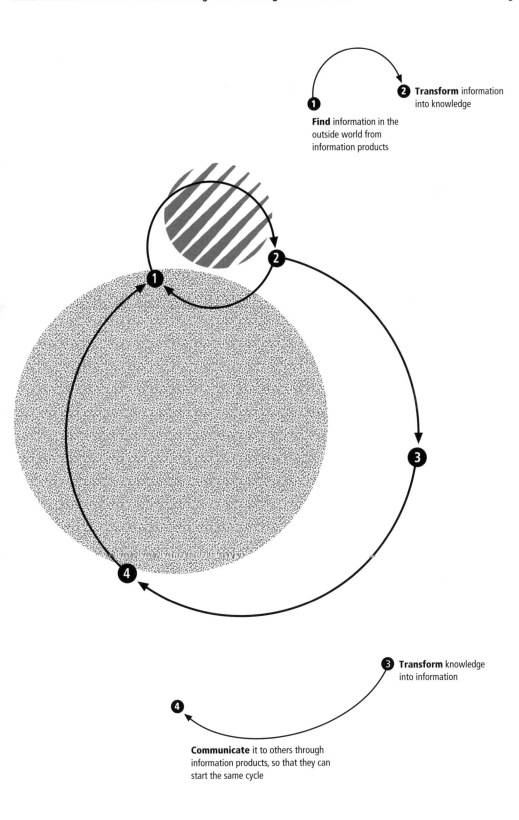

2 **Transform** information into knowledge

1

Find information in the outside world from information products

3 **Transform** knowledge into information

4 **Communicate** it to others through information products, so that they can start the same cycle

As this general definition of information implies, the information required to feed knowledge has to be selected to meet the requirements of what we need to do with it – and they depend on our aims, purposes or objectives. The information that individuals and institutions need in order to maintain their knowledge will consist of different elements, according to their understanding of what they most need to do, that is, according to their value system.

Information is often spoken of today as a valuable resource, but in applying this description we need to be aware of some peculiarities and unique features which distinguish it from other material resources, and which are relevant to its value:[1]

Given those characteristics, organizations, including museums, need to be aware of the importance of interchange and negotiation among those with a stake in information. For examples of promoting interchange and negotiation, see the case studies of LASSI p170, the National Maritime Museum p190 and the V&A p259. They also need to know what their information assets consist of, and to realize their potential for adding value and avoiding risk. See Chapter 5, p68 for an example of an 'audit' of a museum's information assets.

Why organizations need to define information for themselves

For most organizations, the idea that they need to define information in their own terms, or indeed that they need to define it at all, is an unfamiliar one. Most discussion of information systems, information resources, etc. assumes that everyone knows what information is, and that they all agree on what it is. But the definitions that emerge by implication from what organizations say about themselves, or explicitly from the answers of managers if they are asked what information means to them, are mostly rather thin and impoverished, usually with an emphasis on such things as IT, MIS (management information systems), or financial results. And there is no agreed organization-wide definition – individuals will define information in differing ways, from the point of view of their own immediate experience, and some people may not recognize that they actually use information at all, because their understanding of the concept is so restricted. Richer, more comprehensive and so more useful defin-

---

[1]This description of the peculiarities of information is based on Orna (1995).

1. In order to have value, information has to be transformed by human cognitive processes into human knowledge, without which no products of tangible value can be produced or exchanged.

2. If it is hoarded for the exclusive use of a limited number of people, it can actually fail to achieve its full potential value for those who hoard it, but if it is exchanged and traded, the value resulting from its use increases for all parties to the transactions.

3. Information has no inherent value of itself. 'Its value lies in its use' (Abell, 1993, p53) and the parable of the talents is applicable to it.

4. Information is a diffused resource, which enters into all the activities of organizations and forms a component of all products and services. As McPherson (1994, p203) puts it, 'Information permeates all organizations; it is the raw material of cognitive activity … and … the means whereby the organization obtains its window on the world.'

itions start to develop only if organizations ask themselves: 'What do we need to *know* to survive and prosper'?

Aims and their knowledge implications – an example

A typical set of aims or objectives for a museum might be expressed in terms similar to those in the left-hand column of Table 2.1; shown on p24. The right-hand column sets out the 'knowledge-about' and the 'know-how' which it needs to have – in the minds of the people who work in the museum – in order to act effectively to achieve its aims. For other examples of museum objectives, see the case studies of Callendar House, Falkirk p151, National Maritime Museum p190, North Somerset Museum p223, and the V&A p259.

Questions essential for survival

A complementary way of arriving at a museum's knowledge requirements is to list the questions to which it needs to know the answers in order to survive.

The collections
1 What is in the collections?
2 Why was it collected?
3 Where did it come from?
4 Where is it now?
5 What has happened to it since it came into the museum?

People on whom the museum depends
1 Who are the visitors to the museum?
2 What do they do there?
3 What questions do they ask?
4 Who are the potential visitors?
5 Who does the museum need to influence?
6 Who are its key contacts?
7 Who are its suppliers?
8 Who are its 'competitors' and its potential 'collaborators'?
9 Who are its 'customers' and 'markets'?
10 What knowledge and expertise do its staff possess? What else do they need to know about?

Finance to support the museum
1 What are the museum's present sources of funding?
2 What is its financial situation?
3 Where can it find additional funding?

Aims	Knowledge required to meet them
Displaying collections	Of collections themselves Of technologies relevant to display of museum objects Know-how relevant to display
Adding to them via gift, transfer, purchase	Of potential and actual donors Of other potential sources Of market prices, vendors, etc. Of 'acquisition history' of items in collection Of value of items Of the terms of gifts
Documentating, researching, publishing collections; encouraging development of scholarship	Of collection, and of subject background; of developments in scholarship in relevant fields Of modern documentation practice, and of technologies to support it Of 'history' of all items since they became part of the collection Publishing know-how
Providing suitable housing and storage, in keeping with modern conservation requirements	Of modern conservation techniques, environmental requirements of materials/object
Complementing the collections by loan exhibitions from other museums	Of collections of similar museums, in all countries
Interpreting the collections so as to engage the interest of visitors, provide education and inspiration and encourage them to continue to visit	Of the subject areas of collections, of collections themselves, of 'visitor profile', of interpretation methods Of the education system Know-how in presentation of information
Promoting the museum to a range of audiences, from first-time visitors to scholars	Of actual and potential visitor profile (including local population) Of strengths of collections, and ways in which they can engage interest of different audience Of PR know-how and skills
Securing resources from a range of sources to allow maintenance and development of the museum's activities	Of museum's actual financial and other resources, and of its financial position Of potential sources and methods of approaching them Of relevant legislation
Observing and contributing to the development of standards which affect the museum's field of interest	Of existing standards, requirements, regulations, legislation Of bodies concerned with developing and maintaining standards

Note: The aims in this table are based on those of the Tate Gallery, as set out in the gallery's *Forward Plan/Biennial Report.* Permission to use them in this context is gratefully acknowledged

Standards and obligations
1. What legal obligations does the museum have to meet?
2. What standards must it meet?
3. What conditions must its collections be kept in?

Scientific and technological support
1. What areas of scientific knowledge does it need to keep abreast of?
2. What is the state of the relevant technologies to support its work?

The knowledge base and the information to support it

We can describe the knowledge which a museum needs to master if it is to achieve its objectives as its 'requisite knowledge base'; it forms a useful standard against which to test its 'actual' knowledge base. We can also derive from it a statement of the kinds of information which it needs to take in so as to maintain its knowledge, and again, that forms a standard against which to set the *actual* information which the museum collects and uses in its work (see Table 2.2 on pp26–27).

The heart of the knowledge base

At the centre of the museum's requirements for knowledge and information are the collections; all the other kinds of knowledge and information which any museum requires depend on them. If that core is not properly maintained, none of the aims can be achieved; instead of a rich store which justifies and rewards all the promotional, interpretive, commercial, financial and administrative uses of information, there will be a black hole in the middle. Current developments in the technology will certainly bring new ways of using collections and of creating 'offerings' based on them, and their form may also change, but they will still remain the core.

A threefold store of information and knowledge

We can think of the core of a museum as a threefold store of information and knowledge, as shown in Figure 2.2 on p28.

The immediately visible store is what confronts us as soon as we enter a museum. Within that store – in art treasures, objects of daily life, machinery, mineral specimens, or dinosaur bones – is a store of 'embodied' information: what artefacts are made of, who made them, how, where and for what purpose they were made; where natural objects originate from, how and when they were formed, the material of which they are composed; how once-living organisms functioned, where and when they lived. Behind that again is an invisible store of knowledge in the minds of the people who are responsible for the care and presentation of the collections – supported by information sources that feed their knowledge, and made visible in the form of products

Requisite knowledge for meeting aims	Information required to feed the knowledge	
	Information content	Container or vehicle for information
Of collections themselves	Comprehensive and complete details	Records, manual or in database
Of technologies relevant to display of museum objects. Know-how relevant to display	Current developments	Periodicals, conference papers, communication with professionals
Of potential and actual donors	Comprehensive and complete details	Records, manual or in database
Of other potential sources. Of market prices, vendors, etc.	'Current awareness'	Press, conversation, contacts databases
Of 'acquisition history' of items in collection	Comprehensive and complete details	Records, manual or in database
Of value of items	Valuations plus 'current awareness'	Records, manual or in database; other documents
Of the collections, and of subject background; knowledge of scholarly developments in relevant fields	Past and current literature	Books, periodicals, conference proceedings – held in libraries and personal collections; communication with professionals
Of modern documentation practice and of technologies to support it	'Current awareness'	Periodicals, conference proceedings, products of specialist organizations
Of 'history' of all items since they became part of collections	Comprehensive and complete details	Records, manual or in database
Pulishing know-how	'Current awareness' of developments in technology; past and current literature	Periodicals, books, trade literature, training courses, communication with professionals
Of modern conservation techniques, environmental requirements of materials/objects	'Current awareness' of scientific and technological developments	Periodicals, books, communication with professionals
Of collections of similar museums, in all countries	'Current awareness'	Periodicals, conference proceedings, communication with professionals

Note: This table, like Table 2.1, is based on the aims of The Tate Gallery

Requisite knowledge for meeting aims	Information required to feed the knowledge	
	Information content	Container or vehicle for information
Of 'visitor profile'	Complete and comprehensive	Records; survey results details of visitors
Of interpretation methods	'Current awareness' of methods	Periodicals, conference proceedings, communication with professionals
Of the education system	'Current awareness' of developments in curriculum, teaching methods, etc.	Press, periodicals, communication with professionals
Know-how in presentation of information	'Current awareness'	Books, periodicals, training courses
Of actual and potential visitor profile (including local population)	'Current awareness' of local demography, employment, etc.	Local press, local organizations
PR know-how and skills	'Current awareness'	Communication with professionals, training courses
Of museum's actual financial and other resources, and of its financial position	Complete and comprehensive financial details	Records of transactions; accounts
Of potential sources and methods of approaching them	'Current awareness'	Press, contacts databases
Of existing standards, requirements, regulations, legislation Of bodies concerned with developing and maintaining standards	'Current awareness'	Government publications, published standards; database of organizations

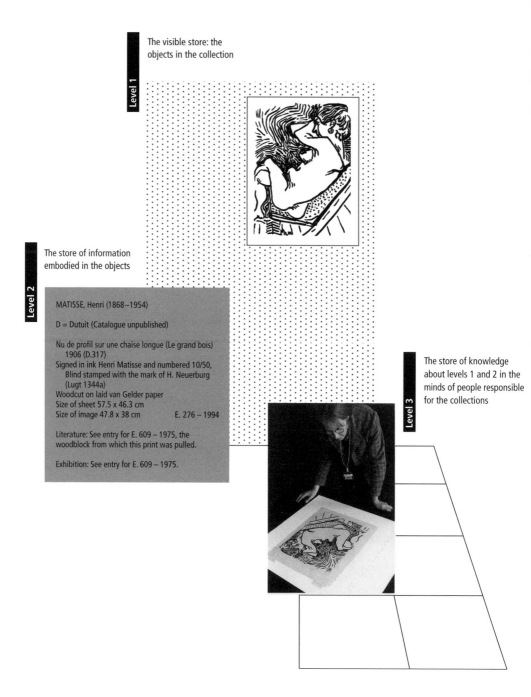

Level 1

The visible store: the objects in the collection

Level 2

The store of information embodied in the objects

MATISSE, Henri (1868–1954)

D = Dutuit (Catalogue unpublished)

Nu de profil sur une chaise longue (Le grand bois) 1906 (D.317)
Signed in ink Henri Matisse and numbered 10/50, Blind stamped with the mark of H. Neuerburg (Lugt 1344a)
Woodcut on laid van Gelder paper
Size of sheet 57.5 x 46.3 cm
Size of image 47.8 x 38 cm   E. 276 – 1994

Literature: See entry for E. 609 – 1975, the woodblock from which this print was pulled.

Exhibition: See entry for E. 609 – 1975.

Level 3

The store of knowledge about levels 1 and 2 in the minds of people responsible for the collections that help visitors to relate to what they see before them, from captions and labels to catalogues, from interactive displays to guided lectures.

Similar ideas were expressed by Lytle (1981) in his 'recommendations for development of information resources at the Smithsonian Institution': 'The Smithsonian Is Information ... Museums select objects because they convey information. Artifacts, specimens, models, paintings, photographs and texts all are chosen because they convey information through their uniqueness or representativeness, their historical significance, or their aesthetic appeal. Museums conduct research to add information to their holdings, whether by identifying them more precisely or by discerning more accurately their relationship to human society. Museums disseminate information through scholarly and popular publications, films, lectures and exhibits. One objective in their educational programs is to bring objects together in a way which increases their information content.'

The full range of knowledge and information as described in Tables 2.1 and 2.2, and not merely that relating to the collections themselves, is essential if the threefold store which forms the core of museums is to function properly. The relationship between information about the collections and information about the visitor profile, or sponsorship funding, or the latest interactive multimedia technology, is one of mutual support – not only are all the kinds of knowledge and information essential, they have to interact if the museum is to gain full value from them (see Figure 2.3 on p30).

Who owns museum information?

There is a good deal of fairly loose talk at present about 'ownership' of information in organizations. If we define knowledge and information as they have been defined in this chapter, we can perhaps arrive at a clearer view of who owns what. Besides the concept of owners of information, we also need to consider two other groups – 'stakeholders' and 'guardians'.

Ownership
The museum is the owner of all *information* that it acquires and generates as an institution (though it must pay due regard to copyright in the case of what it acquires). Individual *knowledge* is the property of the person who holds it in his/her mind. The *information products* into which individuals who work for the museum transform their knowledge in the course of their work become the property of the museum.

'Guardians' and 'stakeholders'
The museum as an institution delegates responsibility for managing certain kinds of information to particular individuals or groups. In exercising responsibility for particular types of information (for example, information about donors, or about enquiries received), they have authority over acquiring, re-

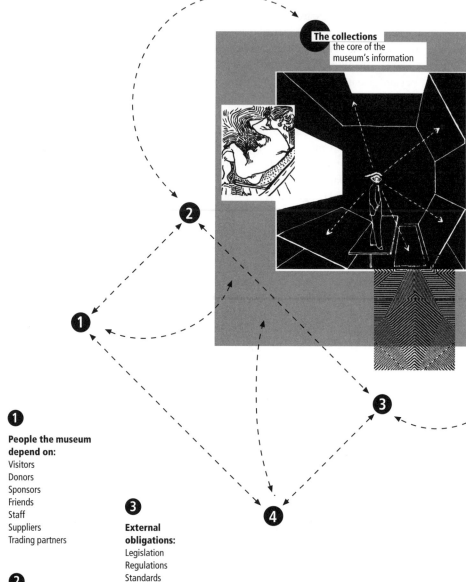

The collections
the core of the
museum's information

 1

**People the museum
depend on:**
Visitors
Donors
Sponsors
Friends
Staff
Suppliers
Trading partners

2

Finance:
Income and expenditure
Grant-giving bodies
Sources of
sponsorship/donations
Commercial activities

3

**External
obligations:**
Legislation
Regulations
Standards

4

**Scientific and
technical support:**
Display
Storage
Conservation
Information management systems
Publishing

cording, and amending the information in question, and oversight of the ways in which it is used. They are, in effect, the 'guardians' of this information.

In addition to the guardians of any particular kind of information, there are usually many people who have a vital stake in it, because they need it in order to maintain their essential knowledge for doing their job. A documentation department, for example, may be the guardian of the master records of the objects in the collection. The stakeholders will include curators who provide cataloguing information, the registrar's department which is responsible for the inventory, acquisition and accessioning aspects of the records database and for keeping movement and location information up to date, conservators who provide conservation details, and the fund-raising department which needs information from the database for developing its strategy and products.

Organizations of all kinds should take into account the position of guardians and stakeholders in relation to information, but often their 'organizational culture' does not recognize it, and the way in which they are managed does not provide a forum where stakeholders and guardians can negotiate about their access to and use of essential information. That creates the potential for conflicts of interest and brings the danger of information not being well used to support the aims of the organization. It is essential for those who manage museums to be aware of the multiple and legitimate interests of information stakeholders and guardians, and to develop equitable organizational forms which ensure that they meet one another and negotiate over the information they need.[2]

Applying this chapter in the small museum

This chapter is primarily about asking yourself questions, thinking, and applying what you know in answering them. Everyone can do that, no vast resources of technology are needed, and indeed small institutions have something of an advantage here, simply because fewer people are involved and the number of things they need to take into account is not too daunting. This is a case where 'small is manageable', so all you have to do is draw on your knowledge and write down the answers as briefly as possible!

[2] While the ideas set out here arose from discussions with colleagues in museums, they find an interesting echo from the world of business in a report from the Hawley Committee (1995) on the use and value of information assets by businesses, which also distinguishes the roles, rights and responsibilities of three groups of people: owners, custodians and users of information.

Summary

The essential points of this chapter:

1. The 'requisite knowledge base' of the museum consists of what it needs to know, about itself and its outside world, in order to achieve its aims; it forms a standard against which to compare what it actually knows.

2. Information from the point of view of the individual museum means whatever it needs in order to maintain its knowledge base. Once that has been defined, it too forms a standard against which to compare the information it actually possesses.

3. The people with an interest in the museum's resources of information and knowledge consist of 'guardians' who hold responsibility for particular kinds of information, and 'stakeholders' who have a special interest in particular kinds of information. They need to negotiate with one another over the use of information, and senior managers need to provide a forum where they can negotiate.

References

ABELL, A. (1993), 'Business Link Hertfordshire', *Business information review*, 10 (2) 48–55

ARGYRIS, C. & SCHON, D. (1978), *Organizational Learning; a Theory of Action Perspective*, Addison Wesley

BELKIN, N. (1990), 'The cognitive viewpoint in information science', *Journal of Information Science*, 16 11–15

BROOKES, B. C. (1980a), 'Informatics as the fundamental social science', in P. TAYLOR (ed.) *New Trends in Documentation and Information*, Proceedings of the 39th FID Congress, University of Edinburgh, September 1978, London: Aslib

BROOKES, B. C. (1980b), 'The foundations of information science, Part 1. Philosophical aspects', *Journal of Information Science*, 2 125–133

CHECKLAND, P. B. (1969, 1985), 'Systems and science, industry and innovation', reproduced in *Journal of Information Science*, 9 171–184

EASON, K. (1988), *Information Technology and Organisational Change*, London: Taylor & Francis

FARRADANE, J. (1980), 'Knowledge, information and information science', *Journal of Information Science*, 2 75–80

FIOL, C. M. & LYLES, M. A. (1985), 'Organizational learning', *Academy of Management Review*, 10 (4) 803–813

GARRATT, B. (1994), *The Learning Organisation*, HarperCollins

GINMAN, M. (1988), 'Information culture and business performance', *IATUL Quarterly*, 2 (2) 93–106

HAWLEY COMMITTEE (1995), *Information as an asset. The Board Agenda. A consultative report*, London: KPMG Impact Programme

INGWERSEN, P. (1992), 'Information and information science in context', *Libri*, 41 (2) 99–135

LYTLE, R. (1981), *Recommendations for development of information resources at the Smithsonian Institution*, Washington DC: Smithsonian Institution

McPHERSON, P. K. (1994), 'Accounting for the value of information', *Aslib Proceedings*, 46 (9) 203–215

ORNA, E. (1996), 'Valuing information: problems and opportunities', in D. BEST (ed.) *The Fourth Resource: Information and its Management*, Aldershot: Aslib/Gower

SARACEVIC, T (1992), 'Information science: origins, evolution and relations', in B. CRONIN & P. VAKKARI (eds) *Conceptions of Library and Information Science. Proceedings of the first CoLIS Conference*. Tampere, Finland, August 1991, London: Taylor Graham

SENGE, P. M. (1990), 'The leader's new work: building learning organizations', *Sloan Management Review*, 32 (1) 7–24

The users of information
in museums

In this chapter

Who are the users of museum information?

Museums are generally considered to be storehouses of objects, but they are also, or have the potential to become, powerhouses of information. As has been shown in the previous chapters, collection information is only one aspect of the information needed to run a modern museum efficiently. But when it comes to looking at volume of usage, it is collection information that forms the bulk of transactions with an integrated information system. Therefore it is this aspect which is addressed in this chapter. The other aspects of museum information are covered in the information audit section of Chapter 7.

There are a multitude of levels at which museum collection information may be accessed (Sledge and Case, 1995) and a multitude of uses to which the information may be put. One person can at different times be many different types of user. Users may need information about a given subject area, such as modern art, contemporary pottery, Etruscan artifacts or South American butterflies. They may have a functional need, as curators, conservators, research students, etc., and the type of use will also vary, from general browsing to detailed research and analysis. Pettitt (1994) details the multiple uses to which natural history collections are put, all of which require access to comprehensive information about the collection. Apart from taxonomic research, he lists environmental studies, biochemistry, evolution and behaviour, archaeology and ethnology, and history as research areas that use the collections. Non-research users include the general public, teachers, hospitals and doctors, local authority enquiries from health, planning and weights and measures officers, aiding law enforcement and import control, commerce, agriculture and fisheries, and fine and decorative art users. Curators know that collections in other disciplines also have multiple uses about which the general public, and sometimes the senior museum management as well, are often ignorant.

Anyone is potentially a user of museum information, even though the information may sometimes reach them in such a roundabout and mediated way that they may not realize its true source. Thus a bird watcher using a field guide may well not realize that the only way the artist could produce such a detailed picture of the bird in question was by painting from a preserved museum specimen, or that much of the information on the geographic distribution of a species is also derived from museum records. Similarly, a viewer watching a television programme on ancient Egypt might well not realize, unless the credits are carefully perused, that much of the information, and most of the illustrative material, will have been derived from museum-based research.

The information pyramid

Museum collection information provision is like an inverted pyramid; at the bottom are a small number of curators and researchers converting raw to refined information, information that is then used by a larger group of people, who with the curator produce mediated information that is used by an even larger group of people. It is important when planning an information strategy to have a clear view of the pyramid for which you are going to provide (see Figure 3.1 on p35).

Users of primary or 'raw' museum information

These are people who need to access the raw information in the museum. This may be on the collector's labels, in accession books, site records or field notebooks and so on; this is the curatorial function. Then there is the information inherent in the objects themselves, to be extracted by detailed examination and comparisons with other similar objects; this is part of the research function. Of course the same person can, and often does, fulfil both functions within the museum. The purpose of these functions is to make the raw information more accessible to a wider audience in what may be considered a 'refined' form.

The curatorial function

The first curatorial function is to ensure that none of the primary written and spoken information about an item, available at the time the item enters the museum, is overlooked or lost. Written information will usually come on labels or documents associated with the items, but the curator must also ensure that all other documentary information is acquired, such as field notebooks, excavation plans, maps marked with collecting sites, correspondence about the material and so on. This is particularly important when items are entering the museum from someone other than the original collector, a relative or an executor for example. Such people may well be unaware of the importance of such associated documentation, even to the extent of destroying it as 'rubbish'. Thus the curatorial function can extend to the period before an item enters the museum, in making secure arrangements with an intending donor that whoever finally hands over the material is fully apprised of the necessity to pass on all the information as well.

Having got the items and the information into the museum, the next function of a curator is to ensure that the integrity of both remains intact. Thus not

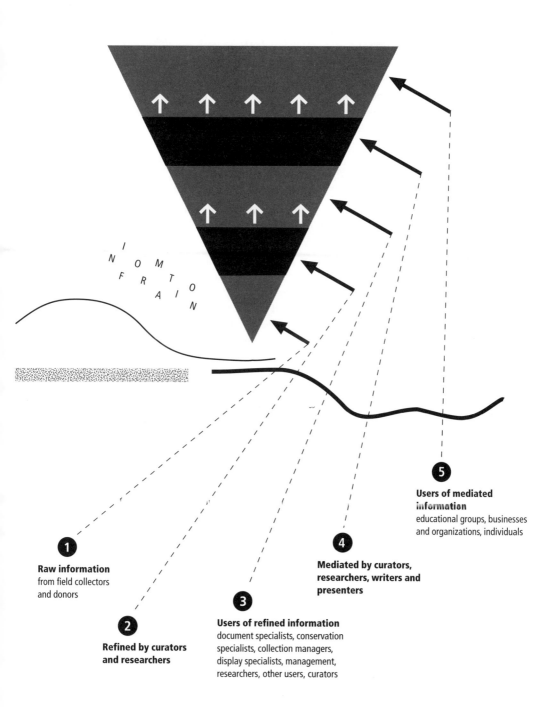

1
Raw information
from field collectors
and donors

2
**Refined by curators
and researchers**

3
Users of refined information
document specialists, conservation
specialists, collection managers,
display specialists, management,
researchers, other users, curators

4
**Mediated by curators,
researchers, writers and
presenters**

5
**Users of mediated
information**
educational groups, businesses
and organizations, individuals

only must the items be safeguarded against loss or damage, but the curator must ensure that the information about them remains securely associated with the items. One of the best ways to do this is to make as complete a copy of all the important information. Textual information can be scanned or typed into a computerized system, allowing multiple copies to be readily stored against the risk of any one copy being lost. Non-text information, such as maps, drawings and photographs, can also be readily scanned into a system, though this does significantly increase the amount of computer storage required, and photocopies may be a more cost-effective way to ensure the security of such documentary information.

Using a computer system to copy the information also allows curators to discharge their third function, that of making the primary information accessible. Computerized records can be accessed by more than one person at a time, and it is also possible for people to access the information at a distance, over a network. Increasingly the curatorial function of access provision is becoming one of ensuring that the information is recorded in a logical and easily retrievable way on a computer system. Naturally someone using the information may need to see the item itself, so the second part of access is to ensure that the items themselves can be found readily when required.

Using well-organized computerized records for item information can also permit the ready collation and comparison of information about several objects in a way that enables meaningful choices to be made by investigators.

The research function

Curators almost invariably do more than merely record the information that arrived with the item. They will add value to that information by using their specialist skills to elicit additional information from the object itself; this can be assigning an authoritative modern name to the item, establishing the use of an object, identifying the materials from which it is composed, deciding on the authenticity, or otherwise, of its professed provenance, and generally classifying the item. All these activities are part of the research function of curators, athough not seen as such by some benighted managers and funding bodies.

Curators, when they can get access to the necessary facilities, also often do more 'mainstream' research on the items in their charge; chemical, spectrographic or biotechnological analyses such as computerized tomography, for example. And curators can show remarkable ingenuity in getting access to the facilities, so such research can often happen in quite small museums, with the assistance of the local college or hospital or a benevolent large firm. All of this work adds more and more detail to the information which the museum has about its collections.

Users of refined museum collection information

These are the people who, to obtain the knowledge they seek, will normally need to access the published or computerized information sources, produced by the curatorial and research workers. They may be other professionals with-in the museum, involved in aspects of the collections such as documentation, display or conservation, they may be curators or researchers from outside the museum tracking down material to aid them in interpreting other collections, or they may be the curators within the museum using the refined information they have produced to help them answer an enquiry or service a loan request. In the list that follows it is possible that a curator, especially in the smaller museums, having generated the refined information, will then don alternative 'hats' and use the information in a number of the roles defined below. How-ever, it is useful for these roles to be treated separately when considering the uses to which the information is being put.

Documentation specialists as users of refined information

Where a museum has a registrar or database manager, their interest in the refined information made available by the curator is likely to be in incorporat-ing the information into the integrated information management package. For this they need access to the information in machine-readable form, either input by the curator directly, or typed in by data-input staff. See Chapter 9 for more information on data capture and entry. Documentation specialists will also need to make and check the necessary interlinking of the data in the system, making sure, for example, that any necessary entry receipts or transfer of title forms have been correctly completed, safely filed and are referenced in any computerized system. Information on paper will remain important in mu-seums for the foreseeable future; the paperless museum seems as unattainable a goal as the paperless office that was much vaunted a decade ago.

Collection managers as users of refined information

Collection managers are a new but increasing breed of museum professionals. Where they exist, in essence they are responsible for overseeing such matters as the location and movement of items in the museum, and for liaising with other users within and outside the museum to supply the items themselves for various uses. To enable them to do this efficiently and safely they need access to the refined information that stands proxy for the items concerned, and they have to be able to update the records as items are moved. They also need an additional specialist subset of information about items, such as any restrictions on handling or essential packing information; for large objects the size and weight are also important.

Conservation specialists as users of refined information

Conservators will need access to the refined information when they are plan-ning the treatment of an item or group of items, but what will interest them will be the age of the item and the materials of which it is made. The latter will sometimes be implicit; for example, if it is a mollusc shell it is likely to contain aragonite and calcite. For cultural objects this may not be apparent, and often in treating the object the conservator can further refine the information;

whether a 'metal' handle is iron or steel, for example. So they need access in order to change some parts of the existing information, and also to add another subset of specialist information to the record, noting the treatments the item has received, and the apparent results of those treatments. Such records are going to become increasingly important as more research is done on the long-term preservation of items, and also the prior treatment they have received may in future decide which items in the collection are used for what research projects. Conservators are usually responsible for condition reports on items leaving or entering the museum, and therefore the information system will need to accommodate these in a way which is securely linked to the items concerned.

Display specialists as users of refined information

Designers of exhibitions have tended until fairly recently to rely on information mediated by the curator. As computerized systems expanded, the use of computer-aided design (CAD) has become more common in museums, and thus not only are designers much more computer literate, they also tend to want information on-line about potential items for forthcoming exhibitions. Since they are largely visual people, the provision of images is high on their list of desirable information, particularly images which they can 'grab' and manipulate within their CAD package, or in graphic design of catalogues, guides and posters. Normally they have no requirement to be able to change or add information to the database, though where the designer also deals with incoming loans for a temporary exhibition they will need the facility to record information about those items.

Curators as users of refined information

Curators themselves frequently require access to the refined information they have generated about the collections in their care, to enable them to answer enquiries and loan requests, and to permit them to explore and enhance the information resource represented by their collection.

Because they are already familiar with refined information about collections, curators from other institutions will normally expect access to the detailed records about the collection. Not only can they usually successfully navigate around such rich information sources, often they can offer enhancement information. How this is to be treated can pose interesting logistical and access questions. Should all such information be submitted separately, when the local curator then has the task of tying it in with the existing records, or should a non-staff member be permitted to add information directly to the record, where that exists in machine-readable form? With the growth of the Internet, and of museum collection databases on it, these questions are going to have to be addressed soon. It is possible that the security measures being developed to allow secure transmission of credit card details and the like over the Internet may be adaptable in time to permit secure registration of trusted curators to access parts of other institutions' databases and to use their specialist knowledge to add value to the information.

Researchers as users of refined information

Much of what has been said in the last section also applies to researchers using the collection databases. But researchers, who may of course be curators too, usually wish to see the items in which they are interested. For them an image, while useful in narrowing down which items they wish to see, is as yet unlikely for some time to be of sufficient resolution to stand proxy for the item itself. However, again, while searching for items of interest, a researcher is likely to spot errors or omissions in another's database, and to wish to offer a correction.

Research loans are a common feature of the interchange of information between museums. The detailed research on an item, usually with comparative material to hand from the relevant museum and several other institutions, and often using modern technology, can add significantly to the store of refined information about that item. It is most important to ensure that all this 'value-added' information is returned with the item when the research loan is terminated.

Management as users of refined information

Managers' interest in the refined collection information produced by curators is generally restricted to summaries. 'How many plants, or archaeological objects, do we have, and where does that place us in the pecking order of museums?' is the sort of thing they want to establish. Other information that will need to be extractable for management use is statistical, the 'how many of ... did we ...?' type to query. Loans out, broken down by discipline and by countries served, number of items conserved last year (and the cost), number of new acquisitions in the last year, and how many still await accessioning, are the kind of information that managers tend to require. Accountability audits are another common use of the refined information by managers (Gardner, 1995).

Other users of refined information

Expert 'amateurs', volunteers or docents and college-level students can also have a valid need for access to the refined information, and the first two at least may well be able to add value to the information.

Users of mediated museum information

For many users even the refined information is too detailed and 'rich' to help them; they need the information to be mediated or interpreted in various ways before they can extract the knowledge they desire from it. Mediated information can take many forms, from the gallery label interpreting an exhibit, though worksheets for school groups, gallery or special exhibition guide-books, to a published book or article on some aspect of the collections. This last may be scholarly or 'popular' in content. Mediated information can also be oral, as when curators answer enquiries from non-subject specialists, or give interviews to the media about some news item that impinges on the museum's expertise. They will then pitch their response at a technical level suitable for that audience.

Educational groups as users of mediated information

The main educational group which uses mediated information is schools, both primary and secondary. The teachers look to the museum to be a resource to further their work imparting knowledge of a defined curriculum of ideas. Thus to make their collections useful to schools, the information has to be mediated with this approach in mind. Where a museum enjoys the luxury of an in-house education section, much of this work will be done by the teaching staff there. In most museums, however, it is the curator who has to provide this information, and this is often done partly by the choice of gallery displays, by the use of restricted reading age for the text on the gallery labels (them-selves usually mediated versions of the information in the detailed database), and by the production of worksheets aimed at specific age groups and curriculum aspects, for use by school parties visiting the museum. If a school loan service is run, then mediated information has to be prepared to go with the items on loan.

As more and more schools become connected to the Internet, museums will be expected to put up mediated information on the Net for schools to access without the expense and complications of a party visit. Such use of museum information is in its infancy, though growing rapidly, and many museums with access to the Internet are currently experimenting with ways to satisfy this demand. The problem is that unless you have very unique collections, a local school could as easily make a virtual visit to a rival museum at the other end of the country, or even on another continent, if their offering is superior to yours. This aspect of competition is only just beginning to be realized, and any decisions to make information available on the Internet should be subjected to rigorous cost–benefit analysis. At the end of the day a museum's strength lies in the fact that it is the only place where people can see, and even sometimes touch, real things.

Businesses and organizations as users of mediated information

As already mentioned, many colour-plate books contain a large number of illustrations prepared from museum objects and specimens, and publishers need access to the mediated information to assist in the choice of institutions from which to borrow material. As image databases become more common, such use for selecting potential illustrations may be expected to grow, not just by main-stream publishers, but also by companies looking for interesting illustrations for their annual reports, or advertising agencies wanting an unusual object to feature in a campaign. Television companies already borrow some material for their shows, but image databases, with mediated, easy-to-read information, can again be expected to increase this demand on museums. Museums can be an extremely valuable resource for media researchers (Kocjancic, 1995).

Individual visitors as users of mediated information

Again, virtual visits on the Internet are likely to increase rapidly, and though nothing is certain, the best use of museum information in this context would seem to be the presentation of a well-mediated subset to intrigue viewers and encourage them to visit in person to see real things.

Defining the needs of users as a basis for planning

Before you can define the needs of your users, you must establish who your users are –what 'client groups' you are setting out to serve. Most of the likely groups have been mentioned above, and the first task is to decide which groups are likely to be relevant to your museum. Once this is done, a preliminary idea of the needs of each group can be gleaned from this chapter, but nothing can replace the need to establish from the people who will actually be using your museum what it is they want.

This can be done in part by going and talking to them, and listening to what they say. Never pass up a chance to talk to a local group, be it a school speech day, a rotarian lunch, a local society, or the staff club of a large local employer. Such occasions should always be seen as two-way streets. You can inform your public about what you have to offer; from their questions, and, particularly, from their comments during the informal chat that hopefully happens before and after the talk, you can often pick up ideas for new ways to produce and provide information about your museum and its holdings. Visitor surveys can also be a fruitful source of information about the needs of your client groups.

Having established the facts about who uses your museum, and what they wish to learn from it, it becomes much easier to prepare a strategy setting out the steps to be taken to satisfy your users. Doing the groundwork well will help significantly when you then have to 'sell' the strategy to your governing body. More importantly, it should help you to obtain the necessary resources to implement the strategy, if the funding body can see that the whole strategy is firmly rooted in the real world. Chapter 5 gives more information on preparing such strategies. Griffiths (1995) presents a useful case study of the cost and the value of collections information to various users.

Summary

The essential points of this chapter:
1. Different people, at different times, need different types of information.
2. In creating an information policy it is vital to have a clear view of who, in relation to your museum, requires which information for what purposes.

Chapter 3 has shown the range of users of museum information, and has indicated the great variety of ways in which they need and wish to use that information. This chapter looks at what these needs and wishes imply for the ways in which museums should manage their resources of information.

References

GARDNER, R. (1995), 'The auditor's perspective', in FAHY, A. and SUDBURY, W, *Information, The Hidden Resource, Museums and the Internet,* Cambridge: Museum Documentation Association, 79–86

GRIFFITHS, J. (1995), 'The cost and value of collections information. A case study: the Apollo 10 Command Module', *in* FAHY, A. and SUDBURY, W. *Information, The Hidden Resource, Museums and the Internet,* Cambridge: Museum Documentation Association, 267–277

KOCJANCIC, G. (1995), 'The media researcher', in FAHY, A. and SUDBURY, W. *Information, The Hidden Resource, Museums and the Internet,* Cambridge: Museum Documentation Association, 93

PETTITT, C. (1994), 'Using the collections', in STANSFIELD, G., MATHIAS, J. and READ, G. *The Manual of Biological Curatorship* (Chapter 6), London, HMSO, 144–166

SLEDGE, J. and CASE, M. (1995), 'Looking for Mr Rococco: Getty Art History Information Program Point-of-View Workshop', *Archives and Museum Informatics,* 9 (1) 124–129

Managing information to make it accessible

Chapter 3 has shown the range of users of information, and has indicated the great variety of ways in which they need and wish to use that information. This chapter looks at what these needs and wishes imply for the ways in which museums should manage their resources of information.

In Chapter 2, we listed questions to which museums need to know the answers in order to survive. Answering such questions is essential in making decisions about what to *do* with information to ensure that everyone who needs it can get at it and use it, in ways that meet their needs and are congenial to them. (That is what information management for access means.) The first part of this chapter looks at the implications of the answers in this light; it also considers the common ground between museums and other types of organization, and identifies some features that are special to museums. In the next section, we take a step back in time, and consider the origins of information management in museums and elsewhere, to see what if anything remains valid, and what has been changed by modern developments – particularly those brought by the diffusion of information technology. The final part of the chapter brings all this together, by considering appropriate methods and tools for managing information to meet the needs of particular museums.

The vital information, its users, and what they need to do with it

This section looks at the various kinds of information which we identified in Chapter 2 (see pp23–27) as being essential to museums; for each, it lists the questions that the museum has to answer, the people to whom the answers are vital, and what they need to do in order to manage the information for the benefit of the museum.

Information about the collections
1. What is in the collections?
2. Where did it come from?

3 Where is it now?

4 What has happened to it since it came into the museum?

This is the most essential knowledge for museum directors, administrators, curators, registrars and conservators, and the registration standards of the Museums and Galleries Commission are designed to ensure that museums achieve it.

SPECTRUM, the Museum Documentation Association's standard[1] for documentation (GRANT/MDA, 1994) for museums seeking to meet the standards, outlines:

- The procedures that museums need to provide which will enable them to answer those questions
- The implications for how museums need to be able to use the information. The procedures cover: object entry; loans in; acquisition; inventory control; location and movement control; cataloguing; condition checking; conservation; reproduction; risk management; insurance management; indemnity management; valuation control; audit; exhibitions and displays; despatch; loans out; loss; deaccession and disposal; retrospective documentation. The examples which follow examine, for two of these areas, how people need to use information, and what that implies for information management.

LOCATION AND MOVEMENT. The people concerned with this aspect of the museum's work need to be able to:

1. Assign an object to its place when it enters the collections. That implies links with storage and display locations, and with the people responsible for them (it should be noted that at this point the *nature* of the links and the means used to create them are not specified; there are many factors which have a bearing on these decisions).

2. See quickly and accurately, from whatever form of record is used, where it usually is and where it is if it is not currently in its usual place. That implies:

- Being able to look up all objects by name or by accession number, or by donor name, etc. and to go straight to the normal location
- A means of ensuring that whenever movement takes place it is recorded on whatever form of master record is used.

3. See what is in any particular location (gallery, room or store). That implies being able to search under location name and to find there a comprehensive list of everything displayed or stored in that location.

4. See at a glance a summary of the movement history of an object, and move from that to related documents. That implies:

- A master record which provides for these links
- A system that enforces the recording of movement and of links between the record and such documents as correspondence, movement forms, etc.

5. Know who has been involved in moving objects. That implies a system

[1]For more about SPECTRUM and its development, see the case study of the MDA, p181.

which enforces entry of the names of those who have done the actual moving and of those who have authorized it (Figure 4.1 on p46 illustrates the requirements).

CATALOGUING. This example is based on an actual analysis of information management requirements in an institution which was planning to acquire a new system. The analysis started, sensibly, by looking at how people carried out the essential procedures at present, what obstacles the existing system placed in the way of doing the job, and what features were therefore necessary/desirable in any new system.

The major problems identified in the existing system were:
1. Catalogue records did not embody the history of items since they had come into the collections (e.g. movement, conservation, loans, photography).
2. Difficulties in indexing, partly related to the limited time available for getting to know and using the capabilities of the software currently in use, and partly to problems with authority files (deficient in some areas, and where they did exist not easy to access while creating catalogue records). The inherent richness of content of pictorial materials also created particular problems of indexing the collections of photographs and topographic prints.

The staff and the consultants working with them on producing a specification for a new system defined the main information management requirements in this area in these terms:
1. The system must allow development of a master catalogue record embodying the total history of items within the institution.
2. It must permit the derivation from the master record of records needed for such special purposes as conservation.
3. It must make it possible to treat cataloguing and indexing as a single operation: cataloguing recording factual information about items; indexing adding value based on curatorial knowledge.
4. It must support software which helps build and maintain authority files.
5. It must be possible to hold standards and authority files on-line and to consult them without moving out of the cataloguing and indexing module.
6. It must be capable of automatically converting non-standard data elements into standard forms.
7. It must be capable of adding to place or area names in a record the relevant grid references as index terms.
8. It must provide the facility for adding images of items to catalogue records.
For examples of system specification, see the case studies on Beamish p140, LASSI p170, the National Maritime Museum p190, the RAF Museum p232 and the V&A p259.

Information about the people on whom the museum depends
1. Who are the visitors to the museum?
2. What do they do there?
3. What questions do they ask?
4. Who are the potential visitors?

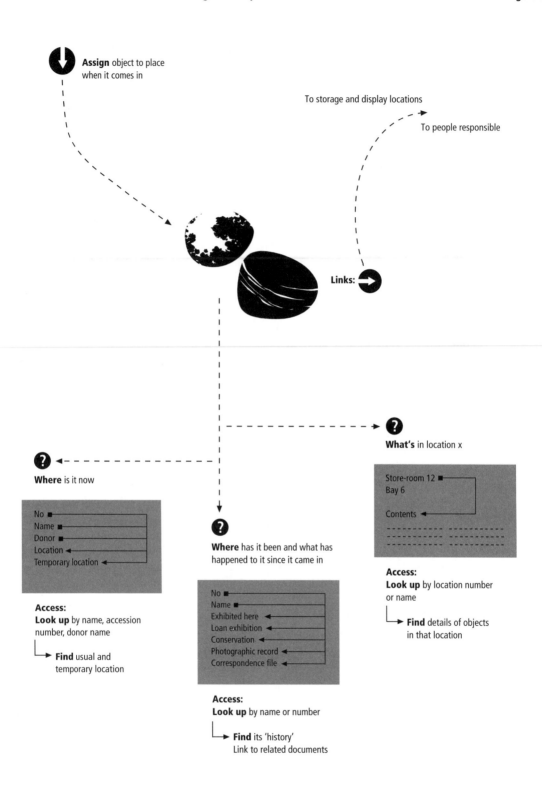

Assign object to place when it comes in

To storage and display locations

To people responsible

Links:

What's in location x

Store-room 12
Bay 6

Contents

- - - - - - - - - -   - - - - - - - - - -
- - - - - - - - - -   - - - - - - - - - -
- - - - - - - - - -   - - - - - - - - - -

Access:
Look up by location number or name

→ **Find** details of objects in that location

Where is it now

No
Name
Donor
Location
Temporary location

Access:
Look up by name, accession number, donor name

→ **Find** usual and temporary location

Where has it been and what has happened to it since it came in

No
Name
Exhibited here
Loan exhibition
Conservation
Photographic record
Correspondence file

Access:
Look up by name or number

→ **Find** its 'history'
Link to related documents

Answers to these questions are essential for management, administrators, curators, research, education and display staff, and those responsible for publications. They need it in order to make sensible decisions about the use of resources to meet the needs of actual visitors, and to reach and draw in potential visitors.

The information management requirements are to:

1. Record the numbers visiting, and gather data on where they come from, why they came and their responses to their experience of the museum.

2. Record and index the questions put by visitors and enquirers and the answers given.

3. Record information about potential sources of new visitors, and about action taken to reach them.

4. Access the recorded information, collate it and create reports as a basis for policy decisions, e.g. on exhibitions, forms of display and access, publications, outreach activities. For examples of visitor surveys and other activities to gather information about the museum's public, see the case studies of the Ceredigion Museum p158, North Somerset Museum Service p223, and the V&A p259.

Information about the people whom the museum needs to influence

Knowledge about the museum's key contacts is required especially by directors, and by financial managers, as the basis for policy decisions on dealing with funding agencies, governmental and other organizations, and potential donors.

The information management requirements are:

1. A unified, authoritative, centrally managed base of information about contacts, and about the museum's interactions with them.

2. Agreed procedures for contacting and updating.

3. Access to up-to-date information on the museum's relations with all its contacts, to help in preparation for meetings, production of the annual report, decisions on approaches to contacts, preparation of bids for funding, etc.

Information about markets, competitors and collaborators

1. Who are the museum's suppliers?

2. Who are its 'competitors' and its potential 'collaborators'?

3. Who are its 'customers' and 'markets'?

This knowledge is needed by directors, financial managers, commercial and purchasing staff, as the basis for decisions on the use of resources, market initiatives and collaborative ventures.

Information management requirements include:

1. A unified, authoritative and centrally managed base of information about actual and potential suppliers of goods and services.

2. Access to information about specific organizations, businesses, etc, and about the museum's dealings with them.

3. Intelligence gathering about potential products, markets for them, and commercial collaborators (e.g. CD-ROMS of reserve collections for special-

interest groups and businesses specializing in their production and marketing), and about the activities of other museums in this field.

4. Ability to bring relevant information together and produce reports to aid decision making.

The museum's human resources

1. What knowledge and expertise do its staff possess?
2. What additional knowledge would be beneficial?

This information is needed by management and the personnel function for planning the best use of the museum's human resources, and for making decisions on staff development and training programmes.

Information management implications include:

1. Records of staff expertise and of training they have undertaken.
2. Ability to access these records in planning new developments, so as to make the best use of staff knowledge, locate people with appropriate skills, and identify new training and development requirements.

Information about finance to support the museum

1. What are the museum's present sources of funding?
2. What is its financial situation?
3. Where can it find additional funding?

Directors and financial managers need to know the answers as part of the basis for strategic planning. The information management implications include:

1. A centrally managed and accessible base of information about present sources of funding and about the museum's current financial situation.
2. Intelligence gathering about possible additional sources of funding.
3. Ability to bring this information together in planning approaches to seek funding for new developments, meet the requirements of fundings bodies.

Information about scientific and technological support

1. What areas of scientific knowledge does the museum need to keep abreast of?
2. What is the state of the relevant technologies to support its work?

The people with an interest in this area include directors, registrars, documentation specialists, systems managers, conservators and exhibition designers. The information management requirements are:

1. Provision for science and technology monitoring and intelligence gathering as a specific job responsibility.[2]

[2] This is something that is, rather late in the day, coming to be recognized as necessary by business: 'To ensure that they always get the most out of IT, companies need a ... team of technical experts to help them stay on top of changing technology, changing business needs, and the changing capabilities of ... IT providers ... Another of the team's primary responsibilities is to assess emerging technologies. New technologies ... may sound very tempting, but will the company really be able to take advantage of them? The answer is no or not yet in a surprising number of instances.' (Lacity et al, 1995).

2. Ability to access relevant information for use in decision making about IT strategies, use of interactive media, exhibition design, etc.

Integrated management of information

In addition to all these information management requirements for the many separate domains of museum activity, there is one more – that the interdependence of information from all the domains should be recognized, and that all the systems for managing their particular kinds of information should be able to work together to provide their users with information that creates a whole picture as a basis for sound decisions. For example, those planning revenue-raising multi-media products need to be able to draw on knowledge about the strengths of the collections, potential markets for the products, visitor information, the results of technology monitoring, information about potential commercial partners, and information about what the 'competition' is doing (see Figure 4.2 on p50). Specifications for new documentation systems need information not only about the current technology and the vendors – they cannot be properly planned without knowledge of the kind of questions which visitors, researchers and curators ask about the collections, and of the current procedures for managing the collections. Bids for funding for new developments are more likely to succeed if they can draw on information resources about the collections, the actual and potential range of visitors, the museum's financial situation, the activities of 'competitor' or 'collaborator' museums, and the background of the individuals who will make the decision on whether to give funding.

It has to be said that this is a requirement which no museum, so far as we know, has yet managed to meet, and one of which many are not even conscious. The obstacles lie less in the potential of the current technology than in organizational culture and management structures (there is, however, some evidence that the process of specifying and starting to use modern collections' information management systems is making the museums concerned see their potential for integrated information management). For examples of the effect of this process, see the case studies of LASSI p170, and the V&A p259.

Common ground between museums and other organizations

All organizations – including businesses and institutions of every kind – need to be able to answer a similar set of questions to the ones just posed in relation to museums, and to act appropriately on the answers in order to survive and prosper. They need to know the state of their resources – material, financial and human; they need to know about their customers, competitors and suppliers; they need to know the legal and quasi-legal obligations placed on them; and they need to keep a watchful eye on the economic, social and technological environment in which they operate.

While even the most intelligently managed and successful businesses are not much further forward than museums in the integrated management of

Sources for answers ↓

*What technology should
we be looking at?
Who else is using it?
Who are the vendors?*

Specialist press
Professional contacts
Technology monitoring

*What are the essential
features the product
should have?*

Market information
Visitor surveys
Analysis of other
existing products

What are the risks?

Professional contacts
↑ Technology monitoring
Specialist press

*What have we got
that would make a
saleable product?*

↓ Curatorial knowledge
Collection records
Museum's publications

*What are the strengths
of the collections?*

What's the market?

Market monitoring
Sales records
Visitor inquiries
Knowledge of specialist groups
Knowledge of educational
institutions

*How do we find a
commercial partner?*

Specialist press
Information about suppliers
Technology monitoring
Information about own and
other people's joint ventures

*What will it cost us?
What returns can we
expect? When?
Can we afford it?*

Information on museum's
finance
Expenditure and revenue from
other commercial products
Information about other
museums' experiences

Sources for answers ↑

What's our way
forward on
multi-media

different kinds of information, museums can benefit when they appreciate the common ground. They can learn much about good practices that are standard in well-managed businesses, which can protect them against risk when they enter new areas – particularly commercial ones – and engage with new concepts in their own work. This is especially true of accountability, inventory control, risk assessment in relation to new ventures, and market information. Organizations like museums, to which the 'market economy' is a new and, to some, stimulating concept, are sometimes in danger of burning their fingers by embarking on risks that experienced businesses would not touch.

Areas with special requirements

In spite of the common ground with other organizations, museums are in some respects unique and special, and those special characteristics have a decisive role in decisions about information management.

In the first place, the objects which museums handle are mostly one-off, each unique in itself and distinct from others in the same category, in contrast to the printed documents which form the material resources of libraries, or to the products of manufacturing. (The significance of manufactured products to their manufacturers and to museums is indeed very different, and so is the approach to handling and recording them.) This has implications for the nature of the records that represent objects and the ways in which they are used. Although the kinds of use made of the records are not unique to museums (businesses need stock inventory, valuation, document management and mailing lists, for example), museum records need to allow for complexity of a kind that goes far beyond that of catalogue records for books, or of most records which other institutions or businesses need to maintain – in order to allow for all the things that need to be done as part of collections information management. In addition, museum records have the fairly unusual property of being open ended – there is always the possibility that new information about the objects they represent will have to be added.

The objectives of museums, whether formulated in detail or accepted by implication, also distinguish them from most other organizations. Besides the traditional safe keeping of the collections in their care (implicit in the job titles of 'keeper' and 'curator'), and the more recent obligations of accountability and of providing 'keys' to their records in the form of indexes, many museums today place increasing emphasis on access of an interactive kind which in principle allows users to take initiatives in seeking information, and to choose their own ways through the 'threefold store' of objects, the information embodied in them, and the museum's knowledge resources.[3] See Chapter 2, p28. Meeting objectives which relate to access indeed provides some of the most interesting

[3] There is a parallel here with enlightened thinking about business management. Norman & Ramirez (1993) suggest that the goal of modern businesses should be 'to mobilize customers to create their own value from the company's various offerings' (i.e. products and services).

challenges in information management. As Jones (1996) expresses it, 'We manage collections in order to make them accessible', and the particular characteristics of museums mean that the process of management requires a 'balance between control, care and access'.

Assisting access

As McCorry and Morrison (1995) point out, little research has been done on the questions actually asked in museums, whether by visitors or by those who work there. Their own analysis of a sample of about 1000 questions asked by visitors in 100 museums found that the most common enquiries were for information about specific types of object, or individual objects. Next came requests for 'associated information' on places or named individuals. Enquiries for objects with a particular subject content were most common in art galleries and museums with photographic collections, but represented a very small proportion of the total; so did those relating to physical characteristics of objects. This study provides some useful pointers to the 'ways in' which many visitors to museums seek, and so to some of the essentials that information management in the form of record structure should provide. McCorry and Morrison suggest, in the light of their findings, that: 'Since what, where, who, when comes out ahead and these are the questions that database management systems are good at answering, we should be looking at ways to standardize and simplify how we do this rather than worrying about nuances of description and setting ourselves impossible tasks of terminology control' (p7). However, their sample is small, and biased in the sense that questionnaires were sent only to people known to the authors, and it contains few examples of the questions which museum staff ask in the course of their work. Questions that remain to be investigated include: what 'ways in' are most important for museum staff? Are there other questions that people would ask if they thought they were answerable? What are the implications of access to information through images of objects (like 'thumbnail' images of pictures and photographs)? How should words descriptive of subject content and associations be used to give access to the images?

TERMINOLOGY AND ITS CONTROL.[4] The question of terminology control is one that recurs in the case studies – it is a problem round which museums, and the Museum Documentation Association, have over the years performed a kind of dance with much advancing and retreating; and today there seems to be a

---

[4] For examples of various approaches to terminology control, see the case studies on the RAF Museum, Falkirk Museums, the V&A, Hampshire Museums Service and Ceredigion Museum. Standards for thesaurus construction are published by the British Standards Institution (1985, 1987) and by ANSIO/NISO (1993).

renewed movement towards it. For an account of recent MDA initiatives, see the case study on p181.

If we want all kinds of users to be able to use collections documentation for themselves, so that they can make their own decisions about what they want and find their way to it, terminology control is an essential tool. It is probably fair to say that when users seek to get into the museum's store of information as represented by whatever forms of access are offered to them, they would wish to be able to:

- Come in through their own particular concerns
- Move freely through the store
- See what it offers that meets their requirements
- Pick up the 'goods' they want
- Come out again with them quickly, ready to get on with pursuing their own interest, or move on easily to find new things.

By the same token, they are likely to be displeased by:

- Finding no way in that matches their own interest
- Being offered goods they don't want, mixed up with those they do
- Tedious sifting to find what they want
- Coming out empty handed.

The commonest cause for the negative experience is probably still the lack of enough 'ways in' – from collections which offer only an accessions list, and perhaps a donor index, to those which have a classification but no index to it (see below, p59). This is the problem identified 120 years ago by Antonio Crestadoro (1856) in respect of books at the British Museum library:

'How can an alphabetical Catalogue on the existing plan of joint inventory and index, or one entry and one heading, satisfy enquirers that seek the same book from different data, and for different purposes? ... Freedom is, in all things, an essential condition of growth and power. The purposes of readers in search of a book are as manifold as the names and subjects, or headings under which the book may be traced. Entering the book only once is giving but one of its many references and suppressing the remainder; – it is serving the purpose of one reader and defeating that of others. So far the book is withdrawn from the public, its light is extinguished and destroyed'.

If that particular obstacle is removed, by using technology that allows multiple ways in to the documentation – for instance by means of information-retrieval software that permits free-text search on multiple criteria – another is liable to take its place. The new difficulty arises from the sheer richness and variety of language. There are so many possible ways of describing things and of expressing concepts that, even when we have a tireless electronic slave that will find any word or phrase we ask for, what it brings us may be only a fraction of what is relevant, because some records which we would find useful don't contain the exact words we have asked for; or it may be quite irrelevant, because the people who created the records used our words in quite a different sense from the one we intend.

To make words help rather than hinder the users of museum documentation, we need to help users to:

- Get from the words they use to all the things they need, whether the words they use are the same as the ones used in the records or not
- Find exactly what they want at the most precise level of detail they need, without having to sift through a lot of things they don't want
- Find everything relevant to a generally formulated interest, without having to guess at the detailed elements that make it up.

And we need to remind them of related things that may also be useful. These are the standard kinds of help that thesauri seek to give; they do it by providing a strongly structured terminology, with well-thought-out links between terms and guidance on using them.

The interesting and difficult question is what is the cheapest and most effective way of helping:

1. The people who create the documentation to use tools of terminology control to help the users?
2. The users to put their questions and take control in interacting with the documentation?

It will be noted that the *users* have to take control – it is the terminology that has to be controlled, not the users, and the mechanism of terminology control should be invisible to them; it should help them unobtrusively and never ever give them negative or incomprehensible messages. A conventional thesaurus in all its glory is an alarming sight, even for some information professionals, let alone non-specialists. We have to find ways of making its benefits available without revealing the works. Experience with making other kinds of information accessible to a wide public suggests that people untrained in information search find it reasonably easy to cope with a 'keyword out of context' index, based on a thesaurus, with very simple displays of related terms and more precise terms, which allows them to select any term – including non-preferred ones – and to go direct to the relevant records (Orna, 1986).

As to help for the people who create the documentation, more and better support than ever before is available to them today, both as part of total collection information management packages, and as stand-alone software to help in creating and maintaining thesauri. For examples of the use of software for creating and maintaining thesauri, see the case studies of Callendar House, Falkirk p151, LASSI p170, the RAF Museum p232, and the V&A p259.

Desirable features for thesaurus software:

1. It should allow you to integrate the building and use of a thesaurus with the creation of records.
2. It should let you link as many entry (non-preferred) terms as you wish to relevant index (preferred) terms, so that they can be used interchangeably. This means that:

- When you are creating records, the software will let you use any of the entry terms, and will index the record with both that term and the relevant index term
- When any one of a group of terms linked in this way is input as a search term, the software will retrieve records containing any of the terms, starting from the ones where the term actually input has been used in indexing.

3. The software should allow you to set up authority lists for different fields, and to call up in a window the lists for different fields – e.g. periods of time or materials – as you are creating records. Then you should be able to scan through them and select those relevant to the record you are working on, so that the software automatically assigns them as index terms for it. For an actual example of a specification for thesaurus software as part of the operational requirement for a collections information management package, see the case study on the RAF Museum, p232.

Something else that is urgently needed is more off-the-peg smallish thesauri for specific subject areas, available in machine-readable as well as hard-copy form, which museums could buy and extend to meet their own needs, rather than facing the problem of starting from scratch, which usually means never starting at all. It is to be hoped that the MDA's project on terminology control will lead to such developments. See p185.

Another much needed development that is surely now almost within reach is a thesaurus that combines text and images, so that users can move from:

- Word to related image
- Image to related images
- Image to related words.

A backward glance – the origins of information management in museums

Before considering potential modern approaches to the information management requirements outlined in the earlier part of the chapter, it is worth reminding ourselves of the basic conceptual problems which have always confronted those responsible for managing any sort of collection. (This section draws on Chapter 2 of the first edition of this book – the lapse of time has not invalidated the ideas here!)

The central problem

'Those whose business it is to house and care for physical objects ... always come up against the inconvenient fact that an object can physically be in only one place at a time. This is inconvenient because, in order to be able to think about an object purposefully in relation to other objects ... it is necessary to bring together and manipulate the information content of the objects. This means finding some way of representing objects which allows them to be moved around freely, by proxy, as it were, so that they can be brought together in any way that suits the kind of thinking we want to do about them ... The problem is essentially one of getting the maximum freedom of access to the useful information ... at the minimum cost in terms of time, effort and money.' (Orna & Pettitt, 1980, pp6–7).

Moveable representations

The proxy for the objects themselves which was devised (initially by librarians) was the moveable representation in the form of records. It long ago became well-established practice to multiply the records and organize them in differently arranged sequences for greater freedom of access and more power for users – as in traditional card catalogues.

The pursuit of freedom and power led to consideration of two further problems: the content and structure of records, and the ways of gaining access to and manipulating the records for useful purposes – the 'keys' to the store of information.

Records

'The importance of the record cannot be over-estimated; it represents the object and so carries a central responsibility in any system of handling information. What has not been put into the record cannot be retrieved. Inconsistencies in the presentation of information in the record, for example calling similar objects at one time by one name and at another by a different name, or spelling the same author's name differently on different records, will lead to failures to find like objects, or to delays and confusions.' (Orna & Pettitt, 1980, p9).

The implications are that there should be careful thinking in the planning stage about the information content of records, and established and scrupulously observed rules and procedures for preparing them. This is the motivation for the librarians' Anglo American Cataloguing Rules, and for the intensive and necessary investment of effort by the Museum Documentation Association during its early years in developing cataloguing cards and rules for completing them. The need to think about record content and structure has not been superseded by any advance in technology so far.

'Keys' to the information store

Two powerful and complementary approaches to getting into the store of information represented by records had been developed by the end of the nineteenth century – one depending on a fundamental feature in the way the human mind stores and accesses its knowledge, and one on the simple fact that in literate societies there is fairly universal agreement on the sequence of characters in the alphabet. In other words: classification and indexing.

CLASSIFICATIONS. The idea of deciding the relative placing of things and the records representing them on the basis of grouping like with like derives from the oldest human principle of managing ideas in the mind. The biblical account of creation is of an exercise in classification, so too is the first occupation of Adam and Eve in Paradise in naming the creation, and Noah's embarkation arrangements for the inhabitants of the ark. As McArthur (1986) reminds us, the 'taxonomic urge'[5] was inherent in society from the earliest days: it got into its stride with the development of writing, and became the structural principle of the great compilations of knowledge of the ancient and medieval worlds, and of the Renaissance and Enlightenment.

But this noble principle has an in-built problem: by bringing groups of things together on the basis of one set of shared features, it separates individuals in one group from individuals in another with which they have other features in common (a problem quaintly known in library circles as that of the 'distributed relative'). A simple example makes the difficulty clear. If a social history collection in a museum classifies tools by the materials of the crafts in which they are used, tools of the same basic form which are used in different trades are separated from one another: a flint knapper's hammer from a silversmith's, a thatching needle from an upholstery needle. So anyone who wants to compare the form of all hammers in the total collection has a long task. He will have to think of all the possible hammer-using crafts and go to the appropriate section of the classified catalogue and scan card by card, looking for hammers. (Orna & Pettitt, 1980, p16). Figure 4.3 on p58 illustrates the predicament.

The other awkward fact about human classifications is that, while we all classify from our earliest years, as part of learning to make our world manageable, we each do it in different ways, according to what we see as significant. That still doesn't stop people – even people in museums – from trying to make what they describe as an 'intuitive' classification the only principle of arrangement of records.

INDEXES TO COMPLEMENT CLASSIFICATIONS. From the realization of the in-built problem of classification described above came the development of another, much later, tool, the alphabetical index – a principle of arrangement which we owe to the early compositors who quickly found the advantages of sorting their types alphabetically. Even so, according to McArthur (1986, p77), 'it took more than 100 years after the advent of printing for alphabetization to establish itself as a serious and regular tool in the world of reference' and

---

[5] McArthur argues that 'classification and thematization' are driving forces in the development of human society and culture: 'Classification and thematization have many forms, but the key forms appear to be only two: first, the making of categories or groups', and then the creation of a hierarchy ... through which to systematize the categories or groups.' (p34). For further insights into how we categorize see Edelman's (1992) brilliant study of 'the matter of the mind' – 'categories are heterogeneous in origin: the actual properties humans use to determine category membership are interactional and they depend on different biological, cultural, and environmental variables' (p236).

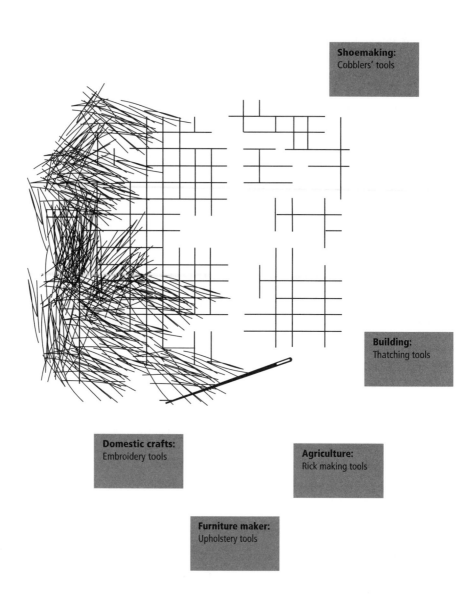

Shoemaking:
Cobblers' tools

Building:
Thatching tools

Domestic crafts:
Embroidery tools

Agriculture:
Rick making tools

Furniture maker:
Upholstery tools

indexes became firmly established only around 1600. There is still an inherent problem in indexes, however: that of agreement between those who make them and those who use them on which words to use for specific things or concepts – the problem which thesauri seek to solve (see pp53–55).

The increase in power that could be gained from harnessing indexes and classifications together was probably not realized until the late nineteenth century when Dewey developed the 'relativ index' to his decimal classification, which he himself described (Dewey 1885) as 'the most important feature of the system'. The combination is indeed one that gives the maximum power and freedom of access that can be attained in manual systems.

Libraries quickly learned the power of this double tool both for arranging items and records and for finding those which were relevant to particular requirements for information – developing the use of both indexes to whatever classification scheme they were using ('indirect' indexes), and 'direct' indexes to specific collections of information. Some museums followed their lead, but it is probably fair to say that the role of indexing as a complement to classification was not always appreciated (the comparative neglect of indexing was indeed one of the reasons for writing the first edition of this book), nor was the importance of consistent use of words in indexing. (See Figure 4.4 on p60, for an example from a museum classification.)

The trade-off: input effort vs ease of access
Table 4.1, on p61 and Figure 4.5 on p62 summarize the argument of the preceding pages and suggest the trade-off that exists between, on the one hand, investment in aids to finding required objects and, on the other, speed and success in the task.

The impact of IT

In 1980, it was possible to predict that specialized classifications would probably continue to be a useful intellectual tool to support thinking about collections, and that developments in information technology already under way would relieve some of the rigours associated with constructing and applying them, while the way into information handling through indexing would become the easier one. Events have more or less borne out that prediction.

Table 4.2, on p63, suggests what has remained unchanged, what has changed, and what has become less significant in information management thanks to the developments in the technology.

Choosing the methods and tools to manage information

As the previous sections of this chapter have shown, the information needs of museums are many and varied, ranging well beyond the 'simple' cataloguing of their collections. Deciding on the best way of managing this information

Index terms	Notation	Classification
comb, pocket	3.54	Section 3.　Personal Life
		3.5　　　Toilet
		3.54　　Hair care
		eg Pocket comb
comb, tortoiseshell, manufacture	4.596	Section 4.　Working Life
		4.596　　Ivory, Bone, Horn,
		Shell etc Products
combat jacket, military	1.81.41	Section 1.　Community Life
		1.8　　　Warfare and Defence
		1.81.41　Uniform and Armour
combinations, men's	3.3242	Section 3.　Personal Life
		3.3　　　Costume
		3.32　　Men's
		3.324　　Underwear
		3.3242　Combinations

	Tools to help in finding them	What they cost the user
1	Objects alone	No initial cost; go straight in; but it could mean a long walk
2	List of objects, with their locations	Low initial cost; scanning may take a long time; but a shorter walk Cheap to maintain
3	List turned into record cards: 1 card = 1 object ordered in one way, e.g. accession number	Slightly higher initial cost; if you know the number of the object you want, you can go straight to the right record; and a short walk to the object But if you want to find objects meeting any other criterion, bad luck; no better than 2 Fairly cheap to maintain
4	> 1 card to 1 object, ordered, e.g. one set by accession number, one set by donor	Slightly higher initial cost; if you want to find objects by accession no. or by donor name – straight to the right record, and a short walk to the object But if you want to find objects meeting any other criterion, bad luck; no better than 2 Fairly cheap to maintain
5	A classification, and an extra set of records ordered by classification group	Much higher initial cost – you have to assign records and objects to their place in the classification scheme; and a more complex route to the objects: find the right bit of the classification –>to the records with that class code –> scan till you find the right sub-section and locate the records you want in it –> with luck a short walk to the objects But a good classification opens many doors into the collection and adds greatly to freedom of access. More costly to maintain
6	As 5, but the classification has an index	Puts up initial cost a bit, but index makes assigning classification codes to records more consistent, and you can go straight from index to the right batch of records in classified catalogue, so shorter scanning time, and a short walk to the objects (provided they are arranged in something like classified order) Maintenance costs as 5
7	As 6, but with supplementary 'direct' indexes to allow other ways of indexes of artists' names, associated places, events	Adds again to initial cost. The path now goes from supplementary index –> records meeting the requirement > of objects. So, a more complex path, and the objects you want may be widely distributed, so it may be a long walk More costly to maintain
8	As 7, but with a thesaurus to control the terms used in all indexes	Adds yet more to initial cost, but thesaurus makes for consistency in what things are called, and so a higher proportion of relevant records should be found Adds another stage to the path: find the right term in the thesaurus –> index(es) –> relevant records –> objects Much more costly to maintain
9	*Limit of manual methods* Back to 1 record = 1 object. But this time the record is electronic, in computer database; it contains full history of objects, before and after entry into collections, and there is an on-line thesaurus	High initial investment cost, but all the ways in provided by 3–8 are built into the system, so the path to the relevant records and objects is simpler and shorter, and there are multiple means of access Reduced maintenance costs Diversity and complexity have merged into simplicity (if you've been clever in specifying what you want from the database!)

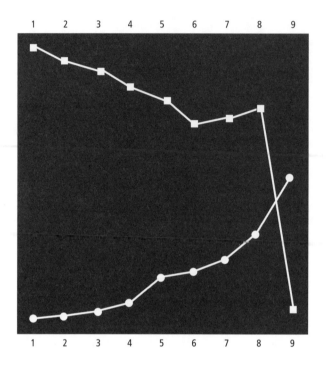

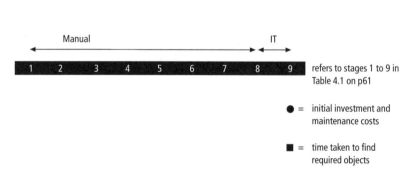

refers to stages 1 to 9 in
Table 4.1 on p61

● = initial investment and
maintenance costs

■ = time taken to find
required objects

Change			No change
New	**No longer needed**	**Reduced significance**	
Rapid searching of all records in database	Multiple record sequences	Classification: still a useful analytical tool, but can become just one field in a record – in effect a top-level index term	Need to think about: • Ways in • Record structure • Terminology
Full-text searching	Separate indexes		
Help with managing terminology	Searching separate sets of records, using different methods		
Links between records and images/sounds			

requires a clear idea of what information management means. Information first has to be gathered, in a way that is cost effective and ensures that it is correct and complete. The information then has to be recorded, and filed in a form that permits its later retrieval in a convenient way to allow the information to be interpreted to solve problems and inform decisions.

At present most of the 'administrative' functions of a museum are best served by a series of separate files, which may well all be paper based, all computer based, or, more usually, a mixture of the two. This information about staff expertise and training, because of an element of personal confidentiality, might well be kept as paper files with restricted access, but nowadays very few institutions would attempt to manage their finances by a series of manual written ledgers. How the information is best gathered and, just as important, kept up to date, on the topics outlined in the previous part of this chapter will depend on the nature of the individual museum, and thus on the sources available to it.

Gathering the information

For budgetary control, and to keep track of suppliers of goods and services, for instance, it may be possible in local authority or university museums to tap into this information from the governing body, who may also supply the necessary software (and, if you are really fortunate, the hardware) to make use of the information. Such a course is not usually open to independent or national museums, who therefore would need to provide their own software for these purposes.

Collaboration in information gathering can be most cost effective. For example, keeping abreast of advances in information technology can be time consuming, but by periodically meeting with other people in charge of IT in museums a great deal of useful information and advice can be transmitted between the participants in a very short time. Then when the IT specialist re-

returns to his or her own museum a brief report to interested colleagues quickly disseminates the information relevant to the institution, while any IT database can be updated with the latest 'peer-reviewed' information on database management packages, support organizations and so on. In the UK, the Museum Computer Group meets twice a year at different venues around the country, and is an important source of up-to-date information and experience. Other, regional, forums have been established where local museum staff who are res-ponsible for documentation and information technology, but who are unable to justify attending a distant national meeting, can get together for mutual support and to get guidance on specific problems.

Approaches to organizing the information

While well-organized paper files of, say, information on markets, competitors and collaborators might be fairly easy to compile, without indexes efficient retrieval will be difficult. Even more problematic is that such files are relatively inaccessible to more than one person at a time, and may be physically scattered around the institution, often wherever the person responsible for their compilation happens to be based. This can make the gathering of different aspects of information of relevance to a given problem both time consuming and inefficient. It is therefore suggested that as far as possible institutions should endeavour to make all relevant information available in computerized form, and that networked connectivity is used to ensure that everyone who has the need can easily and quickly access the information they require to inform decisions for which they are responsible.

Deciding what it is *relevant* to put on the computer will exercise the brains of all the staff involved. Take the example of 'markets, competitors and potential collaborators': here much of the information gathered may be in the form of brochures, annual reports, press articles, etc. It would be unnecessarily tedious and expensive to digitize all this information; what is needed is for an intelligent precis of the information to be placed on the computer in a structured form, but with links back to the published information held on file. Exactly what goes into the computer precis will depend on the uses envisaged. One use may be comparative – 'How are we doing compared to our competitors?' – so annual and/or seasonal visitor totals might be one criterion, and these will need to be held for several years to show changes. This requirement would govern the type of database software required, so the decision on the information needs has to be taken before deciding on the software to use. The institution's own figures are probably recorded on a daily or weekly basis, and might well be held in the form of a spreadsheet for short-term monitoring and analysis. Thus a simple way to transfer totals from that spreadsheet to the database used for the 'competitor' information is another requirement to be borne in mind when choosing both the spreadsheet and the database management system.

Use the tool for the job

In practical terms the various facets of the museum's information will be held in separate databases, and though if networked these are accessible by colleagues, for someone actually to make connections between the various items of information will usually require the retrieval of different information from the separate databases and making the interpretation and assessment 'off-line'. While very sophisticated 'corporate' database management systems are available that might allow the totality of the museum information base to be held in one package, the cost and complexity of support needed would put them out of reach of all but perhaps the largest national museums. The recently completed large-scale systems initiative (LASSI) by a consortium of major UK museums has now agreed on an all-embracing collection management package, Multi-MIMSY. See p170 for a case study of the LASSI initiative. However, this is still expensive relative to many museum budgets, and does not cover finance (other than valuation and insurance), personnel or other institutional management information. For the smaller museum, it is much more cost effective to use a simpler, cheaper and easily supported database management system, but to ensure by careful design of the various databases that the disparate information they hold is presented to the user in as consistent and comparable a form as possible.

Access control

While ensuring that *necessary* personal, commercial and academic confidentiality is protected, the approach of management should be to make as much information as possible available to as many staff as possible at all times. Naturally some restrictions will need to be placed on access, and probably these should be largely role determined, on a 'need-to-know' basis. Thus the marketing manager should have free access to the information needed for the job, but re-stricted access to, say, salary information.

With paper files access is controlled physically by keys to locks on filing cabinets, etc. The same principle applies to computerized records, only here the 'keys' are user name permissions and passwords. Access to computer information can usually be refined to give various levels of access, from read only; through read and add information; read, add and change; and, at the highest level, read, add, change or delete records. In a networked environment the level of control can be quite sophisticated; not only can read, write, edit and delete be permitted to whole files, but often they can be restricted for given users down to individual 'fields' of information within a single database. Stakeholders would normally need only read or read-and-write access, while the guardians would have read, write and edit access. Deletion of records from databases should normally be reserved to the system manager only.

Applying this chapter in the small museum

Collections information

Follow SPECTRUM for the minimum essentials. Go for the simplest you can get away with in recording and indexing; be guided by your knowledge of how people want to look for information; apply it consistently; aim to get everything to same basic level, and then upgrade as opportunity offers. Use MDA training services. See the case studies of small and medium-sized museums in this book for some examples of successful approaches.

People information

Collect only the basic minimum, and then keep it up to date, and act on what you learn from it – don't collect anything that you can't use. See the North Somerset Museums Service case study p223 for an example of productive use of visitor information.

Card indexes are fine for contacts – provided one person is responsible for them, and they are conscientiously kept up to date (the same goes for contacts databases!).

Human resources

Volunteers can make an invaluable contribution, provided their work is well managed. For useful examples see the Ceredigion Museum, and Norfolk Museums Service case studies pp158 and 214.

Appropriate technological support

Resist having hardware and software wished on you! Define what you require to help you do the things you really need to do, and seek advice from other museums with similar needs, and from MDA.

Integrated use of information

Being small is an advantage here; just make sure there is a 'forum' where everyone concerned can exchange information informally and negotiate action on it. See the Ceredigion case study p158 for an example. Remember that small improvements in using information are not to be sneezed at; something useful is always better than nothing.

Summary

The essential points of this chapter
1. Museums have multiple and complex needs for information management in order to make productive use of the knowledge they require to achieve their objectives and prosper.
2. They also need to manage this diversity of knowledge in an integrated way in order to get the best out of it.

3. Their information management requirements are similar to those of most other organizations, but they have certain special requirements which arise partly from the nature of the things they handle, and partly from their specific objectives.

4. They can learn useful things about information management from other organizations.

5. They still need to use the traditional 'tools of the mind' in thinking about what they have to do with information.

6. But, so long as they do that, there is a great deal of help available from modern information technology.

7. Information sharing with colleagues in other museums about developments in IT pays off.

References

ANSI/NISO (1993) *Guidelines for the construction, format and management of monolingual thesauri,* z.39.19–1993, Bethesda, Maryland, USA: NISO Press

British Standards Institution/International Standards Organization (1985), *Guide to establishment and development of multilingual thesauri,* BS 6723 : 1985 (ISO 5964)
    (1987), *Guide to establishment and development of monolingual thesauri,* BS 5723 : 1987 (ISO 5964)

[CRESTADORO, A] (1856), *The art of making catalogues of libraries or, a method to obtain in a short time a most perfect, complete, and satisfactory printed catalogue of the British Museum Library by A reader therein,* London: The Literary, Scientific & Artistic Reference Office

DEWEY, MELVIL (1885), *Abridged Decimal Classification and Relativ Index for Libraries, Clippings, Notes etc,* Second edition, Boston, USA

EDELMAN, G. (1992), *Bright air, brilliant fire,* HarperCollins (London: Penguin Books, 1994)

GRANT, A. (ed.)/MDA (1994), *Spectrum: The UK Museum Documentation Standard,* Cambridge: Museum Documentation Association[1]

JONES, SHAR (1996), Personal communication

LACITY, M. C. *et al,* (1995), 'IT outsourcing: maximize flexibility and control', Harvard Business Review, May/June 84–93

[1] A second edition was published in 1997: COWTON J. (ed)/MDA (1997), *SPECTRUM: The UK Museum Documentation Standard,* Cambridge: Museum Documentation Association

McARTHUR, T. (1986), *Worlds of Reference,* Cambridge: Cambridge University Press

McCORRY, H. & MORRISON, I. O. (1995), *Report on the Catechism Project,* Edinburgh: National Museums of Scotland

NORMAN, R. & RAMIREZ, R. (1993), 'From value chain to value constellation: designing interactive strategy', *Harvard Business Review,* 71 (4) 65–78

ORNA, E. (1986), 'Information management by design: improving information retrieval on Prestel', *Information design journal,* 5/1, 61–68

ORNA, E. & PETTITT, C. (1980), *Information handling in museums,* London: K G Saur, Clive Bingley

Useful organizations

Museums Computer Group
Fiona Marshall, *Registrar*
Leicestershire Museums
County Hall
Glenfield
Leicester
LE3 8TB

Multi MIMSY User Group
Rosa Botterill & Terry Corbett
National Maritime Museum
Greenwich
London
SE10 9NF

Chapter 5

A strategy for using information

In this chapter

Relating information needs and activities to museum objectives and policies

Any information-based organization, which museums are, must have a coherent policy for information management; strategy then follows as the way to get there. Information management, properly addressed, will involve a significant proportion of available resources, whether being implemented in a small, single-staffed local museum, or in a large national institution, and the interests of the information strategy must be represented at an appropriate senior level. Before beginning to plan a strategy for such a major investment, it is therefore sensible to be clear as to what are the real needs for your museum, and what are the underlying objectives and policies your institution is trying to achieve. Orna (1987) covers in detail the development of museum information policies.

Nowadays the mission statement of the institution is usually the starting point for this discussion, coupled with any policies already written, such as those on acquisition, collection management and access; if a business plan exists for the museum then that must also be referred to. If such policies or plans do not exist, then they will need to have been prepared, at least in outline, before attempting to decide on information management matters. Fortunately the registration process of the Museums and Galleries Commission makes it probable that most museums will already have these policies in place. While drawing up the information management strategy, every section should be referred back to the mission statement and to the various policies, to ensure that there are no conflicts and that the information strategy meets all the declared aims and objectives of the museum. For discussion of one area that needs attention – integrated management of information – see p49.

An information audit

If no information already exists on the existing pattern of use of present information systems in the museum, an 'information audit' is called for.

A good model for such an audit is the one recently done at the Natural History Museum in London.[1] There the information policy group set out three stages for such an audit:

1. Identify what information the museum holds
2. Identify who needs what information, and what of that information is not currently held by the museum
3. Identify projects designed to enable easy access to the required information.

Ten information 'domains' were identified for audit, that is areas where appropriate information and its successful use were seen as critical. These domains were:

1. People and institutions.
2. Museum collections (and associated information and archives).
3. Museum projects and products.
4. Museum fabric.
5. Official documents and correspondence.
6. Statistics.
7. Finance.
8. Training.
9. Diaries.
10. References/directories/indexes/lists.

The survey of the existing information and purposes revealed some problems in defining and interpreting objectives. This gap acted as a catalyst for the development of a 'corporate information plan'. All the above headings would have some relevance in any museum, no matter how small, though, of course, some of them, such as museum fabric and finance, may be dealt with entirely by the governing body.

An important part of the 'people domain' referred to above is the users of museum information, and their use and expectations must be established. Doing this can range from looking back through a daybook at the types of enquiries actually dealt with in the last few years, to a full-blown survey of all staff and visitors. The sort of questions to ask could be: what loans have been requested in the past, and how readily were they serviced? Has anyone had difficulty finding suitable suppliers, or addresses of related institutions? Have the needs of gallery display and temporary exhibition caused any problems? Often asking one question will throw up a new line of enquiry into another area of information use.

Past 'group' users, such as schools and local societies, should be included, to determine whether there were any desired aspects of information which they felt were not provided on their previous visits. Don't neglect receptionists and

---

[1] For more about information auditing, see Booth & Haines (1994), Dimond (1996), Haynes (1995), Orna (1990), Robertson (1994)).

gallery staff; they generally field a lot of questions during the day that the curators rarely get to know about. Time spent establishing what people really
want to know about your museum and its collections will rarely be wasted,
but it can help to prevent wasting resources on designing and implementing
an information management system that either under- or over-performs the
necessary task. See Chapter 3 for more information about the users and use of museum
information.

Of course, you also need to know about people and institutions, so what
information you hold about your visitor profile, competitors, suppliers, and
what information is gathered already on visitor numbers, loans in and out,
temporary exhibitions past and planned, publicity contacts and so on, should
be included in the audit. At the end of the day what you need to know is all the
various types of information the museum already holds, where and how it is
stored, who has access to it (in reality, not in theory), what use has been made
of it in the past few years, and what information needs have not been satisfied
in that period.

While doing the information audit it is a good idea to get curators to identify which parts of the collections in their care they consider candidates for computerization. See Chapter 9 p121.

Developing information strategies to support overall museum policies

Having established the information needs of the museum by means of an
audit, a strategy is needed that will draw together all the existing sources, sup-
plement them with necessary additional information, and make sure that
everyone has access to the information store in accordance to their needs, in
line with museum aims and policy.

Developing a strategy that meets these conditions can involve dealing with
some problems of conflicting priorities, and it is worth looking here at one
critical problem of this kind, before we go on to discuss the practicalities of setting up a strategy.

Information management versus access? [2]
The mission statements and objectives of many museums, as can be seen from
the case studies in this book, require both management of information about
the collections and maximum access for the widest range of users. In practice,
as some of the case studies indicate, museums sometimes get into something
of a tangle in trying to reconcile the two, especially when their resources are
not adequate for all the things they are committed to doing.

The result can be a conflict between outward-oriented activity (especially
the kind with commercial links) designed to attract the public and provide

[2] Much of the material in this section is based on
Orna (1994), with acknowledgments to the
Museums Association.

exciting forms of access, and the work which is carried out entirely within the walls of the museum to record essential information about the collections and make it accessible. If the tension is not resolved, there is little chance of arriving at an information strategy that repays the effort of putting it together.

A museum can be said to offer access in the fullest sense of the word if:

- It enables people to think, for purposes they have defined for themselves, about the objects in the collections and the subjects dealt with by the museum
- It allows users to approach and move through information about the collections in ways appropriate to what they want to achieve
- It lets them take their thinking to the limits of the detail available in the museum's resources of knowledge about its collections, and offers them the opportunity of dialogue with the museum in which they can contribute their own knowledge and ideas.

These criteria can and should be applicable at every level and to all kinds of users, from visitors who want to see if there are any pictures of the street where they lived in childhood, to researchers in pursuit of the finest detail of their subject.

An earlier chapter (see Chapter 2, p19) used the metaphor of a threefold store of information and knowledge as the core of the museum: the immediately visible one, the information embodied 'within the objects themselves, and the invisible store of knowledge in the minds of the people responsible for the care and presentation of the collections. If museums are to offer full access, they need to make use of all three stores. And the essential means for achieving this is information management – of every kind of information that contributes to the museum's resources of knowledge about itself and the outside world which it serves. Integrated use of the whole range is the best guarentee of fruitful access for the whole range of users.

The kind of access on offer today, and the level at which it is available, varies greatly from museum to museum. Holm's survey (Holm, 1993) found that 25 per cent of West Midlands museums had no means of searching for items by any attribute other than accession number. Morrison (1994) found similar problems in Scotland. Even those museums with potential for access in multiple ways actually often find it difficult to exploit the potential, usually because their systems hark back to the 1970s and 1980s, with their rigid demands on users – the case studies contain at least one example of a system (now happily superseded) which put near-insuperable difficulties in the way of finding answers to multiple-feature questions.

In most museums there still seems to be a mismatch between the access that users need and the access that is actually on offer. And that mismatch could have something to do with a lack of connection between thinking about collections information management and documentation on one hand, and about 'access' (especially IT-based) on the other. Figure 5.1 on p72 represents four typical situations.

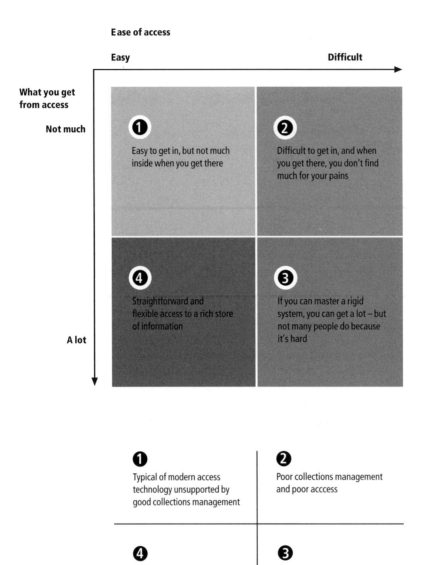

Ease of access

Easy   Difficult

What you get from access

Not much

❶ Easy to get in, but not much inside when you get there

❷ Difficult to get in, and when you get there, you don't find much for your pains

❹ Straightforward and flexible access to a rich store of information

❸ If you can master a rigid system, you can get a lot – but not many people do because it's hard

A lot

❶ Typical of modern access technology unsupported by good collections management

❷ Poor collections management and poor acccess

❹ Collections management and access technology co-operating on the basis of understanding the access needs of users

❸ Thorough (perhaps over-through?) collections management con-strained by traditional IT access

Fortunately there is a growing number of examples (some of them described in the case studies) of how technology that helps good collections infomation management also benefits access. The work described above at the Natural History Museum and the case study of the National Maritime Museum (p190), for example, show how careful basic thinking combined with appropriate use of technology can allow the emergence of new information, give new perspectives through the information store, and offer new 'information opportunities' for making 'implicit information' explicit. For more about the potential for creative interactions between people and technology, see Chapter 7 p103.

There are less happy examples of access projects initiated and taken forward without communication between the people responsible for them and their collections management colleagues; and of museum managements who are so sold on interactive multi-media public access, and so unaware of the fundamental role of collections information management that they starve it of resources, foster mutual ignorance and suspicion, and downgrade the significance of curatorial knowledge.

Both kinds of situation point to the fact that you cannot achieve balance and mutual help between collections information management and access without addressing deep organizational issues. There are two main organizational conditions for success. First, the museum's knowledge base must be protected from ignorant administrative intervention. Without that, there is the danger of forward-looking technology giving access to static, backward-looking information, because the knowledge base represented by experienced people has been under-valued and lost to the museum. Secondly, those who have knowledge need to be confident that, even when it has been embodied in a system, it still remains theirs, and they can go on developing it; that confidence is a necessary condition for willingness to let others have access to their knowledge and use it for their own purposes.

To meet the conditions, it is necessary to think about the museum as a whole organization, the purposes for which it exists, criteria for evaluating its success in achieving them, and new ways of using resources – collections, knowledge embodied in people, money, technology – to enhance each other, without destroying anything useful. All decisions about collections information management and access should contribute towards the aim of using the 'third store' of knowledge as effectively as possible to support both collections management and access. This should be one of the main issues addressed by any strategy for using information. It is not an easy task, and carrying it through is harder still, but there are enough hopeful developments to show that the aims of managing collections information and providing access are not mutually antithetical, that you can't have one without the other, and that they can actually support each other to the benefit of museums and their users.

Steps to drawing up an information strategy
The task of drawing up an all-embracing strategy can seem pretty daunting

even in a small, single discipline museum. But as with most complex tasks, by breaking it down into smaller steps, and tackling these one by one, the job can be made manageable.

Start with a preamble, covering the background to the information needs, how they are relevant to the mission statement, and a brief review of how documentation and information provision have developed at your museum. Cover major decisions for the future, such as all documentation procedures to conform as closely as possible to those given in SPECTRUM (1994), and how the information management is itself going to be managed in the future. For example, is one person going to be responsible, or will an information and documentation panel be appointed? The level of expertise within or available close to the museum should be noted.

General decisions should be recorded here, such as whether to support museum-wide access, whether a computer system is contemplated, whether it would be networked, whether the information system will be text only or whether images are to be included, particularly for the collection-based parts.

The existing infrastructure should be reviewed, such as the nature of existing information sources (manual or computerized) and an outline of any information technology equipment available. Some indication of future resource needs should be noted, whether this means budget reorganization or the seeking of additional funding, and how these needs are seen to dovetail into the general development plans for the museum.

Next, each of the 'domains' mentioned above should be addressed, and the subsections within each identified. For the collection information domain SPECTRUM provides a well-thought-out series of headings. For the others the information audit should provide details of how to 'break down' the domain relative to your museum. Statistics, for example, will nearly always include visitor and loan numbers, but other statistics may be required by your governing body.

Having established the sections to be addressed by the strategy, each should be drafted in a reasonably standard way. One advantage of this 'modular' approach is that different sections can be drafted by different members of staff. Not only does this spread the workload, but it also assists in getting staff to 'take ownership' of the finished strategy, which itself can greatly ease the implementation of something that may require considerable changes in established working practices throughout the museum.

A suggested model for each section is as follows, based on that adopted at The Manchester Museum (MM). An example of the completed section for labelling and marking items in the *MM Documentation Plan* is shown in Figure 5.2, on p75.

CURRENT POSITION. A brief summary of what happens at the moment, with reference to any existing information documentation. Copies of any extant forms, lists of instructions and so on should be included in the strategy document as numbered appendices, and cross-referenced here.

7   Marking and Labelling Items

7.1   *Current Position:* At present it is normal practice to mark the
            accession number on all items in the humanities and geology
            departments when practicable, and to have the number on the
            label attached or closely associated with all biology specimens.
            Some staff have attended a course on labelling and marking
            run at the MM in June 1993 by the North West Museums Service
            in association with the MDA.

7.2   *Objective:* The formulation and implementation across all depar-
            ments of MM of a unified labelling and marking procedure by
            the end of 1996.

7.3   *Implementation Strategy [A]:* The methods in use to mark and/or
            label items will be reviewed before the end of 1996 in association
            with the Keeper of Conservation, to confirm that appropriate mater-
            ials and methods are now being used throughout the Museum.

            The section on labelling and marking in the MM documentation
            manual will be written and implemented by the end of 1996.

7.4   *Resource Implications:* One week each for the Keeper of Conser-
            vation and of the identified IT officer to perform the review of
            methods and materials,and to write up the results as a Manual for
            reference by all staff.

OBJECTIVE. One sentence only, encapsulating what it is intended to achieve under this section of the strategy. Whenever possible a target date for reaching the objective should be given. Once the strategy has been approved and adopted by the governing body, the existence of these 'deadlines' can sometimes be used to squeeze a budget enhancement to enable the objective to be met on time.

IMPLEMENTATION STRATEGY. A paragraph summarizing how this objective is going to be achieved. Each step of the implementation should be mentioned, and if possible each step should be given a target date for completion. Without these dates, monitoring the implementation of the strategy becomes very difficult. This paragraph should include details of any new documentation, forms, thesauri or other tools to be produced to assist the implementation of the strategy. Sometimes drafting the strategy will highlight gaps in the policies of the museum, and plans to introduce these can meaningfully be included in the strategy. Occasionally two or more sub-sections may be addressed under a single objective, and then separate implementation strategy paragraphs should be drafted for each; this is less prolix than raising every sub-section to a higher level, especially where a single objective covers them all.
Each implementation strategy should be graded as follows:
A. The strategy is well within the current means of the museum, and can be achieved within two to four years.
B. The strategy can only be achieved by the reallocation of a significant part of the museums resources, but could be achieved over a 5–20-year period.
C. The strategy is well beyond the means of the museum to achieve, and relies on the success of a bid for additional resources (to Area Service, Heritage Lottery Fund, etc.)
Thus *all* aspects should be covered, even if there seems at present no way that they can be achieved. The cohesive strategic plan thus set out can be used to help get the funding required to accelerate level B and make feasible level C strategies.

RESOURCE IMPLICATIONS. Here should be estimated, as accurately as possible (get quotations), the costs of materials and processes needed to achieve the given objective. In addition, the staff resources required must be specified, including an allowance for time needed by all staff involved in consultation and revision of procedures and documents.

Adoption, implementation, review
Once all the identified sections have been covered they can begin to be drawn together into a unified whole, and any internal inconsistencies removed. It is most important that the final draft goes for comment to as many members of staff as possible. This will help to identify omissions, errors or impracticalities that may only be apparent to one person. It will also enable the person responsible for overseeing the introduction of the strategy to meet and reassure staff who express reservations about the implications of the policy for them, which

should then smooth the implementation of the strategy. The finished strategy, probably with an 'executive summary' and an overview of resource implications, will need to go to the governing body of the museum for approval and adoption. Once it has been adopted all that remains is to get it into place, and hopefully watch the improvements that flow from an integrated information strategy appropriate to the work of the museum. The implementation phase should be carefully monitored, to ensure that the various steps along the way happen in the right order, by the agreed date and within the agreed budget. The entire strategy should be reviewed to ensure it is still fully relevant. This should be done by a representative group of staff, initially every year, though once it has been fully implemented a longer period may be suitable.

Summary

The essential points of this chapter:

1. Before starting to design an information strategy it is important to know, by means of an information audit, what information the museum already holds and in what form.

2. An information strategy should be built by designing modules to cover each domain of information, making sure each section supports the mission and policy statements of the museum.

3. Information management and access must be allies, and the information strategy should be designed to achieve this.

References

BOOTH, A. & HAINES, M. (1994), 'Information audit: whose line is it anyway?' *Health Libraries Review*. 10 (4), 224–232

DIMOND, G. (1996), 'The evaluation of information systems: a protocol for assembling information auditing packages', *International Journal of Information Management*, 16 (5), 353–368

GRANT, A. (ed)/MDA (1994), *SPECTRUM. The UK Museum Documentation Standard*, Cambridge: Museum Documentation Association

HAYNES, D. (1995), 'Business process reengineering and information audits', *Managing Information*, 2 (6), 30–31

HOLM, S. A. (1993), *Let's Set the Record Straight: A report on the state of documentation in the museums of the West Midlands*, West Midlands Area Museums Service, £10 from the Museum Documentation Association

MORRISON, I. (1994), 'Towards a National Database of Museum Collections in Scotland', *Managing Information*, 1 (1), 35–38

MORRISON, I. (1995), Museum Information for Documentation, *in* FAHY, A. and SUDBURY, W. *Information, The Hidden Resource, Museums and the Internet*, Cambridge: Museum Documentation Association, 39–45

ORNA, E. (1987), *Information policies for museums*, Cambridge, Museum Documentation Association, Occasional Paper No. 10, 48pp

ORNA, E. (1990), *Practical information policies*, Chapters 4 & 5: Aldershot, Gower

ORNA, E. (1994), 'In the Know', *Museums Journal*, November, 24–27

PETTITT, C. (1994), 'Using the collections', *in* STANSFIELD, G., MATHIAS, J. and READ, G. *The Manual of Biological Curatorship* (Chapter 6), London, HMSO, 144–16.

Human resources in information management

'People are gregarious and social beings. We need to interact with each other and we do our best work when we do. The work place is not a machine, despite all of the 19th century metaphors to the contrary. It is a community and social practices make it work.' Boast (1994).

In accordance with this insight, which comes from a museum professional, this chapter deals with what people need to do with information in museums, the role of human resources in achieving successful change, the kind of support people need from systems in using and communicating information (and how to ensure they get it), maintaining the museum's knowledge store, human resources as an element of the museum's information strategy, and principles for effective use of human resources in managing information.

The really essential resource

There is plenty of lip-service paid today to the importance of people, but not much grasp of the simple and self-evident fact that the only agency which can turn information into knowledge, and act constructively upon it, is the human mind. It is only human beings who can make sense of information and manage it to good purpose. Unfortunately, human minds are a costly resource, and the value of what they do with information is intangible and hard to calculate in concrete terms, as are the costs of failures in performing these tasks effectively. This probably accounts for the fact that talk about the value of human resources is often accompanied by action in the form of 'down-sizing', replacing human work by information technology, short-term contracts, and various other 'cost-saving' devices, whose main effect is to undermine the sense of self-worth, create insecurity and deprive organizations of the value that is added through the exercise of human knowledge, experience and skills. Yet there is a well-established body of thinking by respected practitioners in business management which points to 'invisible assets' (including information and knowledge resources, corporate culture and management skills) as, in Itami's

(1987) words: 'the most important resources for long-term success'. Money cannot buy:

'an instantaneous change in corporate culture or employee morale. Accumulation of these resources requires on-going, conscious, and time-consuming efforts; you cannot just go out and buy them off the shelf ... The important features of invisible assets – they are unattainable with money alone, are time-consuming to develop, are capable of multiple simultaneous use, and yield multiple, simultaneous benefits – make it crucial to carefully consider strategies for accumulating them ... People are important assets of the firm ... because much of the invisible assets of the firm are embodied in people; people carry and exchange the information necessary for strategic fit.' (ibid. 13–14).

The case studies in this book would not have been possible without interaction with the staff of the museums – through conversations, demonstrations of how things are done, and reading documents composed by people. The experience goes to underline that organizations are indeed 'socio-technical' systems in which the 'socio' element comes first, and in which human knowledge, human interactions, and people's perceptions of the organization, of their colleagues and of themselves, are critical to what the organization can achieve.

What people need to do with information in museums

Chapter 2 (p23) took a typical set of museum aims as the starting point for an outline of the knowledge the museum required in order to meet its aims, and then went on (p25) to define the kinds of information needed to feed that knowledge. We can also use this framework to develop ideas about how *people* need to *act* in acquiring and using the required knowledge to achieve the museum's aims (see Table 6.1 on pp80 and 81).

It is evident from this kind of analysis that people in a wide range of jobs – including curators, collections managers, conservators, systems managers, education staff, financial managers and administrators – are responsible for managing and using significant resources of information. Apart from that, an overall information management role needs to be provided for. The person who fulfils it has to be aware of the full range of the museum's information resources, to know and to communicate on terms of mutual understanding with the guardians and stakeholders of each resource, and to take responsibility for developing the museum's strategy for using information (for a detailed statement of the information manager's role, see Chapter 9, pp120–123). As the case studies show, the people who fulfil this role can be drawn from many different functions and backgrounds, and have various job titles; and they can, in smaller institutions, combine their overall management of information with a number of other tasks. It is essential, however, if the job is to be done properly, for the holder to be at a level of authority which matches the responsibilities that go with it.

Aims	Required knowledge and information to support it	How people need to act to use knowledge and information
Displaying collections	Of collections Of display technologies Records, 'current awareness', professional contacts	Maintain awareness of current developments by reading, and interaction with colleagues inside and outside the museum Apply knowledge in developing display; learn from response of visitors
Adding to them	Of potential and actual donors Of other potential sources Of market prices, vendors, etc. Of 'acquisition history' Of value of items in collection	Negotiate with donors, vendors colleagues Select, make decisions on what to accept/purchase Maintain records in the light of knowledge
Documenting, researching, publishing; encouraging scholarship	Of collections, and of subject background; of developments in scholarship in relevant fields Of modern documentation practice, and of technologies to support it Of 'history' of all items since they entered the collections Publishing know-how	Maintain awareness of current developments by reading, and interaction with colleagues inside and outside the museum Tell other people with an interest about relevant developments; contribute to decisions about new systems and uses of technology Maintain records in the light of new knowledge Co-operation between publishing, curatorial, marketing staff Negotiation with commercial partners
Providing suitable housing and storage	Of modern conservation techniques, environmental requirements	Apply knowledge in planning/ maintaining conservation schedules Interaction between conservators, documentalists Contribute to development of systems, and to decisions on housing/storage
Complementing the collections by loan exhibitions	Of collections of similar museums, in all countries	Co-operate with colleagues in decisions about loan exhibitions Negotiate agreements with lending institutions Produce catalogues and related publications
Interpreting the collections	Of the subject areas of collections, of collections themselves, of 'visitor profile', of interpretation methods	Interaction/information sharing between curators, education staff, marketing, visitor-information services Use information from interaction with visitors in planning interpretation policy and activities

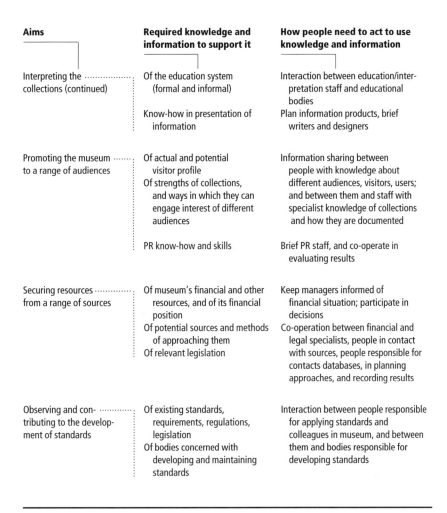

Aims	Required knowledge and information to support it	How people need to act to use knowledge and information
Interpreting the collections (continued)	Of the education system (formal and informal)	Interaction between education/interpretation staff and educational bodies
	Know-how in presentation of information	Plan information products, brief writers and designers
Promoting the museum to a range of audiences	Of actual and potential visitor profile	Information sharing between people with knowledge about different audiences, visitors, users; and between them and staff with specialist knowledge of collections and how they are documented
	Of strengths of collections, and ways in which they can engage interest of different audiences	
	PR know-how and skills	Brief PR staff, and co-operate in evaluating results
Securing resources from a range of sources	Of museum's financial and other resources, and of its financial position	Keep managers informed of financial situation; participate in decisions
	Of potential sources and methods of approaching them	Co-operation between financial and legal specialists, people in contact with sources, people responsible for contacts databases, in planning approaches, and recording results
	Of relevant legislation	
Observing and contributing to the development of standards	Of existing standards, requirements, regulations, legislation	Interaction between people responsible for applying standards and colleagues in museum, and between them and bodies responsible for developing standards
	Of bodies concerned with developing and maintaining standards	

It is also evident that, if a museum is to achieve its aims, the people who work for it need to:

1. Be aware of the aims, and of the museum's interpretation of the knowledge and information it needs to support their achievement.

2. Define for themselves, in co-operation with management and colleagues throughout the museum:

- What their own knowledge and information requirements are
- What they need to do in order to meet them
- How they need to use knowledge and information in their own work
- The support they can get from and give to colleagues
- The interactions they need with the museum's 'outside world'
- The support they need from information systems to maintain and use their knowledge effectively.

3. Take and implement decisions to ensure that they get what they need and use it constructively.

4. Monitor the process and negotiate changes to make it work better, and to keep it in line with developments.

There are probably no museums where this has been undertaken as a formal process, just as there are few if any organizations which have taken time to define what 'information' means in their context. On the other hand, there are museums which have considered some of these requirements in the course of planning for major changes, for example in specifying what new information systems should provide, in moving towards revenue generation, or in developing an information policy or IT strategy. For examples, see the case studies of the National Maritime Museum p190, the RAF Museum p232, Scienceworks p252, and the V&A p259. As many museums are engaged in changes of this kind, it is worth considering what makes for successful use of human resources in the process.

Human resources for successful change

Any major organizational change process entails a succession of activities, involving people from different functions within the organization, and often people from outside as well; the degree of success depends critically on how they co-operate in the various stages, and how the handover from one stage to the next is managed. The first edition of this book contained an example of the use of human resources in developing an information system. It showed the process 'as it should be' and 'as it sometimes is'. The 'as it should be' sequence ran from a first stage in which the 'stakeholders' contributed to the initial decision, through their participation in defining information needs by analysing their own work areas and the information problems in them, and in developing a 'user specification'. It continued with management discussing the financial implications with them, agreement on the overall pattern of the system to be procured, staff participation in detailed planning for its implementation, and establishing training for the people involved in each phase of implementation. The final stages brought staff into monitoring the progress of implementation, using the results in subsequent phases, and acting as trainers and 'consultants' to colleagues in those phases. The end result was new skills for staff, and confidence in their 'own' system, with a basis established for co-operative development towards an 'integrated information system for all museum activities'.

The parallel 'as it sometimes is' sequence, which drew on some real-life events of the time, was characterized by failures of communication on the part of management, lack of control of outside agents, and demoralization among people who had to endure the consequences in their work. Such a tale of disasters, in all its crass disregard of common sense, would probably not happen in many institutions today. The risks of taking arbitrary decisions about information systems without involving the people who will have to implement them are now better known. It takes a very benighted management to believe that systems can work by virtue of the technology without any contribution of human thought, and consultants and vendors are usually regarded with a more critical and better informed eye (though it has been pointed out that some World Wide Web developments show the old melancholy sequence).

In fact, as some of the case studies seem to suggest, the dangers are now perhaps better realized in relation to information technology than to other aspects of change in organizations (though it is far from universally recognized yet that, as Drucker (1995) expresses it, 'in knowledge-based work especially, additional capital investment will likely require more, rather than less, labour').

Many museums are now contending with large changes concerning administrative structure, traditional roles of staff, and relations with their outside world of visitors, researchers, grant givers, financial sponsors, business, commercial partners. All these changes involve the way in which information is used and the people who use it, and what Davenport (1992) describes as the 'politics of information', as well as the 'stories' (Macdonald & Silverstone, 1990) that museums use to describe what they are about. It is as well to realize that success in these initiatives, too, depends on understanding and commitment from the whole range of people who will be called on to make the changes work, and on recognition from management of their interests and of the knowledge they can contribute.

For all projected changes, there should be the widest possible identification of people with a stake in them (thirty years' experience of organizations of various kinds has convinced the present author – sometimes rather painfully – that the commonest mistake is failure to take into account all the people who need to know, and have their say, about proposed changes). They need an opportunity, before ideas have become too fixed and firm commitments have been made, to learn what is proposed from those who are initiating it, with maximum openness. They need time to consider in depth the likely impact on their own work, both threats and opportunities; they need a guaranteed opportunity to ask questions and express anxieties, and to receive honest answers. The majority of people who work in museums are knowledgeable and committed to their work; they merit on that account respectful treatment from decision makers, who should be prepared to justify their change proposals, and allow staff to make judgements. And there should be a proper forum for constructive negotiation, allowing the people whose work will be affected in any way by the changes to contribute from their knowledge and experience. People from different functions and different areas, whose 'stake' in the changes differs, need to be brought together to explain their interests to one another, and to negotiate if possible ways in which there can be as many 'winners' and as few 'losers' as possible from the changes.

Once the form of the changes is established, the education and training essential to support the people involved should be planned, with their participation. Phases of implementation should be agreed, and the people involved in them should jointly decide the criteria to be used for judging whether the planned results are being achieved. A forum for review of the process should be established, with a senior manager responsible for convening it and for feeding in the results to the relevant policy-making body. Change itself needs to be capable of further change in the light of organizational learning; failure to provide for that is the source of some of the gravest risks and the heaviest costs to organizations.

This is not an easy recipe; gaining commitment to change takes a lot of time, and because it touches on the politics of information the process can be an uncomfortable one. As Davenport *et al* (1992) say 'Explicitly recognizing the politics of information and managing them constructively is a difficult, complex, and time-consuming task. It will not happen by itself, nor will the problem go away. Effectively managing information politics requires a shift in organizational culture; new technology and even new executives alone are not enough to make this happen.' Time spent on thinking and interchanging ideas is, however, still quite a cost-effective investment compared with the alternatives.

Systems to support people in using information

One factor worth serious attention in the planning of information systems is how they can support people in the kind of interchanges just described, as well as in those involved in normal day-to-day working. If systems make it easy to get at information which is managed by a different department, to tell colleagues what we are doing, or to ask them for help or information, they are likely to promote habits of using them for that purpose. There are still not many which do this, but there are plenty which impose every possible obstacle – management information scattered around a variety of incompatible systems acquired at different points without any co-ordination, conservation databases and photography records which cannot be reached from the main database, or networks which exclude significant groups of staff.

So, when new systems are being planned, the planning should take account of the interchanges of information which people need to make in order to achieve the museum's objectives. As Chapter 2 pointed out, the various kinds of information that museums handle have a relationship of mutual support – 'not only are all the kinds of knowledge and information essential, they have to interact if the museum is to get full value from them' (p29). And that interaction has to take place through people, supported as far as possible by the available technology. So we can re-draw the picture which was used in Chapter 2 (Figure 2.3) to show the kind of interaction needed among different kinds of knowledge and information, this time to show what people need to do with information and knowledge in order to sustain the museum's knowledge base (see Figure 6.1 on p85).

The activities are drawn from column 3 of Table 6.1 (pp80 and 81); they fall into two main categories:
1. Those concerned with acquiring information and transforming it into knowledge.

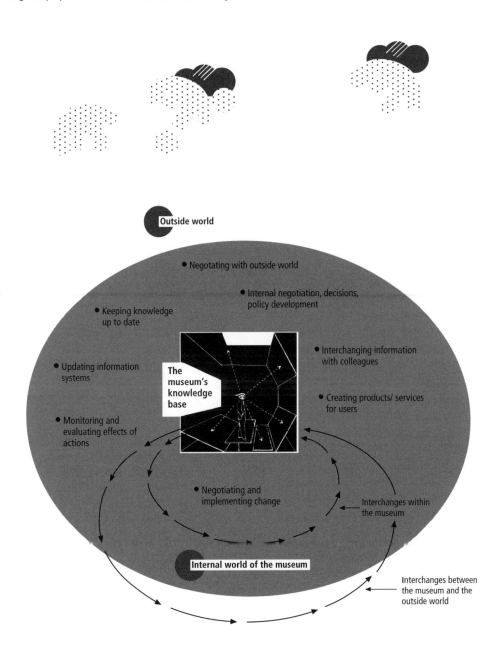

Outside world

Negotating with outside world

Internal negotiation, decisions,
policy development

Keeping knowledge
up to date

Interchanging information
with colleagues

The
museum's
knowledge
base

Updating information
systems

Creating products/ services
for users

Monitoring and
evaluating effects of
actions

Negotiating and
implementing change

Interchanges within
the museum

Internal world of the museum

Interchanges between
the museum and the
outside world

2. Those concerned with diffusing the knowledge to others, so that they can absorb it and use it in their own work.

(These activities are represented in terms of 'transformations' in Figure 2.1 (p21), and in terms of 'codification' and 'diffusion' in Figure 6.2 (p87). Either way, they are the foundation of 'organizational learning').

Taking care of the museum's knowledge store

The metaphor of the museum as a threefold store of information and knowledge was introduced in Chapter 2 (Figure 2.2, p28); behind the visible objects which immediately meet the eye is a store of 'embodied information' in the objects themselves; and behind that an equally precious store of knowledge in the minds of people. That knowledge is deep, widely spread, and of great diversity. It embraces not only the objects themselves and their cultural, social, historic or literary context, but also the disciplines that illuminate them; it also extends to the way they are cared for, displayed and made accessible; to how the business of the museum is run; and to the potential for educational use, in the broadest sense, of the museum's resources of objects and human knowledge. It resides in the minds of people doing the whole range of jobs in the museum – from curators to marketing staff, from documentalists to those in everyday contact with visitors – and in the minds of many people outside the museum with whom they are in contact.

Knowledge in the human mind is a wonderful, dynamic force, with amazing potential for making connections and speedy retrieval and application. It is, alas, also a desperately fragile, vulnerable, and easily wasted resource, as we may see from daily experience in all kinds of organizations. Museums are not exempt. Curators with valuable knowledge in their own discipline, who have also devoted time to acquiring IT skills, can find themselves with a choice between being wholly diverted to trouble-shooting on the technology for their colleagues, or struggling to do their curatorial work on top of additional tasks which form no part of their original job description. Such expedients may achieve the required short-term saving of n per cent on the budget, but they offend against the sound economic principle that people should spend the largest possible amount of their working time using the specialist knowledge for which they were employed, and represent a long-term loss.

And what is one to say of a local authority museum committee which has recently closed a popular social history museum with particularly valuable textile collections, ostensibly to bring fire protection up to standard, but with every possibility that it will be a permanent closure. The saving of a comparatively trivial sum on the current year's budget will then be achieved at a cost of dispersing a body of curatorial knowledge, and making the collections to which it has been very effectively applied until now permanently without use or value?

An aspect of knowledge not often considered is provision for the transfer of the 'tacit knowledge' acquired in the course of experience in the job, as part of

The process of organizational learning. Reproduced, with permission of the publishers, from *The Learning Organization* by B. Garratt (1964), published by HarperCollins

Figure 6.2

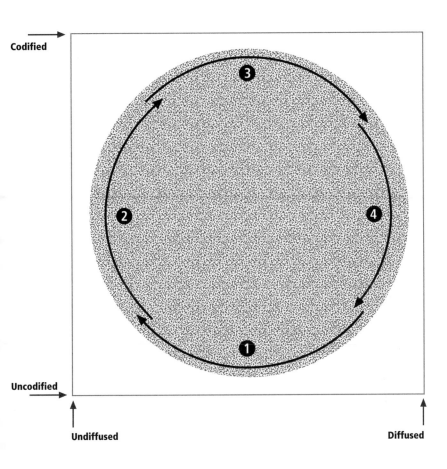

❶ Scanning	❸ Knowledge diffusion (knowledge transformed into information)
❷ Knowledge creation (information transformed into knowledge)	❹ Knowledge absorption (information transformed into knowlege)

the process before people leave the museum where they have worked. Some organizations have a policy for retirement preparation which includes 'succession planning' and briefing by the retiring job holder of the person who will succeed him or her. This, while useful, leaves out of account people moving to other jobs, or taking early retirement, or made redundant, whose knowledge effectively goes with them. It would be worth considering a negotiated 'transfer of knowledge' contract in such cases. It could take various forms: for example, the training of less experienced colleagues; written or electronic products embodying knowledge; 'knowledge-elicitation' sessions of a more productive kind than those conducted by non-specialists trying to embody expert knowledge for artificial intelligence purposes. The purpose would be to put the 'tacit knowledge' into the outside world, where it would be accessible for transformation to knowledge within the minds of others and embodiment as part of the organizational knowledge base. An important part of the knowledge that should be transferred is that which constitutes the organization's memory of its own history, a resource whose value is today beginning to be recognized in the business world (see, for example, Palmer, 1995, and Hebrail, 1995).

The institution of a contract of this kind would help to preserve the continuity and relevance of the knowledge base, to avoid risks arising from lack of essential knowledge, to prevent the costs of re-creating lost knowledge and of finding new information sources. It would also mitigate the losses that arise from the demoralization of both those who leave and those who are left behind (at the time when this was being written, the press was reporting British Gas's 'gains' from dismissing large numbers of its staff before the electronic system designed to replace them was working properly, which left fewer people, who had no cause to feel confident in their employers, to run the old system, with the inevitable result of financial loss and customer dissatisfaction).

Human resources as part of information strategy

When museums are developing an information strategy, it should embody a supporting strategy for the use of human abilities and knowledge. These aspects of human resources should be taken into account:
- The resources of human knowledge and skills which the museum needs in order to achieve its aims
- The existing resources of knowledge embodied in the people who work in the museum (a 'knowledge audit')
- How to maintain the continuity of knowledge resources, and protect them from loss, in the face of normal changes in the composition of the museum's staff, and of major developments in policy and ways of working
- The groups of people who need to co-operate in using knowledge
- The organizational structures to allow and encourage the co-operation
- The education and training that the museum needs to provide for its staff in order to develop and maintain their knowledge

- The role of technology in supporting the people in using and interchanging knowledge
- The promotion of 'organizational learning' – the capacity for the organization as a whole to learn from experience, and to apply it in developing its work[1] (see Figure 6.2 on p87).

Such an approach, it is worth noting, is consistent with ideas being developed (by the World Bank among others) about the need for 'national balance sheets measuring the stock of the nation's physical and intellectual capital' (Hutton, 1996). GDP measures, which leave out of account all non-market transactions – both those which add value, and those which (like the waste of skills of unemployed people) are in effect a loss – 'offer only an indifferent guide to policy'. The World Bank's new 'wealth accounting system' includes, besides natural capital and produced assets, human resources and 'social capital'.

Burack *et al* (1994) make a similar point in relation to the individual business: 'New paradigm companies recognize that ... business strategies require counterparts for human resources, often involving significantly changed roles for the human resources function.' So institutional policies which take account of the value of people in managing their resources of knowledge are realistic rather than utopian.

Applying this chapter in the small museum

This is another case where good practice is probably easier to achieve in smaller than in larger institutions. Where few people are involved, there is a much better chance of bringing the knowledge and abilities of everyone together to work for good information management, and the process can be an agreeable and enjoyable one as well. In large organizations it requires very intensive efforts to avoid the misunderstandings that can get in the way of good use of human resources, but in small ones, as doing the case studies has shown us on many occasions, informal and cordial, but productive, interchanges of information are constantly going on, among people at all levels, including clerical and front-of-house staff and volunteers.

---

[1] The concept of organizational learning, or the 'learning organization', is based on the idea that organizations can learn, just as individuals can, and that when they master the ability to do so, the effects are greater than the sum of individual learning. Figure 6.2 (Boisot, 1987, reproduced in Garratt, 1994) shows two processes essential for organizational learning at work:

'Codification' – a psychological process by which people bring in ideas from the outside world, work on them, and turn them back into some form of intellectual property, which can be productively used in relations with the outside world.

'Diffusion' – a sociological process, by which codified knowledge gets to other interested parties inside the organization, who can then take ownership of it and use it. The processes are similar to the transformations of knowledge to information and information to knowledge described in Chapter 2 (pp20–22).

Summary[2]

The essential points of this chapter:

1. Only human beings can make sense of information and manage it to good purpose, so museums should know of the abilities, skills, knowledge and potential of all the people who work for them, and should seek to use them to the full, so that they contribute fully to the museum's objectives and at the same time develop their own careers.

2. Jobs should be structured so that people spend the maximum possible proportion of their time using their abilities, skills and knowledge at the highest level.

3. Organizations are socio-technical systems; human knowledge, human interactions, and people's perceptions of the organization and themselves are critical to what they can achieve.

4. People in many different jobs in museums need to interact with one another and with the outside world in using information; museums also need to provide for an overall information management role (which is different from that of managing IT or information systems).

5. Success or failure in organizational change depends critically on recognizing the 'politics of information', and on negotiations among the stakeholders in different kinds of information.

6. The uses of technology must be planned so that the technology helps humans to contribute what humans are best at; people should never be distorted to serve technology, and the meeting point between them and technology must be one with which they feel at ease.

7. Investments in technology may well require more rather than less investment in human thinking power to take advantage of them.

8. 'Tacit knowledge' is a treasure not to be wasted. Museums should think of negotiating equitable 'transfer of knowledge' contracts so as to preserve the continuity and relevance of their knowledge base.

9. A musem information strategy should embody a strategy for the use of people's ability and knowledge.

[2] For an example of these principles applied in practice to the development of a collections management system, see the article by Boast (1994) cited at the start of this chapter. (It makes the useful point, incidentally, that it is a great help in system development if museum staff actually like and respect each other both professionally and personally.)

References

BOAST, R. (1994), 'The construction of a community', *MDA Information*, 1 (2) 7–11

BOISOT, M. (1987), *Information and organizations. The manager as anthropologist,* HarperCollins

BURACK, E. H. *et al* (1994), 'New paradigm approaches in strategic human resources management', *Group and organization management,* 19 (2) 141–15.

DAVENPORT, T. H. *et al* (1992), 'Information politics', *Sloan Management Review,* Fall 53–65

DRUCKER, P. F. (1995), 'The information executives truly need', *Harvard Business Review,* Jan–Feb 55–62

GARRATT, B. (1994), *The Learning Organization,* HarperCollins

HEBRAIL, G. (1995), 'The SPHERE project: a step towards more sophisticated information systems' [a system for archiving and giving access to the history of the activities of Electricité de France Research Centre, and for improving communication between researchers], *Journal of Information Science,* 21 (6) 429–448

HUTTON, W. (1996), 'Priceless assets amount to folly', *The Guardian,* 11 March

ITAMI, H. with ROEHL, T. W. (1987), *Mobilizing Invisible Assets,* Cambridge, Mass: Harvard University Press

MACDONALD, S. & SILVERSTONE, R. (1990) *Rewriting the Museums' Fiction: Taxonomies, Stories and Readers,* CRICT Discussion Paper, Uxbridge: Brunel University Centre for Research into Innovation, Culture and Technology

PALMER, C. (1995), 'Lest we forget...,' *The Observer,* 8 January

Chapter 7

Using today's technology to help the people resource

Integrated management of the whole range of the museum's information

For as long as all information was recorded manually, an integrated information system was not a practicable goal. The time needed to analyse, evaluate and disseminate information manually meant that realistically only the most important information, such as that related to money, was so treated. Once computers became widely available to museums the whole climate of information handling changed, and changed fast.

The speed of this technological culture change can perhaps be illustrated by an anecdote. In 1980, the year in which the first edition of this book was published, Manchester Museum purchased its first 'in-house' piece of computing technology. This was a computerized typewriter which could be connected, via an audio-coupler modem (modulator/demodulator) and a telephone, to the University mainframe computer. Until then all data processing had involved a member of staff walking across a busy main road to the computer centre, and going to one of the 'computing labs' where, if lucky, a free teletype terminal (no visual display units, or what we now call 'monitors', in those days) would be found on which the database work could be done.

Therefore being able to access the database files from within the museum, albeit at the (today) incredibly slow data exchange rate of only ten characters a second, was considered to be a great advance! It is interesting to speculate what would have happened if the member of staff involved had said to his colleagues then that within a dozen years not only would they all have on their desks a computer with considerably more power than the mainframe we were then using, but that also they would each of them have purchased, from their own hard-earned money, a similar computer to use at home. If he had added that after only a further three years they would be routinely exchanging electronic messages and documents not only with their colleagues in the museum, but with those around the world, and doing it at speeds of thousands of characters a second, then it is fairly certain that they would have sent for medical assistance in the certain knowledge that their colleague had taken leave of his senses. See Manchester Museum case study in Part 2, p176.

But within 15 years, scarcely the blink of an eye in terms of human evolution, all the things listed above have come to pass! As Sim (1995) points out, today's personal computer has more processing, storage and display capacity for about £1000 than a mainframe computer costing £1 million in the late 1970s. This should give us pause when we attempt to plan for the next 15 years. One thing history teaches us is that it is probable that today's technical standards will be of little value tomorrow.

The power to retrieve

The relation between information and knowledge has been covered in Chapter 2. See p19. It is equally important to realize the difference between information and data. Data are the binary codes held within a computer; only when they are retrieved and output in human readable form, either on a screen or as a document, do data become information, capable of being the food of knowledge. Thus 5.55N 162.25W is merely a string of data to be manipulated and processed while in the memory of the computer; once output, it becomes the information that it is a latitude and longitude reference. But it only becomes knowledge when a human interprets this as meaning that the item in question came from Palmyra Island in the middle of the Pacific Ocean. The intellectual knowledge that this is the most northern known occurrence of the species concerned is interpretation of the information contained in the data, and requires correlation with all similar information known about the species.

However, binary data are useful servants, arguably as important an invention in human cultural evolution as Gutenberg's 'little lead soldiers' (moveable type). Data permit information in the computer to be sorted according to various classifications and to be indexed readily. Given the right software, complex nested indexes are simplicity itself to produce from a computer, and such re-organized data can greatly enhance the information content conveyed to the person reading the output.

But where data excel is in the ability they give to retrieve information selectively. Information on computer can be selected at will according to different criteria, and these selection, or search, criteria can be linked together by logical terms such as and, or, not, greater than, equal to, and so on. Only in the last decade or so has it been feasible to ask museum staff for information of the type: 'What items have you that were collected by Mr X before 1880 in South America?' Using manual systems such queries could be all but impossible to answer; with modern hardware and software the answer to this, or to even more complex enquiries, can be produced from a collection database in minutes, if not seconds.

The power to analyse

There are a number of advantages of holding museum information as computer files. The principal advantage is the ease with which the information can then be reorganized, analysed, selectively retrieved, and correlated with other files of information. Let us take the visitor figures mentioned above. These are usually recorded daily, and if that information is entered into a modern spreadsheet then it is simple for management to see the pattern of visits in various time-frames. Thus all the weeks can be compared, to see which days are consistently busier. (The staff on the galleries could probably tell you that, but could they quantify the effect of closing for a half-day each week, should that become necessary?) Once the power of this analysis tool is realized, it could well be that figures would be collected separately for morning or afternoon, or even hourly for a large and busy museum. Previously such detailed information would have been pointless as it would have been too voluminous to make much sense of.

Similarly, the figures can be analysed month on month, and as the database builds, can also give year-on-year comparisons. Then by linking to a separate spreadsheet giving details of all the public events in the gallery over the year graphs can be almost instantaneously thrown up to show graphically how much each event, such as a special exhibition, an open day or competing events outside the museum, affected the visitor response.

All the above tasks could have been done using the manual records, but they would have taken a lot of time, and would not necessarily have been error free. For these reasons such analysis was rarely done, and at most would consist of an impressionistic review of the figures. Using a computer program to do the work means that, once set up, the analysis can be done in seconds, and will be as detailed and accurate as the input figures permit. Finally, of course, it is simple to make the spreadsheet add the total for the year, ready for the annual report. But that report can also now include substantiated, quantifiable information about visitor trends and responses for the year, and even a graph or two imported directly from the spreadsheet, not only to impress the governing body, but also to enable it to manage more effectively.

The power to disseminate

Traditionally information has also been disseminated via exhibition guides and journal articles. Here again computerized databases can make the production of such material easier, by enabling the relevant information about items to be quickly retrieved, and slotted into a document being prepared for publication. This facility will become even more useful as more images are stored on the computer, so that they too can be quickly downloaded into a document for dissemination.

With intelligent, or knowledge-based, interfaces, it is no longer necessary for the curator to act as direct intermediary in an enquiry (Li, *et al*, 1995, 1996; Petch, *et al* 1995). Visitors, either physically present in the museum or virtually via the Internet, can, if given computer access, easily retrieve information about items of interest to them held in the collection.

The impact of the new technology

It must be recognized that new technology disrupts the routines and rituals of working practice, and may conflict with an individual's self-image. New technology systems impose structural changes within an organization (Somekh, 1995). Museum staff are more likely to work to implement change if they have been involved in the decision-making processes, therefore it is important that staff be fully consulted as part of the process of decision-making about new technology systems. See Chapter 6 p78.

Every effort must be made to reduce the extent to which new technology conflicts with the professional and cultural values of staff. Any new information system must be driven primarily by the needs of the museum, its staff and its clients, rather than being technology-led. In particular the views of the curatorial staff, and the needs of potential users of the collections, are of paramount importance. The IT specialists should be given explicitly clear roles and responsibilities within a new organizational structure.

The world, or a representation of it, is becoming digital, leisure is changing, with an ever wider spectrum of interests, and multi-media is becoming prevalent in many areas of work, education and leisure. Museums need to try to understand the different markets for these technologies, products and services, in order to invest in the right technologies and products at the right time (American Council of Learned Societies, 1993; Omerod, 1995).

The Internet, the World Wide Web and the information superhighway

The Internet started in 1969 with just four computers connected together by the United States Defense Department, and has grown exponentially until today there are getting on for 35 million users, with thousands more joining every day. The Internet is merely the interconnection of many separate local, regional and national networks, but allows any user connected to one network to contact a user or a resource on any other network. The 'information superhighway' is just a subset of the networks within the Internet that have physical connections capable of carrying fast communications (155 million bits of information a second is typical), with a wide bandwidth for images, full video or even 3D virtual reality, and that can also cope with full bi-directional interactivity (see Figure 7.1 on p96). Not many of the current Internet connections can do this yet, but the superhighway links are also growing daily, and soon most users will be able to access it. The World Wide Web (WWW) is one of the major protocol-based utilities available on the Internet, just as electronic mail, or email, is another. Various navigation programs are available for browsing (or 'surfing') the WWW, and these are constantly being updated and improved (Barron *et al*, 1996; Tseng *et al*, 1996). Further information about museums and the Internet can be found on-line at http://www.cidoc.icom.org, the site of the International Committee for Documentation of the International Council of Museums (ICOM-CIDOC).

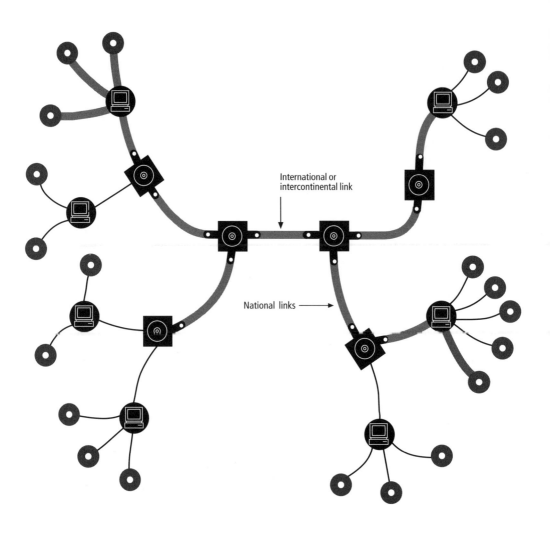

International or
intercontinental link

National links →

Legend

= large computers acting as main switches or routers

← = Fibre optic 'superhighway' (may be specially configured
twisted-pair between local switch and user)

= computers acting as local switches or routers

← = lower speed copper wire connections

= users, client machines. All can access the Internet,
but only those with fast fibre optic connections can
use the information superhighway

The Internet, and the information superhighway, present museums with a unique opportunity to reach broad and narrow, local and international, publics in new ways. For the first time museums are freed from their inherent localism, the physicality that requires their users to be in-person visitors. Reasonable projections suggest that within a few years, most potential museum clients will be able to be an electronic visitor (Bearman, 1995A, B).

For example, in Manchester Museum one database, the Bryozoa, which-some may say is not the most exciting group of animals, was made available on the World Wide Web. Within one month the database had been visited by several hundred people from over two dozen countries, numerous searches had been done (the computer log shows who searched for what terms), and two research loan requests generated. Similar responses have been found when databases on other collections, in different disciplines, were released on the Web. A useful guide to museums on the Web has been compiled on-line by Jonathan Bowen at Oxford (1995); it may be located at the URL (Uniform Resource Locator): http://www.icom.org/vlmp.

However, Bearman (1995A) points out that while each museum considers its holdings to be unique, and at some level this is true, for many purposes cultural heritage holdings are interchangeable from the perspective of most users. Ultimately it will be those who provide successful, value-added services who will benefit, rather than the holders of the objects. He adds that the lesson of the industrial society may have to be re-learned; those who depend on the export of raw materials will not prosper. The more raw material there is available the more it must be mediated, by being surrounded by indexing and interpretation in depth; museums will increasingly be regarded as information centres (Will, 1994).

On the Internet especially, people do not want the things in themselves, they want the meanings they convey. For instance, the associations which gave the object its local relevance must be emphasized over those which give it more universal relevance. The Canadian Heritage Information Network (CHIN) has recently been examining how best to reach the public through electronic products and services, and Sherwood (1995) gives the results of their brainstorming, particularly ways in which institutions can protect their investment in the preparation of material in electronic form.

It is imperative to understand the dynamics of pricing information on to-day's networks and the emerging information highways (Mitchell, 1995). When looking at the usage of on-line information, it is important to know not only how many people looked at it, but how long they spent and what actions they took, such as downloading or interrogating (Lowderbaugh, 1995). It is possible that Broadie (1995) is right in stating that on the superhighway in the future one will buy services not content, just as on television one buys channels not programmes. For most users, however, content is likely to be more important than who supplies the information, and the Museum with a better offering on the WWW will find people beating a path to their (virtual) door. The main arguments about the superhighway will concern access, cost (who will pay, and how much), applications (for what it may be used) and, to some extent, regulation (Stubbs, 1995). Lifelong learning is increasingly the norm and providing distance-learning resources will offer many opportunities for museums (Bearman, 1995B, Ya, 1995).

A potential inhibitor of the mass uptake of information services in galleries and on the Internet is the difficulties which non-technically minded people can experience in coping with the interface software, and designing a really user-friendly interface for public use is one of the major challenges a museum (or other information service provider) has to face (Sim, 1995). Experience has shown that many people have difficulty with phrasing precise enquiries using Boolean logic, e.g. 'this and this, or this, but not that'. Jones et al (1995) point out that general queries for a topographic region such as 'the Vale of Evesham' imply the need for systems to be able to reason with knowledge of the structure of space, and must be capable of being combined with conceptual reasoning allied to classes of information, and with temporal reasoning allied to descriptions of time based on quantitative dates or on qualitative temporal categories related to historical periods and events such as 'World War II'. Such 'knowledge-based interfaces' are being developed, particularly using the burgeoning geographical information systems (GIS) that are becoming available.

Setting up a Web service
Museums wishing to establish a presence on the Internet are most likely to do this by setting up a series of 'pages' on a World Wide Web server. A Web server is a dedicated computer running special software, and naturally needs to be joined to the Internet. However, because of the expense and complications (such as obtaining a 'domain name') of setting up and maintaining such a server, most small or medium-sized museums would be well advised to explore the possibility of putting their pages on an existing Web server, such as one run by their governing body, or by a local academic institution or well-disposed local business.

If a museum decides to set up its own Web server then there are several textbooks available which provide the technical information required; examples are Chandler, 1995, and Ford and Dixon, 1996. Up-to-date information is available at the CIDOC Website mentioned above. There are some pitfalls to be aware of in preparing pages for the WWW. One is that visual design is very important in conveying a good impression of the providing institution. Input from a trained designer should be used wherever possible.

If you provide information that is wrong, and someone acts on it to their detriment, you can be liable for negligence. This can even apply if the wrong advice is not on your home Web site but on one to which yours provides a link (Miller, 1996). As a result, most Web sites now carry disclaimers; liabilities for causing death or personal injury cannot be excluded, but it is to be hoped this is unlikely to arise from the type of information provided by most museums. Note, however that Web site owners will be liable as publishers if their site contains defamatory material. It is most important that a staff member is appointed as 'Webmaster' and made responsible for all the Web pages put up by the museum.

Extending the range of information through newer technology

Image databases

Much work has been done on how best to set up image databases (Black, 1993; Bordogna, *et al*, 1990; Cawkell, 1993A–E; Holt & Hartwick, 1994; Lewis & Draycott, 1993; McCorry & Rees, 1995). Tony Cawkell's series of articles on image processing in particular cover the development of image databases. He points out that, from the first, indexing has been consistently ignored. Yet it is a crucial problem, and how well or badly it is solved will condition the power, freedom and satisfaction with which people are able to use interactive systems which incorporate image databases. As Cawkell says, systems of indexing which aim to match actual image content depend on image recognition, which is still in its infancy. One model is the Micro Gallery at the National Gallery in London (Martin, 1992) which used the gallery's resources of curatorial knowledge in the preparatory stages to anticipate 'ways in' and paths through the information store that would help users make decisions and find what they want. The system is essentially a combination of well thought-out 'traditional' information structuring, sorted by thematic groupings and comprehensive indexes, with sophisticated technology that uses the potential of hyper-media in a very accessible way.

Creative use of digital-imaging technology has the potential to change the nature of teaching and research, two prime functions of museums (Besser and Trant, 1995). It is now possible to examine rare and fragile objects without handling them or moving them from the secure controlled-climate environment of the museum store. However, before a museum can build an image database it must first generate a store of digital images.

Digital images are made up of pixels (picture elements) rather as a newspaper picture is composed of printed dots. The pixels are arranged in rows and columns, and the number present in each defines the *resolution* of the image. The higher the resolution (ie the more pixels used) the greater the detail an image can convey. Each pixel can be a shade of grey for black-and-white images, or represent a particular shade of a colour. The number of shades of grey or of colours available on the system in use determines the *dynamic range* of the image. In a *true-colour* image each pixel can represent any one of 16 million colours, but this requires a great deal of storage space. A more restricted palette, taking up less space, can be used, where each pixel can have only 256 variations of shade or colour.

Digital images are created either by recording the item on film and then scanning in the picture so formed, or else by capturing the image directly with a digital camera; prints, documents and other flat items can sometimes be scanned in directly without going through a photographic stage. With digital video cameras becoming available, it should in future be possible to 'grab' good-quality images from a video recording using a video frame-grabber card in the computer.

As mentioned elsewhere, image files take up a lot of storage space on a computer. This space can be reduced by compressing the image, using specialist software that either combines repeated pixels or by deleting parts of the image that would not be visible to the naked eye. However, for a user to view an image that has been compressed in the first way they must have the right de-compression program, which can restrict the utility of compressed images made available across the Internet.

Irrespective of how the image is created and stored, its appearance to the user will also depend on the resolution of the monitor (again measured in pixels) used to view it, or of the dots-per-inch (DPI) resolution of the printer used to prepare a paper copy. Naturally, the images will need to be accompanied by text to explain and index them, and this will require a database management system that can also handle images.

With the rise of the superhighway the routine dissemination of three-dimensional and 'walk-through' images is becoming increasingly possible (Strimpel, 1995). Paul (1995) gives a brief overview of the available technologies for 3-D geometry data acquisition, with special attention to image-based methods; he pays special attention to the perspective of the non-technical user. Geschke (1995) discusses some of the fundamental issues about incorporating 3-D images in a multi-media presentation. These are why the 3-D information is required, where in the overall concept of the presentation the 3-D element is to be incorporated, and how the incorporation of these elements is to be achieved.

Multi-media and the visualization of data

Multi-media presentations are those that include text, images and sound in a single program (Bearman, 1994B). On the Internet the text is usually hypertext, that is, text written in hypertext markup language (HTML), where various words and phrases can be flagged with links to other parts of the text, allowing a user to jump around within the program in a non-linear way. Such link words are usually shown in a different colour, and HTML also permits text to be highlighted, or for it to flash to attract attention. It is recommended that anyone contemplating becoming involved with the design of such hyper-media presentations attends a short course on HTML if possible, as this will give an understanding of the potential and the limitations of hypertext. Conventional multi-media presentations are usually based on the Apple Hyper-card, and achieve a similar result to those using HTML.

The images may be still pictures, or moving video clips, and be presented at once or only after a user has 'clicked here' with the cursor. The latter is preferable for presentations on the Internet, because downloading images can take a considerable time and it is better that the user has the choice whether to do so rather than being forced to wait while all the images are received. Sound can consist of, for example, bird song, a voice-over from a curator explaining the background to an object, a piece of music, or the sound of a machine operating. Thus, for example, on the *Images of War – the real story of World War II* CD-ROM, produced by a commercial firm with the assistance of the Imperial War Museum there are more than 1000 original pictures, 100 eyewitness accounts, map sequences of the big battles and 30 minutes of contemporary film. Information comes from narration, still images, video clips, changing text boxes and frequent ticker-tape messages. Data are cross-referenced on screen – a click and you can see the specification of the aircraft used to bomb Coventry. One can navigate one's own way through the information, or be taken on chronological journeys through each battle. Also included are profiles of wartime leaders, text of key speeches, and explanations of tactics (Glaskin, 1995). This represents a very good example of what can be achieved with one museum's resources.

Multi-media offers exciting possibilities to museums, but compiling a multi-media presentation is a resource-hungry process, and the specialist knowledge required is non-trivial (Bearman, 1994B). Therefore it is recommended that most museums, particularly small and medium-sized ones, which are contemplating such a move should do so in collaboration either with a consortium of museums jointly able to provide the skills, money and time required, or else with one of the many specialist multi-media publishing firms. If the latter course is adopted, the usual caveats apply of first thoroughly exploring the market before choosing a firm (one that has worked successfully with another museum is to be preferred), of striking a deal that minimizes the financial risk to the museum (museums should not be risk-taking organizations), and making sure that intellectual rights stay firmly with the museum (Wright, 1995).

Cooper (1995) compares interactive multi-media with face-to-face education in museums; interestingly he calculates that the cost per visitor contact hour is almost identical for the two methods of dissemination, though the cost of multi media can be reduced by providing several identical units.

Copyright issues

Copyright on the Internet
As noted by Lawrence (1995, quoted in Stewart, 1995) the sheer scale of the Internet takes the copyright problem into another dimension: 'it is like a vast, unattended shopping mall, full of goods that are freely available, or at best tied down by the flimsiest of knots'. Legal experts consider that the transition from analogue to digital information does not require a wholesale rethinking of copyright laws, but rather an adaptation of existing laws to this new environment (Rees, 1995). However, copyright of electronic information about muse-

um objects is a complex issue that may not be sorted out quickly (O'Brian & Goodrick, 1995). Rees (1995) quotes another author: 'we do need to think about intellectual property in a new way ... how we define these properties, how we value them, how we protect them, and how we exploit them'. When objects are borrowed from another institution, it is important to realize that permission to use them in a gallery display does not automatically confer the right to use them on the Web (O'Brian & Goodrick, 1995). Most museums own very little of what they think they own in copyright terms, so really the issue is not so much copyright as who controls access.

Rees (1995) points out that what one does with information or images is important. Bringing up an image from a CD or the Internet is one thing; downloading that image into a file on your own computer is another. Downloading an image and using it for your Christmas card is yet another, and altering the integrity of the image before so doing is something different again. If you then go on to sell the image in the market place, that is yet another situation.

Copyright, Designs and Patents Act 1988
In the UK this Act governs copyright law; similar laws now apply in most other western countries. Under the Act violating the copyright of computer software is a civil and in some circumstances a criminal offence. The following information is taken from the *Library Association Guidelines: Copyright in industrial and commercial libraries,* but the information applies equally to museums. Neither 'computer' nor 'program' is defined in the Act, but computer programs are included in the definition of 'literary works' and this remains true whatever the physical format of a program: printed matter, tape or disk. The Act makes it clear that 'storing the work in any medium by electronic means' is an infringement (s.17(2)). Any copying or adapting of a program is also illegal unless made incidentally in the course of running the program (s.21(4)). Thus computer programs should not be copied without permission; the Act does not even give statutory permission to make back-up copies of programs, though in practice it is the standard and recommended procedure for which permission is usually given by the program producers. Back-up rights may become part of the next version of the Act, however.

The contents of databases are also literary works and protected by copyright. If made accessible to the public on-line they become 'cable programmes' under the Act, and the on-line database becomes a 'cable service'. Separate copyright exists in the service itself for any such programme, for 50 years from the date it is first put on-line. Downloading from an on-line database is permitted only under the terms of the licence from the database owner. However, provided the public is not charged for admission to wherever the showing is taking place, public showing of a cable programme is allowed. This would seem to mean that, unless it is specifically forbidden by the licence, a museum could make publicly available on-line databases from other sources, but for viewing only, not downloading, provided the museum makes no admission charge.

Copyright and CD-ROMs

CD-ROMs are not made available via a telecommunications system and are therefore not cable programme services. They have no copyright as far as physical format is concerned, but the compiler will have 'literary works' copyright to databases, programs and images thereon; thus the copyright on CD-ROMs is much more akin to that for books.

Protecting copyright

All versions of any publicly available museum-generated information should carry an international copyright declaration: '(C) The XXX Museum'. Where the museum is not a corporate entity in its own right, then the copyright holders should be shown as the governing body, such as 'The Trustees of the Museum' or 'The Metropolitan Council' etc. This should appear on all printed and electronic versions. With CD-ROMs it should appear both on the wrapper and in the electronic information on the disk. If a CD-ROM is sold, the conditions of sale should stipulate the circumstances under which downloading or copying is allowed. It is important to inform users about their precise rights regarding the information they can download from an on-line server (Michard, 1995). In reviewing data-protection techniques for on-line information, he adds that 'absolute security can never be offered by any artificial system, and the highest security levels will only be obtained at a cost, and by limiting the freedom and comfort of users'.

Although the museum may not own the legal copyright to a picture or photograph despite owning the object itself, protecting images from unauthorized copying is likely to become very important in the near future, as museums vie to release image databases on the Internet. One way to protect the image from 'grabbing' for unauthorized reproduction is only to put up thumb-nail, low resolution images. These would be sufficient for a potential user (customer) to establish which images they need, but if downloaded and enlarged would be of insufficient resolution for realistic publication. The user would have to contact the museum to obtain a high-resolution image, either as a photograph or in electronic form, transmitted directly to the user after payment. Images can be further protected by pixel inversion watermarking; the pixel is the smallest unit used to build the image on screen, and programs are available that will invert two or more pixels within the image. Such inversion is not apparent to the naked eye, but if an image is downloaded and used in breach of copyright, the rightful owner can demonstrate the watermark to prove the provenance of the image.

Creative interactions of humans and technology in museums

A recent report (Francis et al, 1992) from the UK Arts Council endorsed the potential of interactive multi-media in museums but warns that while 'interactive is one of the most liberating and powerful devices that we can give to our museum visitors' it is not 'enlightenment itself … and can easily be abused and exploited'. Orna (1993) considers that visitors using interactive access points need to be able to:

- Get into the information, through entry points that they themselves choose
- Move around it freely – by routes they determine, and to the depths they want
- Move on easily from the interaction into the collection to see the objects in the light of knowledge gained, and to extend this knowledge further.

They will not be helped by:

- Over-visible technology at the interface
- Under-developed hyper-media products offering an over-friendly welcome, with loads of buttons and menus, behind which lurks precious little information, and that so poorly structured that it is hard to navigate around
- An absence of links between the interactive system and the museum's 'invisible stores' of knowledge and information.

Physical factors are also important, such as whether people with different abilities can access the interactive system. Pickles (1995) gives a number of useful points on this, such as the fact that for wheelchair-bound people the range of comfortable forward reach is only as far as the line of the front of the footrest, and that semi-sighted people find it easier to read well-contrasted, sans serif, mixed-case lettering.

Thus several inter-related factors seem to be necessary if interactive access is to deliver the goods. There must be full and efficient management of the information embodied in the objects, using the knowledge of the museum staff. Unless this condition is met, any interactive public access system will be pretending to be what it is not, no matter how sophisticated the interface. Clear, detailed objectives for public access to information must be defined, related to the museum's mission, objectives and priorities. The public access system must be integrated into the museum's total development plan, and should contribute to, and not distort, overall developments. It is particularly important to see that the staff concerned with the public access system should not be seen (or see themselves) as separate from the rest of the museum's staff. Then the technology and its method of use should be selected on the principle that it should give access to the collection in new and useful ways not possible by other methods, and that it helps users see new things and make connections they would otherwise overlook. It is important that the technology is developed by people able to reach understanding with those who manage the collections, but who understand the conceptual problems of access associated with multi-media. Users must be empowered to control how they use the museum's resources, but this does not mean they no longer need support from the people who work there.

Interactive displays and Internet presentations should always include options for feedback; the questions of students and casual visitors can furnish frameworks for future presentations (Bearman, 1995B). Anderson (1995) points out that the World Wide Web enables the involvement of otherwise passive recipients of information, and allows the creativity of the public at large to be tapped. His suggestions include a virtual membership category for those who develop an ongoing interest in the museum's affairs, an interactive children's newsletter with bounce-back games and puzzles, and on-line auditoria with members of the museum staff and visiting international experts. The Smithsonian Institution provides message boards to enable people who share interests to find and communicate with each other, has real-time events which give people the chance to speak with Smithsonian experts, offers reference services to allow users to query Smithsonian experts and to receive authoritative answers, and provides email facilities for people to tell the Institution what they want (Lowderbaugh, 1995).

Summary

The essential points of this chapter:

1. Information technology can greatly increase the power of museums to retrieve, analyse and disseminate information.

2. The Internet is rapidly becoming an important channel of access to museums, and the various logistical, ethical and legal problems it presents must be addressed.

3. Interactive displays or on-line services must be designed to give access in new and useful ways, and to empower users to control how they use the museum's resources; support from museum staff will still be essential.

References

ANDERSON, M. L. (1995), 'The museum director's perspective', in FAHY, A. & SUDBURY, W. op. cit. 155–165

American Council of Learned Societies & J. Paul Getty Trust (1993), Technology, Scholarship and the Humanities: the implications of electronic inform-ation ..., Conference held at Santa Monica, CA, in 1992, Getty Art History Information Program, ISBN 0 9632792 1 1

BARRON, B, ELLSWORTH, J. H. & SAVETZ, K. (eds) (1996), The Internet Unleashed 1996, Indianapolis, in: SAMS Net, ISBN 0 57521 041 X

BEARMAN, D. (1994A), 'Automating the future', Museum International, 46 (1) 38–41

BEARMAN, D. (1994B), Hypermedia and Interactivity in Museums, Proceedings of an International Conference, 1991, 1994

BEARMAN, D. (1995A), 'Museum strategies for success on the Internet', in Museum collections and the information superhighway: a one-day conference held at the science museum on 10 May 1995, London: Science Museum, 15–27

BEARMAN, D. (1995B), 'Information strategies and structures for electronic museums', in FAHY, A. & SUDBURY, W. op. cit. 5–22

BESSER, H.& TRANT, J. (1995), Introduction to Imaging: issues in constructing an image database, Santa Monica, CA: Getty Art History Information Program (available on-line at http://ww.ahip.getty.edu/intro imaging/)

BLACK, K. (1993), 'ELISE – an on-line image retrieval system', Aslib Information, 21 (7/8) 293–295

BORDOGNA, G. et al (1990), 'A system architecture for multi-media information retrieval', Journal of Information Science, 16 229–238

BOWEN, J. (1995), 'The World Wide Web Virtual Library of museums', Information Services & Use, 15: 317–324

BROADIE, R. (1995), 'New literacy and the expectations of young people', in FAHY, A. & SUDBURY, W. op. cit. 339–342

CAWKELL, A. E. (1993A), 'Imaging systems and picture collection management: a review', Information Services and Use, 12 301–325

CAWKELL, A. E. (1993B),'Developments in indexing picture collections', Information Services and Use, 13 381–338

CAWKELL, A. E. (1993C), 'Picture-queries and picture databases', Journal of Information Science, 19 409–423

CAWKELL, A. E. (1993D), 'An introduction to image processing and picture management', Journal of Documentation and Text Management, 1 (1) 53–64

CAWKELL, A. E. (1993E),'Visual arts, multi-media publishing and on-line picture databases', IT Link, November 2–3

CHANDLER, D. M. (1995), Running a Perfect Website, Indianapolis, Que Corporation, ISBN 0 7897 0210 X

COOPER, J. (1995), 'A Comparison of Interactive Multi-media and Face-to-Face Education in Museums', in FAHY, A. & SUDBURY, W. op. cit. 343–348

FAHY, A. & SUDBURY, W. (1995), Information, The Hidden Resource, Museums and the Internet, Proceedings of a conference held in Edinburgh, Cambridge: Museum Documentation Association, 424pp

FORD, A. & DIXON, T. (1996), Spinning the Web. How to provide information on the Internet, 2nd edn. London: International Thomson Publishing, ISBN 1 85032 290 2

FRANCIS, R. et al. (1992), Very spaghetti. The potential of multi-media in art galleries, London: Arts Council

GESCHKE, A. (1995), '3D: Who needs it?', in FAHY, A.& SUDBURY, W. op. cit. 295–304

GLASKIN, M. (1995), 'Images of War', The Times, 25 August

HOLT, B. & HARTWICK, L. (1994), 'Retrieving art images by image content: the UC DAVIS QBIC project', Aslib Proceedings, 46 (10) 243–248

JONES, C. B., BEYNON-DAVIES, P., TAYLOR, C. & TUDHOPE, D. (1995), 'GIS, Hypermedia and Historical Information Access', in FAHY, A. & SUDBURY, W. op. cit. 109–113

LAWRENCE, A. (1995), 'Publish and be robbed', New Scientist, 18 February

LEWIS, M. & DRAYCOTT, C. (1993),'The retrieval, display and publishing opportunities for a visual database', Information Services and Use, 13 371–379

LI, C. S., MOSS, A., PETCH, J., COLE, K., YIP, J., JOHNSON., A., KITMITTO, K. & BASDEN, A. (1995) 'Acessing large and coplex datasets, *via* WWW', *Pre-Proceedings of seminar on New Technologies for Statistics (NTTSAE 95).* Nov 20–22, 1995, Bonn: 395–402

LI, C. S., BREE, D., MOSS, A. & PETCH, J. (1996), 'Developing Internet-based user interfaces for spatial data access and usability', *Proceedings NCGIA 3rd International Conference / Workshop on Integrating Geographical Information Systems and Environmental Modelling,* Jan 21–25, Santa Fe, USA, 350–358

LOWDERBAUGH, T.E. (1995), 'Smithsonian on-line: The Virtual Museum as Community Center', *in* FAHY, A. & SUDBURY, W. *op. cit.* 169–174

MARTIN, D. (1992), 'Multi-media milestone', *Museums Journal,* August 36

McCORRY, H. & REES, J. (1995), 'The Item (image technology in museums and art galleries) Database', *Managing Information,* 2 (3) 40–42

MICHARD, A. (1995), 'Data protection techniques for on-line information dissemination', *in* FAHY, A. & SUDBURY, W. *op. cit.* 283–284

MILLER, N. (1996), 'The pitfalls of cyberspace', *Financial Times,* 30 April

MITCHELL, H. (1995), 'Information for Profit? Pricing your Wares for the Information Highways', *in* FAHY, A. & SUDBURY, W. *op. cit.* 261–265

O'BRIAN, C. & GOODRICK, G. (1995), 'Flints and stones', *in Museum Collections and the Information Superhighway: a one-day conference held at the Science Museum on 10th May 1995,* London: Science Museum, 49–50

OMEROD, P. (1995) 'The strategic impact of emerging technologies on the museum sector', *in* FAHY, A. & SUDBURY, W. *op. cit.* 405–411

ORNA, E. (1993), 'Interaction: Liberation or Exploitation?', *Museums Journal,* February 27–28

PAUL, L. (1995), 'Computer-aided methods for 3-D measurement and modelling in culture applications', *in* FAHY, A. & SUDBURY, W. *op. cit.* 285–294

PETCH, J., MOSS, A., JOHNSON, A., YIP, J., BASDEN, A., LI, C. S., COLE, K. & KITMITTO, K. (1995), 'Knowledge Based Interfaces for National Data Sets: The KINDS project', *Pre-proceedings of Seminar on New Technologies for Statistics (NTTSAE 95),* Nov 20–22, Bonn: 342–352

PICKLES, R. (1995), 'A member of the public with a disability', *in* FAHY, A. & SUDBURY, W. *op. cit.* 87–90

REES, J. (1995), 'Intellectual property issues', *in Museum Collections and the Information Superhighway: a one-day conference held at the Science Museum on 10th May 1995.* London: Science Museum, 53–55

SHERWOOD, L. E. (1995), 'The Canadian heritage information network', *Museum Collections and the Information Superhighway: a one-day conference held at the Science Museum on 10th May 1995,* London: Science Museum, 29–34

SIM, S. (1995), 'The Information Superhighway', *in Museum Collections and the Information Superhighway: a one-day conference held at the Science Museum on 10th May 1995,* London: Science Museum, 9–13

SOMEKH, B. (1995), 'Dilemmas of managing technological change: the impact of new technology on the motivation and job satisfaction of people who work in museums', *in* FAHY, A. and SUDBURY, W. *op. cit.* 229–233

STEWART, J. (1995), 'Where is the knowledge we have lost in information?', *in* FAHY, A. and SUDBURY, W. *op. cit.* 419–423

STRIMPEL, O. (1995), 'Museums on-line: Worth the Visit?' *in* Fahy, A. & Sudbury, W. *op. cit.* 181–185

STUBBS, J. F. L. (1995), 'The 4th Information Revolution', *in* Fahy, A. & Sudbury, W. *op. cit.* 311–322

TSENG, G., POULTER, A. & HIOM, D. (1996), *The Library and Information Professional's Guide to the Internet,* London: Library Association Publishing. ISBN 1 05004 151 4

WILL, L.D. (1994), 'Museums as information centres', *Museum International,* 46 (1) 20–25

WRIGHT, P. (1995), 'A strategic approach to multi-media: three roles for the museum', *in* Fahy, A. & Sudbury, W. *op. cit.* 131–137

YAPP, C. (1995), 'Preparing for the information society: making life long learning a reality', *in* Fahy, A. & Sudbury, W. *op. cit.* 373–379

Chapter 8

Procuring and installing a computerized information management system

Agreeing the data standards

Before making any decision on what software to purchase, it is essential to have agreed the data standards to be used, particularly for any collection management package that would probably form the major investment in the system. Developing and agreeing the data standards should be started as early in the process as possible, and certainly immediately after the information audit. See Chapter 5 p68.

Fortunately today for items in the collection much of the work is covered by SPECTRUM, which identifies most of the types of information that should be recorded. However, thesauri of agreed terms, and deciding on the exact syntax to be used, are still significant tasks for the information manager, hopefully backed by a group of interested curators.

A decision must be made at this stage whether to enhance the primary data available with items, for example by adding country of origin where not recorded in the existing documentation, or sort/search codes to permit hierarchical organizing or retrieval (Pettitt, 1990). Most sequences of classification terms are not usually arranged alpha-numerically; for example, with the geological succession Cambrian, Ordovician, Silurian, Devonian, Carboniferous, Permian ... Tertiary, sorting alphabetically would place the first three terms in the correct order, but then the rest would be slotted in to form a geologically meaningless jumble. Any listing arranged this way would be frustrating for a geologist to use, and certainly would not help to impress them with the utility of the new information system. The problem can be overcome by using codes to 'force the sort'. Thus if Cambrian fossils are coded G0, Ordovician ones G1, and so on, then a sort on the field containing these codes would correctly order the entries into the accepted geological sequence. Whether, and if so how, such secondary information is flagged are further important decisions; such flagging is ethically desirable to prevent distant users being misled as to the provenance of presented information. An Association of Systematics Collections report (Anon., 1992) gives a broad spectrum of views on data sharing and ethics that can inform in-house database design. Data standards are also required for any non-collection-based projects, such as administrative or financial information, within the full information system.

Data standards manuals

A complete data standard for a museum will form a substantial reference work, and a copy should be available to everyone concerned with the computerization scheme. Incidentally, the full SPECTRUM data standard can be made available on-line under Windows. It is a good idea, however, to provide cataloguers with a summary of the standards relevant to their particular project; this will save time searching for information in the full manual and, much more importantly, will increase the probability of the standards being adhered to during data entry. If possible, the essentials should be reduced to a single sheet of paper so that the cataloguer can see everything at a glance. Such a 'mini-manual' can carry short lists of codes or preferred terms, but for some projects it will have to be supplemented by term lists or a thesaurus. Organizing these can form a major task for most museums, especially those containing large ethnography or social history collections; the RAF Museum case study demonstrates the emphasis that may be given to thesaurus capability when specifying the system. See the RAF Museum case study, p232.

Data-entry instructions should be kept as simple and unambiguous as possible. Controlled vocabularies should be restricted to those fields from which it is intended to generate an index, or which will be retrieved using a logical search engine. A sophisticated collection management software package should permit much of the standard, particularly term-lists, to be incorporated and available on-line while inputting or editing data.

Choosing and purchasing a computer system

Once the decision has been made to use a computer system to manage the museum's information, then a range of further decisions have to be made. If the governing body has an IT section some of these decisions may already have been taken, but not all.

People available

What expertise is available to manage the information resources? Someone within the museum should be identified as the information manager, even if the IT expertise is to be bought in, or supplied by the organization to which the museum belongs. The manager must be fully conversant with what the museum wants to achieve using the system, and will normally have been responsible for devising the information strategy; they already should be an experienced museum professional. If the identified manager has no previous experience in information handling then some training will be required. This may be possible by secondment to the relevant section of a large museum with a well-developed information service. What IT expertise is available? Note that this differs from the expertise needed to manage the system. The IT person (who may, of course, sometimes be the same person as the information manager) is responsible at the technical level for achieving those objectives, providing the technical infrastructure and support. What cataloguing/keyboarding skills and time are available in-house? – or can be bought in? If employing staff specifically for data entry, it is strongly recommended that a practical test is performed as well as a normal interview; experience has shown that otherwise strong candidates can prove unable to follow a simple set of cataloguing rules for a small selection of typical items. Accuracy and consistency tend to be innate and are difficult to teach, but are vital if the quality of the finished product is to be acceptable.

Other resources available

What hardware or software does the museum already own that could be applied to the new information system? What upgrade paths are available? How much data is already in the existing system? Is it manual or computerized? The information audit, see Chapter 5, will provide this information.

Having got the system agreed, don't be in too much of a rush to procure the hardware and software. Larger museums may opt to employ outside consultants, such as the CCTA (the Government Centre for Information Systems), to do a strategic review of the museum's IT management, systems and future needs (Roberts, 1996). The objectives of such a review should be:

- To identify a systems strategy to meet the museum's information needs
- To provide options for the delivery of the systems strategy
- To define a migration path from the current strategy, including an assessment of staff and resources.

This review should lead to the acquisition process; the CCTA methodology (TAP or the Total Acquisition Process) could be followed with advantage; even smaller museums may find it informative to examine TAP (CCTA, 1995). See also the case studies at the end of the book on the Large Scale Systems Initiative (LASSI) (Grant and Marshall, 1996) p170, the RAF Museum p232, and the V&A Museum p259, for examples of actual procurement exercises.

For most museums a simpler version of this process is more appropriate (and affordable), but make sure that the market is fully explored before placing a firm order. When obtaining quotations for hardware or software it is most important that one compares 'like for like'. Therefore each company being requested to quote should be asked the same comprehensive questions, and their answers carefully collated and cross-checked with each other before arriving at a decision to purchase.

Software choice and procurement

Nowadays the cost of sophisticated software (the computer programs to run on the system), or of multiple licences for even fairly basic application packages such as word processors, can cost almost as much as the total spent on the machines, or hardware. The first advice is do not contemplate creating your own in-house system, even if you happen to have a keen and expert programmer on the staff. Numerous museums have gone down this road in the past, most attempts ended in tears, and pretty well all of them have now migrated their data to a commercial package. Remember that while this 'expert' is programming your system, they are not doing whatever job it was the museum employed them to do, which is a real cost even if a replacement is not employed for the duration. And that may be a long time, a year or more not being uncommon before an in-house attempt even staggers into use. And what happens when your 'expert' leaves? It will be almost impossible for anyone else to support the system, which invariably is left with minimal documentation. The major advantages of a package-based approach include:

- A shorter timescale to be fully operational
- Opportunity to adopt a proven system
- The ability to provide mutual support by establishing common interests with other users of the package.

So the choice lies in which commercial package to buy. There are multitudinous spreadsheets, word processors and database management packages (DBMS) on the market, as a cursory glance at any computing magazine will show. These are mostly quite economical to buy and install, but, for example, all the DBMS then require you to define the field structure for your records, and to make any relational links yourself. Support, though available, will only be to the package itself; no advice on using it for museum operations is available from the vendor. If you decide to use such a package, then try to pick one that is already in use in a few other museums, and which has an active user group to offer help.

However, if you wish to do more than relatively simple indexing and retrieval of collection item records, then a more sophisticated museum collection management package is required. These are considerably more expensive than a straight DBMS, but they usually come pre-configured with SPECTRUM – compliant fields, and some have built-in thesauri. These will not cope with financial budgeting, nor will they do statistical analysis at present, but it is fairly straightforward to export data to a spreadsheet or other statistical package to do such analysis.

The market in software is developing as rapidly as that in hardware, and so it is not sensible to make specific recommendations in a book. To find out what packages are available and suitable for museum use, one option is to contact the information specialist at a large regional or national museum in your country, who will certainly be aware of what packages are currently available, and more importantly, their strengths and weaknesses and which are in use in museums world-wide. In the UK, contact the Museum and Galleries Commission and the Museum Documentation Association, who will be able to offer this advice. On-going support is all important with such a vital part of the system as the collections management package, so again be inclined towards the package(s) that are already up and running at museums with whom you have close relationships, and for which an active mutual-help user-group is already in place. When deciding which package to adopt, the first task is to decide on the objectives it is desired to meet. Recently the Museum of London (MoL) decided its objectives were to:

- Establish and control a comprehensive inventory of the collections, to demonstrate accountability
- Develop catalogue information about the collections
- Improve the efficiency and effectiveness of collections management procedures
- Improve the management of conservation processes
- Provide facilities to incorporate and use images from the collection
- Incorporate elements of the archaeological archive into the core collection.

This is quite a comprehensive list, but your museum may feel the need to add other objectives. When the objectives have been agreed, an operational requirement (OR) should be drawn up for circulation to the vendors of specialized packages. The OR should cover documentation standards, for example whether compliance is required with SPECTRUM and with the International Guidelines for Museum Object Information: the CIDOC Information Categories (*see* http://www.cidoc.icom.org). The OR should also encompass the functional requirements, and these should be categorized as mandatory or desirable. LASSI provides a good exemplar of an OR (Keene, 1995); some of the requirements were:

Mandatory:
- A report writer to generate user-defined reports
- In data entry, allowing the use of short codes to be expanded to full terms
- Supporting the full variety of different forms of museum numbers.

Desirable:
- Ability to produce completed forms, such as for object entry, dispatch, loan agreements, etc., ready for signature
- In data entry, defaulting to choice of imperial or metric measurement units, with automatic conversion of one to the other
- Manipulation of separate elements of accession numbers, and recording superseded object identity numbers.

Even if one is going to adapt a general DBMS package to act as a collection management system, drawing up an OR covering all the basic requirements will help in the decision-making process.

The next task is to shortlist the software that might satisfy your requirements. For general packages, especially for administration use, reading the computer press is suggested; several magazines do tests periodically of various types of software, such as database management systems (DBMS), spreadsheets, word-processing packages, virus-checking or data-recovery programs, for example, and it is always worthwhile purchasing relevant backnumbers up to six months old to study these tests (any older and there is a serious danger that the information will be out of date). Also talk to as many other museums and computer users as possible to canvass their opinions. See whether there is a user group for any package under serious consideration, and contact them. One of the great advantages of being linked to the Internet, and having electronic mail (email) facilities, is the ease with which you can communicate with like-minded people and obtain help (Lowderbaugh, 1995). As one of the subscribers to a specialist on-line discussion list said recently (on the list) 'Where else can I shout in the dark, and be heard instantly by 800 like-minded people around the world?' This is certainly the case with help for packages; one of the present authors recently needed to solve a problem, and in the space of an hour sent and received three messages of discussion and advice with the senior person in the group responsible for the package in use, including sample sections of text. This was despite the fact that one of us was in the UK and the other in New Zealand.

Obtaining quotations for software
If a complex collection management package is to be purchased then a reasonably full OR should be sent to the vendors of all available collection management packages that are within the budget of the museum. All suppliers should be invited to tender for providing the package suitably configured for your museum, and asked to clarify how their packages meet the functional requirements of the OR. By sifting these responses against the mandatory requirements it should be possible to shortlist the most suitable packages and to arrange for demonstrations. Similar questions to those given in the next section will also need to be answered.

For procuring general packages, such as spreadsheets, word processors, etc, it is suggested that a simple form should be drawn up, listing the questions to be asked of each vendor, and the answers noted either on copies of that form, or as a numbered series relating back to the list of questions.

The first information to note is the name and address of the potential vendor, their telephone and fax numbers, email address if relevant, and, very importantly, the name and position of the person giving verbal information on the telephone. Don't accept 'I'm Max' – ask 'Max who?'. Note the date the quote is obtained. Then ask the following questions:

- What version are they selling? (note that versions labelled 6.01 and 6.02 can have important differences!)
- When is the next version expected to be released? How will that be marketed, as an upgrade or as a new package? (the former is usually much cheaper than the latter)
- Can data be imported from other packages under consideration? For example, make sure you can import a table from a word processor into a spreadsheet, or data from a DBMS into a word processor. Because of this it is often best to go for a 'suite' of programs from one manufacturer, then they all should work together

- Price (including VAT or other taxes)
- Does this include the manuals, and if not, how much extra are they?
- Is there a discount for a multi-user licence? How many copies of the manual would be supplied?
- What is the *minimum* configuration of hardware on which this software will run?
- What is the recommended *optimum* configuration?
- Are demonstration copies available?
- If relevant, will the proposed package read data from an earlier package already in use in the museum? If not, does the firm offer data-migration facilities, to transfer data from an existing system into the proposed new package?
- What support and training are available? Who from: the supplier, the software publisher, or a third party? What are the charges?
- Is there a user group for this package, and how can it be contacted?
- If telephone support is offered, for how long is this valid? (Often the first period is free, then either support is unavailable or has to be paid for.)

Hardware choice and procurement

Choosing computers

The minimum specification of the hardware must be decided first, and this will be governed partly by the software it is intended to run, partly by the nature and quantity of data it is expected to handle, and the type of processing intended, and last but not least by the available budget. Be careful not to under-specify to save money, this can prove to be a false economy because demands on a system have a habit of growing. Over-specifying, on the other hand, can yield a degree of 'future proofing'. Which make(s) of computer to consider is another decision; here again the tests run by the computing press can be enlightening, as not all machines with the same specification in practice give the same performance. The occasional user surveys some of the magazines conduct, that indicate which machines have given most problems over a period of time, also can be most helpful in arriving at the short list. Again, any information over six months old should be suspect, as it may be out of date. When adding new machines to an existing provision, try where possible to keep the specifications the same, particularly of the operating system, as this will simplify the maintenance effort needed.

Then it is necessary to decide how many machines are required, by looking at the following factors:

- How many people will need access to the system, and will each require their own machine or can they share?
- Is the system going to be a network, or stand-alone computers?
- If networked, what system is going to be used, and which type of cabling? Installing network cabling is a complex task, and whenever possible a specialist firm should be employed. Approach more than one firm, and make

sure they explain all the options available; try to get advice from other museums or local organizations that have installed networks

- What specification will the machines have? With the rapid advance of technology only the main factors to consider can be suggested here, as any attempt at precise specification would become rapidly out of date. But as mentioned elsewhere, now is always a good time to start – don't delay waiting for prices to fall, or power to rise, further. The factors to consider are size of RAM (random access memory) and hard-disk storage, the speed (in megahertz) and the type (e.g. PC or Macintosh) of architecture, the nature and version of the operating system to use, the size and resolution of the monitor to use, and what internal peripherals (such as floppy drives, CD-ROM players, audio systems and the like) to add. All these choices, and the overall specification of the hardware, will depend on which software you wish to run, and how much data you expect to hold. If images are to be stored, quadruple at least the number you first thought of for hard-disk space. Similar choices have to be made for the file-server on a network
- What system peripherals will be required to enable the information strategy to be followed (such as scanners, printers (dot matrix, ink jet or laser?), fax modems, or an Internet gateway).

Choosing printers for museum use

There are three main types of printer available, dot matrix, inkjet and laser. Dot-matrix are slow but offer cheap output per page. Inkjet printers are cheaper to buy than an equivalent specification laser printer, but the inkjet cost per page is higher than for laser printers as for the best results more expensive, coated papers should be used. Thus an important choice parameter is how much printed output you expect to produce per year. The main factors affecting a given printer price are the resolution – 24 pin is recommended for dot matrix, and 600 dots per inch (DPI) for laser and inkjet – and the speed in sheets per minute (SPM) that the printer can produce – four SPM is much cheaper than 12 SPM, for example.

If the printer output is to be used for collection labels and archive purposes, however, the permanence of the print is of prime importance. Here the only two printers to use are a dot matrix with a carbon ribbon, or a laser with powder toner. Dot-matrix ribbons with alcohol-based dyes, inkjet dyes and liquid toner in laser printers are all light fugitive, and so are not recommended for archive purposes. The only way to make such fugitive print-out permanent is to make xerographic copies, which are permanent. Permanence also requires the use of archive quality paper.

Obtaining quotations for hardware

Once the number, type and specification of all the equipment have been decided, the costs must be assessed. If a network is to be used, quotes will need to be obtained for installing the wiring. Whenever possible buildings should be 'flood wired', that is every work space, including stores and galleries, should have at least one network point installed, to permit maximum flexibility and minimum disturbance later. Quotes will also be needed for the various items of equipment, and the next section outlines how to go about getting them.

When the decision has been made on which vendors to approach, a form giving the relevant questions should be drawn up as for the software procurement. First will come the vendor details as before, not forgetting to be sure to whom you are speaking, then having given the specification of the equipment you are considering purchasing, ask the following questions:

- What is the price (including VAT or other taxes)?
- What operating system is provided (e.g. DOS or Windows, and which version)?
- What other software, if any, is 'bundled' with the equipment (particularly important when buying scanners)? However, with PCs, such 'bundled' software is not free, so unless a major part of the 'bundle' is software you would be buying anyway, then it is usually better to choose a machine offered without the software.
- What extras may be included free (cables, for example)?
- What other items would be needed to get the equipment up and running for the desired purpose?
- And what would the cost of these items be? (Does this include VAT or other tax?)
- What is the cost of delivery? (including VAT again)?
- Who carries liability in transit from supplier to you?
- What is the cost of any necessary transit insurance? (including VAT?)

The answers to these questions should enable you to calculate the total price of getting the hardware into your museum. Note that usually no computer equipment supplier will do more than deliver the boxes. All the unpacking, checking and setting up will have to be done by museum staff, unless extra payment is made to the supplier for such a service.

Although hardware failures are now quite rare, the next set of questions are about what happens if a piece of equipment malfunctions, or stubbornly refuses to work as the manual says it should:

- Does the vendor have a support hotline?
- What hours/days is it open?
- Is it a free-phone number? Local call? Long distance?
- How many support staff are available when?
- What training/experience do they have? (This last might get some dissembling answers, but they can still be informative in helping decide which firm gets your custom – for remember you are the customer, and they are the ones that want your money, so don't be embarrassed to ask searching follow-up questions.)

Warranties and maintenance

The last set of questions to ask are about longer-term warranties for hardware.

- For how long is the equipment covered by the vendor's warranty? (A supplementary question for firms about which you know little is 'how long have you been in business?'. A warranty is useless if the firm offering it shuts down during the period covered by the warranty.)
- What does the warranty cover? Parts? Labour?
- Is it 'on-site' (where the engineer comes to the museum to fix the equipment) or is it 'return-to-base' (where you have to pack up and arrange transport of the defective equipment back to the supplier)?
- If 'on-site' what is the maximum (not the 'average' or mean) response time?
- If 'return-to-base', who pays the transit and insurance each way? What is the maximum time for repair? If repair proves impossible or uneconomic within that time, will a new machine be supplied?
- And, most importantly, does the firm have any expertise available in recovering data from hard-disk crashes? (You will, of course, have been meticulous in your back-up procedures, but Murphy's law dictates that it is the time the back-up is forgotten that the disk will crash with critical information on it!)

Once the purchase warranty runs out it is recommended that an extended maintenance contract is completed to cover key equipment for the next few years. If the museum belongs to a larger organization, such as a local authority or a university, the IT section of the organization may be able to offer on-site maintenance at a competitive rate, but do ask the above questions about parts/labour cover, guaranteed response time, and hard-disk recovery expertise. Compare the answers with those from the vendor, and from 'third-party' companies who specialize in computer maintenance (see the current computing magazines for advertisements from these maintenance suppliers). When talking to the vendor, always ask who does their extended maintenance; sometimes they will name a 'third party' company, and you may find that a direct contract with that company will cost less!

Again you need to establish the price of the maintenance, and if possible get separate prices for each piece of equipment. This allows you to tailor your overall maintenance contract by looking at the cost effectiveness of the charges. As equipment ages the annual maintenance cost tends to rise, while the cost of replacing the older equipment is likely to be falling. At some point, usually around the five-year-old mark, it can be a better deal to move the equipment on to a 'contingency' basis. This means setting aside a sum of money from the budget each year to cover 'contingencies', such as an old computer needing a new hard-drive, monitor or motherboard. If the computer lasts the year, the money can then be used for other purposes, of course. Unlike businesses, the economics of museums usually dictate that machines are rarely replaced until they fail completely.

All orders should be given in writing, and telephone, fax or email orders should be followed by a 'confirmation of order' that specifies exactly what is ordered. Always remember that wherever possible, equipment and software should be specified, at least in part, by a statement of the purpose for which it is sought; for example, state the main software it is intended to run. Then if when it arrives it does not perform as expected, it should be possible to return it as 'unfit for purpose' and obtain a full refund of the purchase price. But ask whether the firm puts any restrictions or charges on any returns.

For example, one museum was setting up a gallery interactive display, and the staff involved ordered a specific computer, by make and model number, and also a heavy-duty tracker ball, again by make and model. When the equipment arrived it was discovered that the tracker ball would not work with the computer. But the suppliers declined to accept responsibility on the grounds that the order had not specified that the two pieces of equipment should be compatible! This mistake cost the museum time and (unbudgeted) money to correct.

Having obtained all the information on the costs of setting up the proposed system, all that remains is the small matter of arranging a budget to fund the work. It is good practice always to build a 10 per cent 'contingency fund' into the budget, to cover the inevitable small items of equipment, software or work that will have been overlooked at the planning stage.

Summary

The essential points of this chapter:
1. Before setting up a new museum computer system, an audit should be done of the people skills and other resources already available, to identify what can be used and what needs to be added.
2. Always use a package-based solution for software, and where possible choose a package for which an accessible museum usergroup exists.
3. Don't under-specify hardware, but build in a degree of future proofing.
4. Make sure you explore the market fully before ordering hardware or software, and be careful to compare like with like when assessing quotations during the procurement exercise.
5. Make sure that all the elements of the system, programs, computers and peripheral devices, will run together without problems, and specify this compatibility requirement when ordering the various components.

References

Ccta (1995), *The TAP Services Guide,* London: HMSO

Grant, A. & Marshall, F. (1996), 'LLASSI comes home – but to what?' *MDA Information,* 3, Winter 1995/96

Keene, S. (1995), *The Procurement Process and System Requirements,* London: Museums and Galleries Commission (LASSI Consortium of UK Museums), 25pp

Lowderbaugh, T. E. (1995), 'Smithsonian on-line: the virtual museum as community center', *in* Fahy, A. & Sudbury, W. *Information, The Hidden Resource, Museums and the Internet,* Cambridge: Museum Documentation Association, 169–174

Pettitt, C. (1990), 'Sort/search codes: a pragmatic approach to rationalising museum information on computer', *in* Roberts, A. R. (ed.), *Terminology for Museums,* Cambridge: Museum Documentation Association, 448–455

Roberts, A. (1996), 'Information technology and documentation initiative in the Museum of London', *CHArt Journal,* in press

Chapter 9

Organizing and running a computerized information management system

In this chapter

Organizing and running the information system

Having purchased the hardware and got it all connected and running, and having installed the software package(s) on it, then you have to organize the system and put the information into it (Roberts, 1985). It should be noted that if the names of living people (such as donors, collectors etc.) are to be included in any computer files or databases, then in the UK the museum must register this usage under the Data Protection Act.

Organizing the system

It falls to the information manager to oversee planning of the operational details of implementing the agreed information plan. In most museums the main task will relate to the collection management software, but other aspects such as the introduction of word processing and electronic mail, and the provision of management information such as budgetary spreadsheets and order/invoice databases must also be addressed. For a medium to large museum the work will involve constant discussions with management, curators and computing staff, both informally and within a series of sub-committees; in a small museum one or two people may have to discharge all the roles. The information manager, with the help of any IT staff or training opportunities, should become familiar with the complexities of the chosen software package(s), and they should gain a user's knowledge of the operating system in use. Overall progress of the plan should be reported back at intervals, either to a specially convened 'information committee' or, with less fuss, as an agenda item at any regular management meeting.

Building the collection management system

The various stages through which information passes may be categorized as:
- Data recording (or capture)
- Data entry (or input)

- Data verification (may be integral with the data entry for some fields)
- Data processing (updating, searching)
- Outputs (reports, information products etc).

The organization of each of these stages is dealt with below in detail. The information manager should now construct a work flow diagram of the proposed system; Figure 9.1 on p122, shows such a diagram for a typical computerized information system. This kind of flow diagram is an invaluable aid to planning, and will help in explaining the system to other staff. In the early stages people's attitudes will tend to range from dismissive to the attribution of totally unrealistic abilities to the information system, and a single person may well fluctuate rapidly from one extreme to the other and back with each perceived small success or failure of the developing system. Coping with these attitudes calls for a great deal of patient diplomacy on the part of the information manager, and to succeed they must be continuously critical of the work in hand, and be the best informed and best able to offer resolutions to the inevitable problems.

Compiling the work schedule

The next main task of the information manager will be to compile the work schedule that sets out precisely the projects that will be included in the first phase of the implementation of the information plan. Management projects and priorities will no doubt have been set, but for that aspect of the plan involving collections, curators will have to identify which parts of the collections in their care they want included in the programme. Much of this information should have been elicited during the 'information audit'. See Chapter 5 p68. It is best to adopt a 'project' approach. Each project must be of a finite size, and achievable within the timescale of the first phase of the overall programme. Apart from current information such as new accessions or visitor numbers, etc, open-ended commitments should be avoided, and every project should be complete within itself, e.g. a single taxonomic group of animals or plants, the finds from a single archaeological site, or a particular collection of drawings. A useful rule of thumb is to aim at projects that will produce between 1000 and 10 000 records, the optimum size varying with the discipline involved. Record length tends to be shortest in natural history, and to become progressively longer through geology, archaeology/ethnology and local history, to decorative and fine art, for example. Alternatively for a large collection a simple inventory-level entry could be prepared first, with the fuller catalogue information being entered later.

A list of the proposed projects should be compiled; this task also could usefully form part of the information audit. See Chapter 5 p68. For each project the following points need to be established:

- How big is the project? Do not trust curatorial estimates; wherever possible determine the exact number of items to be catalogued or inventoried by a full or random-sample count of the collection. This should not take more

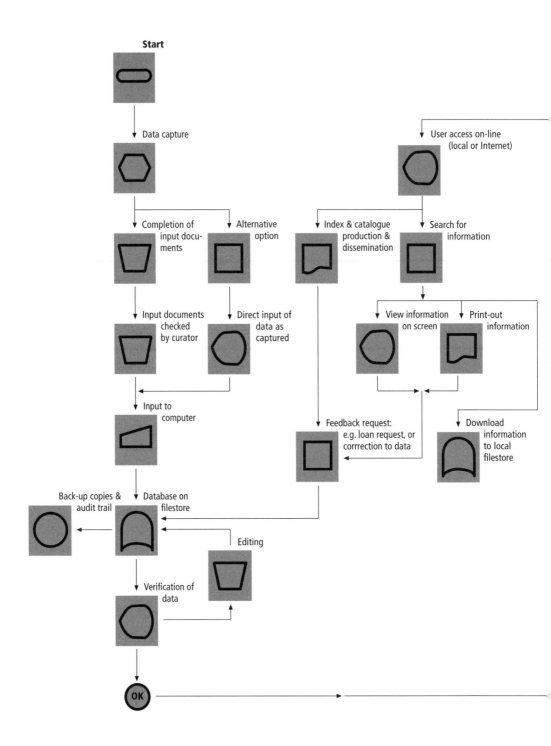

than a day or so, and the time is well spent, because unless the target is known accurately attempts to monitor progress will be meaningless

- How frequently is the material accessed? The more the material is used for loans, or to answer enquiries, etc., the higher the priority it shoud be awarded. Scientifically or culturally important but little-known collections should not be neglected, however, as making the information more accessible will tend to stimulate interest in and work on that collection
- What is the current state of the documentation? Other things being equal, a poorly catalogued collection might take precedence over one possessing a complete card catalogue, for example, but remember that entering existing good records may lead to better access to, and use of, the collection
- How good are the data? Initially at least preference should be given to collections with the data readily available for each item, with a minimum of 'looking up' to do. This will permit rapid results to be achieved, which politically could be helpful in developing the work. Conversely, if the item data are incomplete, or a great deal of background work proves necessary to bring the information to an acceptable standard, it might be better to postpone the project pending further curation of the collection
- What degree of curator involvement is needed? Using their knowledge of each curator's attitude towards the plan and commitment to the collection, the information manager must assess realistically the likelihood of the necessary involvement being forthcoming. It is best to concentrate on the converted at first; once the others see their colleagues achieving good results, the 'me too' factor will come into play
- What resources are needed? The critical ones are the amount of staff time required, and the expected cost of any contracted-out data entry
- What resources are available? Some curators may have a team of docents or volunteers who would be willing to get involved in the information plan work, and this could well be a critical factor in deciding which collections are included.

Having compiled all this information, the information manager should then assign relative priorities to each project, either as A, B, C priorities, or the whole list can be put into ranked order. That order will need the concurrence of the curators concerned and of management, which can mean that the apparent priorities become somewhat distorted by internal politics.

Data preparation

At some stage it will be necessary to enter data into the system (Boast and Chippindale, 1993). As mentioned above, there are three stages to this, data recording (or capture), data entry (or input) and data verification, which together form the data-preparation process.

Before actually starting the work, the staff concerned will need to work out the *modus operandi*. A worksite must be chosen and at it assembled the data standard manual, data-entry documents, any special implements and materials, and any other reference works needed, such as registers, history files, field notebooks, gazetteers or an atlas. It is usually more efficient if the items to be catalogued can be brought adjacent to the dedicated work site, and suitable temporary storage provided. Sometimes for conservation or other reasons the items have to be catalogued in the storeroom, gallery or office; in that event a suitable trolley should be provided to carry the work site to the items. Time spent on simple work study at this stage is rarely wasted, and could well lead to a considerable increase in the throughput of information. To facilitate re-finding at the data-verification stage one approach could be to store them, temporarily at least, in accession number order. It is important that each item is tagged in some way as it is catalogued to prevent future confusion about which items have been dealt with.

Data recording and entry

Data recording is the process of assembling all available information about an item from all sources, including the intellectual input from curators, and ordering it into a coherent record ready for entry.

Recording and entering new data

Although it is perfectly feasible to record data by entering it directly to the DBMS, it is recommended that, for all but the smallest and simplest projects, the data is first assembled on to a data-entry sheet. This is a sheet that has labelled spaces for data, and may incorporate brief notes on important aspects of the data standard. The reasons for not using direct entry are that it allows division of labour and improved efficiency, because:

- For any item data recording invariably takes longer than data entry, which makes inefficient use of the usually limited number of keyboards available, especially as these will also be required for on-line editing and retrieval, whereas data-entry documents and pencils are considerably cheaper than additional computers
- By divorcing data recording from data entry, the two tasks can be done by different people at different times. Thus cataloguers can concentrate on recording, with trained typists coping with the entry stage, possibly between other tasks
- The data-entry sheet enables existing primary data to be recorded by relatively unskilled staff, as it mainly involves just accurate copying. Then the intellectual contribution of the curator can be added at a later stage, and while so doing it also allows the trained eye of the curator to spot and correct obvious errors in the primary data before entry.

Data-entry sheets

The data-entry sheet can be ephemeral, or can form a transaction document, for example entry forms for items coming into the museum, which then form an archival document with a donor's transfer-of-title signature on it, or loan-out forms that are forwarded with the item(s) after data entry. The layout of the entry sheet will be influenced strongly by any secondary use of the document, but it must be recognized that such influence may have a serious adverse effect on the efficiency of the document for data entry. Ideally the document should contain the minimum amount of structure, ie field labels, ruled dividers and instructions. The labelled data spaces on the entry sheet should be arranged in orderly rows corresponding to the data-entry screen of the database application, so that the typist's eye will travel smoothly over them. If the typist's eyes have to skip about the document to find data that is embedded in a mass of ruled lines and printed text, and if the 'tags' identifying the data fields are not clearly shown, entry must be slowed and costs increased; also a badly designed data-entry sheet increases the risk that the cataloguer, the curator or the typist may overlook some item of data. Do not try to crowd too much on to a document; either use a larger format or a continuation document for excess data. Explanatory notes should be as concise as feasible, and grouped at the end away from the data fields. Double-sided documents should be avoided, for reversing such documents slows the typist, and increases the chance that data may be missed. The ruled lines should not be so close together as to cramp handwritten entries.

Provided it does not conflict with the above principles, the order in which the data are entered should be that followed naturally by a curator writing a description of the item.

When computerization using ephemeral entry documents is being discussed, some curators express concern at the lack of a secure 'primary source document'. However, multiple copies of data on-line and back-up tapes, with sets of printed output, are at least as secure a source document as, for example, a solitary bound register prone to all the accidents of fate.

The process is tedious and time consuming, and it is worth taking trouble to get the data-recording stage right for it will almost certainly represent the main museum commitment in terms of time spent on computerization. In addition, if the data recorded are not as accurate and complete as possible, an inferior information system will result. Always remember the GIGO principle: garbage in, garbage out; computerization cannot of itself improve data quality.

Entering existing data

If previously you have been using another DBMS system, then that data must also be migrated to the new system; the feasibility of so doing should have been explored during the software procurement exercise and born in mind when arriving at the latest data standards. Migrating existing data must also be given serious consideration if changing or upgrading other application packages such as word processors and spreadsheets. The software suppliers or a data-processing bureau may be able to do the migration for you, and this may well represent a cost-effective way of transferring large amounts of data quickly and accurately. But the museum's information manager still has to be closely involved in drawing up the specification and contract for the work, so that the museum has adequate safeguards to ensure the finished product is to a satisfactory standard, is delivered on time and within budget. Advice from a user group at this stage can be invaluable. The manager will also be responsible, probably in consultation with the various curators and other staff involved, for seeing that the 'mapping' of the data 'fields' in the existing system to those used in the new system is done accurately.

Data verification

With modern collection management packages, and with some non-specific database management applications, it is possible to control or verify information as it is typed in. This may be by attaching controlled vocabularies to individual fields, so that only terms on the list are permitted, or else by providing 'menus' of terms from which the required term is selected. With both systems it is usually possible to allow 'candidate' terms to be added by the person doing the data entry; these terms can later be accepted or rejected and synonomized by the information manager. The presence of these capabilities would normally form part of the functional requirements of the operational requirement. See Chapter 8 p112.

All modern DBMS packages allow on-line editing of the data, provided the user has been granted 'permission' to change the information (see data security below). Therefore once a quantity of data has been entered into the DBMS, retroactive verification can commence. This can involve the curator studying the information presented on-line in tabular form, so that the data about each item appears on a single line, and each field of data is shown as a column. It is simple then for the curator or other trained person to scan down a column and find the obvious errors. The 'error-spotting' rate can be improved by sorting the entries on each field in turn, as it is checked, because this will help to highlight misspellings and data in the wrong place. Alternatively the information can be printed out for a set of items and then 'call-checked' against the original information. This needs two people, one reading the listing as the other calls out the information on the labels and other source documents. Any errors can be marked on the listing, as in correcting a galley proof, and the 'marked-up' listing then used to update the data on-line.

Some curators are reluctant to put 'their' databases on-line for others to use because they fear the discovery of additional errors that have slipped past the checking stage. However, as McLaren (1992) points out, everyone accepts that curators will not deliberately provide incorrect data, but in the last analysis researchers using a database are responsible for examining items and verifying identifications themselves, for it is only their name that will appear as the author of the research when published. At Manchester several large databases have been put on-line even though the data cleaning is still in progress; a disclaimer to this effect warns users to double check before using the information. The response to this approach has been favourable.

Data processing

Retrieving information

There is no point in expending significant resources entering information into a database without making provision for accessing and using it. The details of how one searches and selectively retrieves information will vary between the different DBMS. Many modern systems support SQL (structured query language) and/or the z39.50 exchange protocol; unfortunately, however, a museum attribute set has not yet been developed for the latter. The type of questions asked can be extremely varied (Sledge and Case, 1995); aspects of information sought are given earlier. See Chapter 3, p33.

Fortunately, however, the way a DBMS handles queries can usually be made transparent to the user; what they are presented with is a screen on which they can enter the attributes or items of interest, and this is then translated by the software into a search instruction. It is often possible to devise a set of 'standard' query screens to assist users to search the database. See several of the case studies in Part 2, p137.

Levels of access

Different users require different levels of access. The information and system managers need to be able to access everything in order to keep the system running; this is usually termed 'supervisor' level access. Individual staff will need access to write and change information for which they are responsible, and usually need to be able to retrieve and read a much wider range of the information in the system. Exactly who should be given what access to which information must be carefully thought through. Non-staff users generally will be restricted to read-only access, and often will be able to retrieve and read only a limited amount of information about collection items, and will have no access to administrative and managerial files.

How access levels are controlled will depend on how the system is configured. If stand-alone machines are in use then access will depend largely on what information is provided on each machine, but who has access to the machine, and the use of control devices such as passwords, will also need to be established. Most network software allows varied permissions to be granted to each registered user, and also allows each file (e.g. a database) to be made available explicitly in varying degrees to each user. Often collections management software will allow or deny access to individual fields within the database.

It is recommended that only copies, or 'clones', of information databases are made available publicly, either in-house or over the Internet via the WWW. This not only allows ready control of what parts of the information are 'released', but also means that should external users manage to corrupt the information then the master database within the museum will be unaffected.

Outputs of information

Information can be obtained, or output, from the system in various physical forms, the most common being by displaying it on a monitor screen, or by printing it on paper. Other outputs are possible, such as writing the information to a file for transfer to another package (from the DBMS to the word processor, for example). Less frequent is output in the form of disks or tape for transporting information to another site; generally such transfers are now done on the Internet. Some specialist outputs, such as microfiche (COM) or microfilm, are still available, albeit generally via specialist external service providers.

The information content of the output also varies. Answers to enquiries often form an important output from the system, as do reports and other information products. Reports are usually subsets of information, information on selected items for example. The software should allow this information to be ordered and presented in the way that best suits the use to which it is to be put. Information products, such as catalogues, indexes, bibliographies etc, can also form very useful outputs from the system. Essentially these too are 're-ports', but generally they will be 'massaged' after initial output, and often will have additional information added to them before distribution.

User training

To make effective and efficient use of the system it will be necessary to invest some resource into training of the in-house users. Training will form part of the remit of the information manager, who in a small museum will probably have to do the training themselves. In larger museums it may well be worth paying the system vendor to provide the training as part of the procurement exercise, although this can prove expensive. A cheaper alternative is to 'train the trainers' by having some lead staff professionally trained, and then allow them to train their immediate colleagues, with the support of the information and system managers.

The importance of data security

Placing a large proportion of the information needed for the efficient functioning of the museum into a computer system, particularly a networked system, can make the system become 'mission-critical'. To decide whether your institution has reached this point, just take a moment to reflect what would be the result if tomorrow when everyone reported for work, it was discovered that all the information in the system was either missing, or corrupt, or had become unreliable through unauthorized changes. If such a doomsday scenario would seriously impede the day-to-day running of your museum, then your system has become mission-critical.

However, long before this happens, indeed ideally from the moment the system is planned, data security should be a prime concern, not only of the system manager, but of all the people using and depending on the system. Threats to data security come under three headings: accident, mischief and fraud. Each of these is examined below; all the illustrative examples have actually happened, so be warned.

Accidents

These can be caused by ignorance – for example, the non-computer-using museum director who, the better to show an important visitor the latest computer acquired by his museum, swung it round on the desk while it was switched on, thereby crashing and ruining the hard-disk drive, and losing all the information it contained. The moral is to make sure that everyone who can get near a computer, and that includes cleaners and stewards, is aware of what constitutes mistreating a computer. The most difficult to guard against are outside contract staff such as window cleaners, who have been known to slosh dirty water all over a running machine, and electricians, who have a penchant for switching off the mains without warning. Sensible positioning of the machines can alleviate the former danger, and notices by all main power switches, instructing who must be contacted before switching that circuit off, can help with the latter. A good rule is not to leave computers unattended while switched on. The unpredictable event, such as the occasion when a museum lost its file-server because a workman accidentally chopped through the power cable to the building, can only be coped with by good maintenance contracts and excellent data back-up procedures. Some accidents are less easy to excuse, like the system manager who crashed his system by blundering into a cable, pulling the ethernet card out of the back of the museum file-server. The moral is, don't leave loose cables draped around, secure everything.

Then there are the accidents that unintentionally corrupt or delete data. Unfortunately power surges, spikes and brown-outs (voltage peaks or reductions) are not that infrequent in mains supplies, and all of these can damage both the data and the hardware. Therefore it is recommended that wherever possible vital equipment, such as a file-server, is protected by an uninterruptable power supply, even though this adds significantly to the cost of the system. Other equipment should be protected by using one of the proprietary spike-suppressing plugs on the market. A further precaution is always to switch on machines that are heavy current users, such as laser printers, before any PCs on the same power circuit. If data are corrupted or lost, a disk-management program is an essential weapon in the system manager's armoury, for they often enable accidentally lost data to be recovered. The cost of such a program can easily be saved the first time you get back some essential information that had taken several days to enter. Even better if it is a senior manager who lost it, as the relief engendered by a successful recovery can often translate into an increased IT budget for the next year.

Mischief 1 – viruses

In computing terms mischief can come in various guises. The mischief that most people associate with computers is virus attack, and unfortunately such attacks are still frequent. The good news is that modern virus-checking programs are extremely efficient, the bad news is that it can be quite hard work persuading people to use them regularly. Therefore wherever possible arrange that when any machine is powered up the virus checker runs to check the hard disk. Memory-resident virus checkers can be used that check every executable file as it is loaded, whether from a floppy or from the internal disk, but these are not to be recommended as they can cause interference with some application programs, and certainly will slow down your system: a case where the cure can sometimes be worse than the disease.

What should be done is to ensure that, as far as possible, every floppy disk that is used on the system is checked for viruses before being accessed for the first time, and re-checked if it is used outside the institution at any time. Some means of identification, such as a stick-on green dot, can help people to keep track of checked disks. An increasing number of organizations are insisting that all disks brought into their premises are checked for viruses on a stand-alone machine at reception before being permitted further into the building. Unfortunately, the havoc that can be wrought in short order by a virus means that such apparently draconian methods are becoming necessary.

The rapid growth of the World Wide Web, and the increasing use of remote file transfer to download data files and software, while amazingly convenient, does bring with it a fresh channel for viruses to enter your system. The only safe course is to ensure that all such files are virus checked before being used on the system, and especially so before transferring them to a network file-server.

Mischief 2 – hackers

To watch actors in some recent television dramas it would seem that just tapping a few keys at random will get you into practically any computer system in the world. This is a nonsense, of course, but hacking is not something to be taken lightly. Kehoe and Stephens (1996) estimate that one computer system on the Internet is broken into every 20 seconds. If your system is connected to the Internet, and if someone really wants to get in and read or re-arrange your data, then quite possibly they can. It will take rather longer than the actor above, but eventually most systems can be 'cracked' by someone with knowledge and persistence, qualities hackers usually have in abundance. The best defence is to isolate your system from the Internet, but increasingly the cost-benefit equation, that is, the dangers of being connected versus the benefits to your organization of access to the global super highway, is swinging in favour of connection.

The next line of defence is to erect a 'firewall' between your system and the great wide world. In essence this is an 'intelligent' computer through which all traffic to the outer world passes. Like any wall the firewall is only as good as its bricks and mortar, the software used to prevent unauthorized access to your system. While useful in some circumstances, firewalls cannot offer complete protection, and need quite specialist setting up. Also firewalls are static by nature, while hackers are continually developing new attack methods. Thus firewalls must be upgraded constantly, as must virus-checking programs, to fend off new forms of attack.

Hacking is now a criminal offence in most western countries, but some hackers may be more criminally minded than others. For this reason it is to be recommended that sensitive information such as value and location are not put into a networked computerized database, at least not in a form that can be clearly interpreted by someone making an unauthorized access to the system. Such information should never be released as part of an on-line public access database (opac), nor should sensitive information such as the field site of endangered species. If valuation information is required for management purposes then it should only be entered in a coded way. This can be done, for example, by placing a brief code string in an apparently unrelated field, to indicate which items have values of, say, more than £500 or £5000. Similarly, while having cupboard and shelf locations on-line can seem attractive, it does mean that any hacker-burglar can readily draw up a shopping list, and know exactly where to find the stuff when they break in.

Mischief 3 – malicious attacks

Regrettably this type of mischief is mainly the result of aggrieved employees, but fortunately in the museum world as far as can be ascertained it is fairly unusual, unlike some large industrial and commercial concerns to whom it is a permanent threat.

The best defence, of course, is treat your people right so they do not become aggrieved. As in most sensitive fields of endeavour, *quis custodiat* ... applies, and it would perhaps be prudent always, where possible, to have more than one person who really understands the system. This is actually a good idea mainly because of the problem of what happens to your mission-critical system if the sole 'expert' is suddenly taken from you? But it also means that two heads are definitely better than one in preventing malicious tampering with the system.

Fraud

Fraud is again mainly a danger from trusted people who have legitimate access to the computerized information. In the 1970s the natural history curator at a main city museum noticed one day that the collection only contained three specimens of a large, showy and quite rare butterfly. The three specimens were neatly pinned in their drawer with no obvious gap, but the curator was still puzzled, so he checked the computerized database, which duly confirmed that there were only three specimens of that species. But the curator was still uneasy, so he dug back through some microfiche copies of the database taken at intervals in earlier years. On one of these the number of specimens became four, confirming the suspicion that someone had not only purloined the specimen, but also altered the database to give fraudulent information. Suffice to say that further investigation led to a police search of the house of a long-serving and previously trusted volunteer, and the finding of a large number of stolen museum specimens.

Therefore it is important to provide an audit trail for information in the database, for this is what the regular microfiche copies offered in the case detailed above. Nowadays audit trails are probably best incorporated into the back-up routine, which provides the ultimate long-stop against losing one's system for whatever reason.

Back-ups – the ultimate data security

The medium

Regularly copying information from the working system, be it a network file-server or a stand-alone PC, on to some form of long-term medium, is the only way to be sure that should the worst happen, the lost data can at least be restored to the state it had at the time of the last back-up session. Back-up media can be of various types. It is still possible to have microfiches made of your data, and the master copies of these are semi-permanent. They also have the advantage that it is very difficult to alter a microfiche without leaving traces. However, this form of back-up does not permit the easy restoration of the data.

The most common form of back-up medium at the moment is magnetic, either as floppy disks or as DAT tapes. Both are cheap in themselves, but while the floppy can be used in the drive that almost invariably is already present on the system, the DAT tape requires quite an expensive dedicated drive to be fitted. The latter can be internal or external; internal DAT drives are usually fitted to network file-servers, but for a series of stand-alone, or peer-networked, PCs the portable DAT drive is to be recommended. This can then be taken round each machine in turn to receive the back-up data.

Write-once CD-disks are now available, and these offer high capacity (holding up to 700 megabytes of data). Each disk can only be written to once; when it is full it cannot be re-written. Although re-writable disks are in development, the write-once-only disk offers audit-trail security because, like microfiche, they are difficult to tamper with without detection.

The market in back-up facilities is a fast-growing one, and the advice is to balance the initial cost of the read/write mechanism, the cost of the individual media, the capacity, and the permanence or otherwise of the data once on the back-up medium. Capacity needs should be determined in relation to the quantity of data likely to be backed up. Backing up a 5 gigabyte file-server disk on 1.44 megabyte floppies is not really a practical proposition, but using floppies to back up just the changed files from a 350 megabyte hard disk on a stand-alone computer is perfectly practical. Remember, provided you keep the master installation disks safely there is no need to back up the applications packages or the operating system, and these usually form a large proportion of the files on a computer. Also there are some very efficient compression programs around that will allow you to back up files that, while occupying a great deal of space on the computer, will take much less space when compressed on to floppies. This is particularly true for databases, where the compressed file can sometimes be only a tenth of the size of the original.

The method

Back-ups should be done at intervals that are governed by the frequency at which data is added or altered on the given system. One should never rely on a single back-up; it is not unknown for a back-up disk or tape to become corrupt, or to be lost. Therefore it is suggested that wherever possible a series of media should be used; for complete protection two such series should be established.

Full data back-ups

Series A, that should consist of at least two tapes or disk sets, is for doing a full back-up of the system. For most museum systems doing this every month would be a reasonable interval to adopt, at least when starting. After gaining experience the interval can be altered to suit the conditions.

The two or three tapes/disk sets should be rotated, so that a different one from the last one written is used for each back-up (see 9.2a, the top section of Figure 9.2 on p134). On each back-up run the previously stored data can be over-written, so the media can, in theory, be used indefinitely; in practice all magnetic media wear out with repeated use and become unreliable, so series A should be replaced at intervals. When doing full back-ups all the data and program files, both old and new, are copied, and the 'new' flag on the files created or changed since the last incremental back-up should be left untouched. The back-up media should be stored well away from the machine backed up, to prevent them being damaged by any disaster affecting the system. If there is a total loss of data on the system, using these full back-ups it can quickly be restored to the state it was in not more than a month previously. In the rare event of the most recent back-up proving unreadable, the previous one can be used, making the 'lost' period no more than two months.

Incremental data back-ups

But even one month's work can represent a great deal of effort lost, and some of the data may not be reproducible. This is where the second series of tapes or disk sets is used. Series B should consist of at least three tapes or disk sets, cycled on the grandfather, father, son principle (see 9.2b, the lower section of Figure 9.2 on p134), and this set is used to backup only those files and programs that have changed or been created since the last back-up. When these files are written to the back-up medium the session should be appended to the ones previously on the tape, and this time the 'new (or changed) file' flag on the computer file should be reset to 'no', or its equivalent (all back-up programs will offer this option). Again, the media should be stored away from the machine(s) backed up, but in this case they should also be kept physically secure, for the serially appended sessions between them form the audit trail men-

Flow diagrams showing the cycle of back-up media. The top section **9.2a**, shows the full back-ups, the lower section **9.2b**, shows the incremental back-ups with the audit trail

Figure 9.

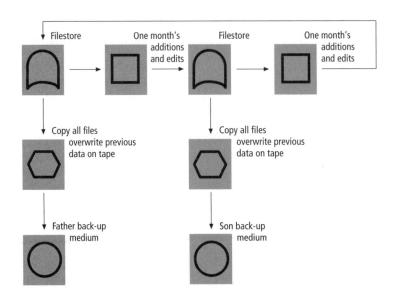

9.2a

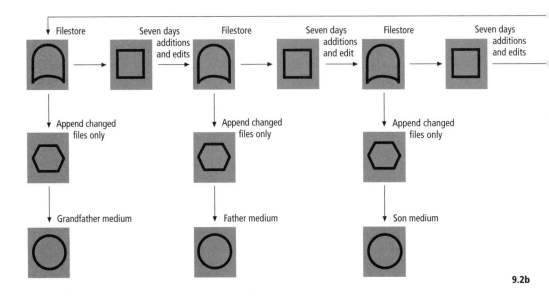

9.2b

tioned above. By looking through these sessions it is possible to examine all the earlier states of a file (and a database is only a file or set of files) right back to the time it was created on the system. Unlike the series A media, series B media will, in time, become full, and a new series of media will have to be set up.

Be aware that tapes are not fully secure storage media, as when left unaccessed for long periods the data they contain can degrade and become corrupt. Therefore it is important that they are stored in an even-temperature, dry and dust-free environment protected from any stray magnetic fields. As a further protection all archival tapes should be read, and ideally re-written, at least once a year.

Finally, all back-up programs also produce a log file reporting what has been done, which files have been backed up, and any errors that may have occurred during the back-up run. These files are normally written back to the disk being backed up. Since they are usually essential for following the audit trail mentioned above, at least two copies should be made, and kept securely apart from the series B tapes that effectively they index. Again this is a security measure, and it is generally best to erase the logs from the system once they have been backed up.

Summary

The essential points of this chapter:

1. Comprehensive data standards must be agreed before an information system is commissioned, for they are the bedrock on which the system rests.
2. Efficient organization and management of the operation of the system are vital for the benefits of the information strategy to be obtained in a cost-effective way.
3. All aspects of data security must be addressed from the start, not only by the system manager but by everyone within the museum who is involved with the information system.
4. Regular data back-ups are essential to safeguard the system against attack, misuse or catastrophic failure.
5. An audit trail, possibly linked to incremental back-ups, should be established to permit all changes to the system to be traced when necessary.

References

ANON. (1992), 'Report from the ASC Workshop on Data Sharing and Database Ethics', *Association of Systematics Collections Newsletter*, 20 (6) 157, 159–165

BOAST, R. & CHIPPINDALE, C. (1993), 'A data day story of cataloguing folk', *Museums Journal*, (February) 93 (2) 17

KEHOE, L. & STEPHENS, S. (1996), 'A hacker's paradis', *Financial Times*, 16 April 1996

MCLAREN, S. B. (1992) 'On database accessibility', *Association of Systematics Collections Newsletter*, 20 (6) 158–159

ROBERTS, A. (1985), *Planning the Documentation of Museum Collections*, Cambridge: Museum Documentation Association, 568pp

SLEDGE, J. & CASE, M. (1995), 'Looking for Mr Rococco: Getty Art History Information Program Point-of-View Workshop'. *Archives and Museum Informatics*, 9 (1) 124–129

Part 2

Case studies

Case studies: topic finder

To help readers to select those case studies which may be particularly relevant to their own interests, here is a list of key topics, with a pointer to the relevant case studies.

Archaeological sites
The Royal Commission on Historic Monuments of England   144

Archive & record management policy
The V&A Museum   259

Archives
Callendar House, Falkirk   151
The Theatre Museum   281

Bi-lingual terminology
Ceredigion Museum   158

Building records
The Royal Commission on
Historic Monuments of England   244

Business plans
North Somerset Museum Service   223

Commercial partnerships
Scienceworks   252

Consultants for systems design
The RAF Museum   232

Contracts
The LASSI project   170

Critical success factors
Callendar House, Falkirk   151

Data capture/entry by volunteers
The Manchester Museum   176
Norfolk Museums Service   214

Data export
The Manchester Museum   176

Distributed processing
The Manchester Museum   176

Documentation plans/policies
The Manchester Museum   176
St Albans Museums   249

FAMULUS software
The Manchester Museum   176

Field archaeology
Norfolk Museums Service   214

GOS software
The National Maritime Museum   190
St Albans Museums   249

Historic monuments
The Royal Commission on Historic Monuments of England   144

Images, computer-based access
BEAMISH   140
Bradford Art Galleries and Museums   148
Hampshire Museums Service   164
The LASSI project   170
Norfolk Museums Service   214
Scienceworks   252
The V&A Museum   259

In-house systems
Portsmouth Museums   229

Information products
BEAMISH   140
North Somerset Museum Service   223

Information systems strategy
The National Maritime Museum   190
The Royal Commission on Historic
     Monuments of England   144
Scienceworks   252

Information policy
The National Maritime Museum   190
The V&A Museum   259

Integrated databases
Callendar House, Falkirk   151

Inter-museum co-operation
The LASSI project   170

International projects
The V&A Museum   259

Internet/World Wide Web
The Manchester Museum   176
Norfolk Museums Service   214
The Royal Commission on Historic
     Monuments of England   252
The V&A Museum   259

Interpretation
BEAMISH   140

BEAMISH, The North of England Open Air Museum

Introduction

The case study about Beamish which appeared in the first edition of this book (Orna and Pettitt, 1980, p155) was written nine years after the museum had opened its doors to the public; it has recently celebrated 25 years of existence. Times have changed in many ways, and the museum faces challenges of a different kind from those described by its founder and first director, Frank Atkinson (1995), which seem mostly to have been posed by Machiavellian intrigues in local government. In other respects, there have been remarkable consistency and continuity in its development, particularly in relation to its approach to information use.

The original intention was to set up an open-air museum for County Durham, and the collection of objects representative of the history of local communities started in the early 1960s – a period of rapid industrial, economic and social change, when much that represented earlier ways of life was being discarded. The impending reorganization of local government led to the idea of a regional museum covering several local authority areas of northern England, as a policy document of the time put it:

'An Open Air Museum for the purpose of studying, collecting, preserving and exhibiting buildings, machinery, objects and information illustrating the development of industry and the way of life of the North of England'. Quoted in Atkinson, 1995, p27.

The museum as ultimately opened on ex-National Coal Board land at Beamish was supported by a consortium of north eastern local authorities.

The site met the criteria that had been established, and offered almost all that could be desired for showing industry, agriculture and community life as they had been in the area in the chosen period of the early 1900s.[1]

It was in the desired size range of 200–300 acres; it lay between the main centres of population in the North East, and had good communications and access; it was based on an existing stately home and had other buildings of historic interest, including two farmsteads; it was basin shaped, so that signs of the present day did not obtrude; and it had a river, woodland and undulating

---

[1] The years leading up to the outbreak of World War 1 were selected because at that time the North East still retained its strong regional identity and culture (1913 was the peak year of coal production in the Great Northern Coalfield). The second period chosen for interpretation was the early 1800s, with emphasis on the 1820s, the period that saw the opening of the Stockton and Darlington Railway in 1825, with Stephenson's Locomotion, the rapid expansion of early coal-mining in Northumberland and County Durham, and the pioneering development of early livestock breeding, particularly the Durham Shorthorn.

areas that lent themselves to development. It even, as a bonus, had a left-over coal deposit.

The most radical change that the museum has had to cope with is in how it gets the money it needs. Initially, it was wholly funded by the consortium of local authorities; now only 10 per cent comes from that source, and the remainder has to come from takings at the gate, and from its own revenue-raising initiatives. While there has been no shortage of business-like and suc-cessful initiatives, the effect has been to make long-term planning difficult, to hold professional staffing to a minimum, and to limit resources for research into the collections. Some of these difficulties have also been met by positive and beneficial initiatives, especially the development of the long-standing role of capable and enthusiastic volunteers in the restoration of exhibits, adminis-tration and interpretation into a very professional operation. Nevertheless, this represents one more example of the consequences of uncertainty in fund-ing, and of the investment balance that needs to be struck between, on the one hand, taking commercial initiatives and, on the other, managing and re-searching the collections which forms the essential basis for outreach and sustained commercial success. See also the National Maritime Museum case study on p190.

The approach to information management

As observed in the case study of the museum in the first edition of this book, the management of information about the collections in relation to the ways in which people wish to make use of them has been seriously considered from the earliest days.

'From the start, the development policy of the museum has included the planning of documentation. Starting from a level of recording which could be consistently maintained by a small nucleus of curatorial and clerical staff, the plan envisaged progress to fuller recording and maximum exploitation of information resources.' Orna and Pettitt (1980) p155.

The sequence of activities described then has remained essentially the same; accessioning and registration remain on a manual basis, though the donor index is held as a computer file. The classification scheme came to form the basis of the Social History and Industrial Classification (SHIC) (Museum Doc-umentation Association, 1993), which is still in use.

The area where major changes have taken place is in the photographic col-lections. Their potential richness as a source of information led me in 1983 to use a sample of the photographic collection in a pilot project for a thesaurus which would complement the classification, and allow searches for photo-graphs of particular subjects, specific places, particular dates, etc. with a de-gree of precision not otherwise possible (Orna, 1983). Circumstances did not allow the project to be followed up, but the museum has now been able to take advantage of developments in imaging technology which allow very full

The photographic archive as it was in 1980	As it is today
Acquisition	**Acquisition**
Record creation Copy negative made	Photographs scanned on to optical disk
Contact print made	
Originals returned to donor	Originals returned to donor
Processing Copy negatives stored in numerical order	
Contact prints stored numerically in albums + information on photographs	
Index entries made	Full details input to database of records: donor, acquisition date, location, subject content, classification number
1. donor/lender	
2. location by county	
3. subject index (based on classification with copy of photograph on index card)	
Retrieval Searches in index	Search on fields & free-text of data-base records, with simultaneous presentation of selected images
Contact prints	
Negatives	Production of prints of selected images

exploitation of the information potential of the photography archive, as shown in Figure 1.1 on p142.

A recently introduced system,[2] designed to a specification drawn up by museum staff, aims:

- To promote wider access to the archive by visitors through access points in the museum
- To reduce the staff time involved in making searches
- To cultivate better searching techniques, enabling the archive to be more effective in providing users with the images and data which they require
- To improve collections management procedures, releasing some staff time for other purposes
- To provide other museums and users with the data from the archive enabling searching to be undertaken away from the museum
- To provide educational establishments with resource material for developing learning materials.

In the system, which is now operating, photographs have been scanned on to an optical disc, and linked to their records held in a database. The high quality of the manual records maintained from the start of the museum allowed them to be used as the basis for the new system. They have been supplemented by additional data (including donor, date of acquisition, and nature and location of related documents) which make them effectively into master records for photographs and other visual materials.

Finding items to match requests is where the system's strength is most manifest – instead of the slow manual process of scanning catalogue cards with the appropriate classification number(s), it is now possible to search quickly on any term in any field, and to make free text searches for single or combined terms. In effect, the system creates an index of significant words and numbers (including classification numbers) from the data input to the records. Access to relevant records is correspondingly rapid, and selection is made easy by the simultaneous presentation of images. See Chapter 4 p56, for a discussion of classifications and indexes.

The photo archive in its old form was already quite intensively used by the museum for promotional activities, exhibitions and publications, and by external customers (including TV companies and publishers) who purchased images for commercial purposes. Material benefits have come quickly from the new system; payments by commercial photo researchers are making an increased contribution to revenue now that it has become so much quicker and easier to locate relevant images.

The system is designed for various levels of access; at present it is available only to museum staff, at the most detailed level, but a version giving less de-

[2] The system is a development of the MUSCAT database software originally developed for mainframe computers; it is used for the curatorial database, but different software is being used for public access workstations.

tailed access, using touch screens, is being developed for visitors. The museum attaches great importance to giving visitors the means of taking their own 'behind-the-scenes' look at the collections, following their own interests rather than having their 'ways in' controlled by the decisions of museum staff.[3] Funding is being sought for a new building dedicated to this purpose, which is seen as essential for ensuring the future of the museum.

The next application of the image system is for the trade catalogues in the library; the main object collection remains on the original cards, but as new objects are acquired their recording is being integrated to the image system.

As the system develops and is more widely applied, it should ultimately integrate accessioning and registration with documentation, using a single-master record which can be accessed and updated in various forms.

Information management and interpretation

One of the striking features of Beamish is the continuity of approach between collections management and documentation on one hand, and interpretation on the other. The organizational structure of the museum helps in this respect; there are only four main divisions: Development, Curatorial, Administration and Marketing. The Senior Keeper in the curatorial section has responsibility for collections management and documentation; of the three keepers – Social History, Industry, and Interpretation – the Keeper of Interpretation is responsible for the supervisors of Transport, Town, Colliery Community and Costume, and for demonstrators, volunteers, etc.

It has always been a fundamental point of policy that exhibits should not be captioned, but should 'tell their own story'. The means of doing that include: contemporary posters on the approach to the new area of Pockerley Manor (which extends the time-span back into the eighteenth century), and documents on the master's desk, such as forms for recording the birth of illegitimate children; a slide show in the Chapel; advertisements in the shops, the garage and the print works; and notices in the school. But above all Beamish is characterized by its strong reliance on personal interpretation by men and women in the costume of the period, going about their work in shops and on farm, engaging in local crafts like quilting, teaching classes in the school. The museum is fortunate in being able to draw on some people who worked in the closing days of local industries, like the ex-miners who introduce visitors to the drift mine, and on many more who are heirs to the ways of life which the museum represents.

The approach to interpretation is very firmly third person – the demonstrators don't 'live the part' to the extent of engaging visitors in conversation as if

---

[3] A parallel to the approach advocated for businesses by Norman & Ramirez (1993): 'the goal is not to create value for customers but to mobilize customers to create their own value from the company's various offerings'.

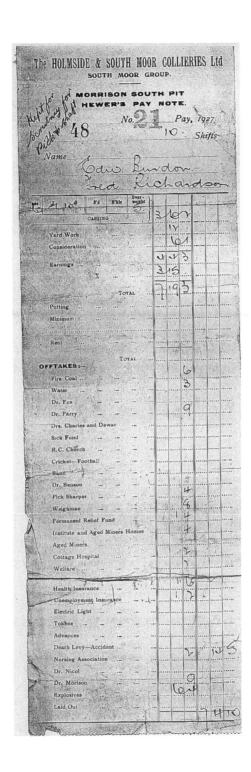

REGIONAL

Glass was made on Tyneside from 1619 and Wearside just before 1700. The fuel was easy to obtain and cheap, the other materials of sand, flint, and potash came cheaply as ballast on the colliers, who could also ship out the finished products.

Sunderland had several works in the early 19th. Century, making bottles and glass sheet especially, but with some good tableware as well, including wineglasses engraved with scenes on the Wear.

The Tyne was similar, and here too the cones were along the river. Production was mainly for everyday ware, although in the later 18th. Century it had been known for its wineglasses, and their very fine decoration by the Beilby family and others.

Some of these glassworks were very large, especially Cooksons of South Shields, said to be the biggest in the country. It was reckoned that more glass was made on the Tyne in 1825 than in the whole of France. The local industry would grow very much from mid Century on, as a restricting tax was removed and new methods developed, especially the pressing of tableware in moulds - a process that could be mechanised.

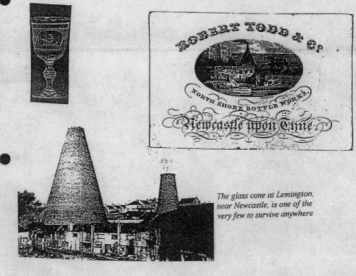

The glass cone at Lemington, near Newcastle, is one of the very few to survive anywhere

SUMMARY

- England was the World's largest producer
- Still a craft industry
- Major growth and mechanisation later in the Century
- North East a major location

they were living in the early twentieth century (a contrast with such institutions as Sovereign Hill, Ballarat's museum of the Australian gold rush), but are free to step into the present to offer contemporary explanations. The explanations are firmly based on relevant information from the collections, transformed by researchers into a series of manuals for each area or building, and on an intensive programme of training for interpretation staff, who are selected for their communication skills. The information flow is a two-way process, as feedback and suggestions come from interactions with visitors. This aspect of information management is, as explained above, the responsibility of the Keeper of Interpretation.

Manuals typically contain details of families and firms associated with particular buildings, examples of documents like pay notes, maps, contemporary advertisements and illustrations from trade catalogues, diagrams of machinery, historical background notes on social movements, public notices, summaries of technological developments such as the early history of the motor car, statistical material (like a table of the output of coal in the great Northern Coalfield in the nineteenth century), and quotations from the trade press of the period. Figures 1.2 and 1.3 on pp145 and 146 show examples.

The *Newsletter* published by the Friends of Beamish is also worth mentioning, as an example of combining information based on the collection with the personal experience of contributors to create an attractive and informative product.

Evaluation

Beamish has had the conviction to maintain a well-founded initial approach to documentation; it has adapted to changed financial circumstances, taking 'crisis as the coin of opportunity'; it is using modern information technology to upgrade and unify its information management; and it realizes the importance of linking its information resources with the interpretation and outreach activities which have won it national and international acknowledgement.

References

ATKINSON, F. (1995), 'The real history of how Beamish began', *Friends of Beamish Newsletter,* 100

Museum Documentation Association (1993), *Social History and Industrial Classification (SHIC),* Cambridge: Museum Documentation Association

NORMAN, R. & RAMIREZ, R. (1993), 'From value chain to value constellation: designing interactive strategy', *Harvard Business Review,* 71 (4) 65–78

ORNA, E. (1983), *Build Yourself a Thesaurus; a Step by Step Guide,* Norwich: Running Angel

ORNA, E. & PETTITT, C. W. (1980), *Information Handling in Museums,* London: KG Saur/Clive Bingley

Bradford Art Galleries and Museums

Introduction

In 1974 UK local government re-organization saw the museums in Bradford, Keighley and Ilkley joined to form Bradford Art Galleries and Museums. There are now some 80 staff; this total includes one documentation person (an assisted placement for a disabled worker) and the equivalent of seven whole-time professional curatorial staff. The collections cover almost the whole gamut of disciplines, archaeology, technology, fine and applied art, natural sciences, and social history, which in Bradford also encompasses numismatics, ethnography, costume, textiles, militaria, musical instruments, and toys and dolls.

The early years

At the amalgamation Keighley museum had a large general collection that was documented in an idiosyncratic way. All had complete accession registers, but really these were 'daybooks' in Keighley for items acquired prior to 1939, and the accession number had not been put on the objects. Prior to 1939 the objects had been numbered in sequence, and an inventory created that tried to map these numbers to the entries in the daybooks – but only for donations! Purchases were recorded separately in the Town Hall, and these records were lost during World War II. In 1979 the Keeper of Social History decided she needed electronic help as all the parameters of collection management were becoming too great to cope with manually. Although some work was being done centrally with environmental recording in the natural sciences, using the local authority mainframe for social history was not considered an option as at the time there was a seven-year wait just for a 'feasibility study', and anyway 'the files would exceed one megabyte and be difficult to handle'! Therefore she looked for alternatives, and discovering that MODES was in preparation decided to continue using the in-house designed cards, which were already known to be MDA compatible, using the MDA data standards as then published.

The present situation

In 1986 the first version of MODES was implemented at Bradford, and this package is now used by all departments for documentation. The Social History Keeper is a MODES advisor for the Yorkshire and Humberside area. All the disciplines are now being computerized as far as possible to the same data standards (the basic 'MODES template' is the same for all), although the over-riding consideration is what each discipline requires to gain from the documentation exercise, so there are individual extensions to the basic template in each department. IT support is provided from the IT section of the Arts, Museums and Libraries Division, based in the Central Library.

Social history had perhaps the biggest problem. Work started from the written records, input by the keeper because discipline knowledge was required to interpret not only the records but such things as whose handwriting a transcription was in, which has allowed many previous queries and problems to be resolved. All new material is now input 'from scratch'. Approximately 37 600 entries are on the database, with about 5000 waiting to be done. The assistant keeper has dealt with the archaeology records. The technology department had good documentation, which is gradually being transcribed and input; the documentation post mentioned above is attached to this department at present, and the work is about one-third complete.

Fine art has some 5500 records on the database to accession register or better standard, with about a third of the entries containing full information at present. This department makes considerable use of volunteers located via NADFAS, the National Association of Decorative and Fine Art Societies, a national body with local branches.

Natural sciences have the largest collection in terms of numbers. At present some 400 000 geology and mollusca specimens are being catalogued, along with some other invertebrates. This department has recently had two posts for three months each year to assist with the documentation on a project basis. These posts have been funded by the Friends organization with matching grants from the Yorkshire and Humberside Area Museum Council.

A subject specialist is appointed each time, and the attachment used for training in museum documentation. These project-based staff are expected to quality control the records, spotting misidentifications for example.

Thus a variety of approaches are being used at Bradford, part pragmatic and part 'horses for courses', but all are working to common standards and with common objectives.

The users

Most of the use of the databases is internal to the museums at present, principally because the curators are unhappy with the overall 'quality' of the data. However other uses are foreseen, such as handlists, checklists, publications and exhibition support. The documentation team is looking at the World Wide Web, led by the fine art department. However, copyright is seen as a problem, in that the museum sometimes does not actually hold the copyright to the pictures it owns. An example is the department's paintings by David Hockney; this artist specifically retains copyright, and this means that the museum may not even digitize the images. Schools and the wider educational establishment are seen as high on the list of potential users outside the museum to benefit from the documentation effort. Specialist groups, ranging from local drama groups interested in costume research to a project to study the history of parasol frame makers, are also seen as important clients.

The level of information to go into the public databases is aimed at supplying the needs of client groups. This starts with collection details, such as the range and the period covered by a collection, but the object-level information will increase in time. A major collaborative project is under way to put on computer information about and images of the large collection of local photographs. The museum's partners in this are the library section of the division, and the Bradford office of the West Yorkshire Archives Service. Other partners may choose to join, for example local newspapers. This project has been held up because of staff shortages; it is intended to make the images available in local libraries local studies sections, but initially only via the staff. Direct public access is not yet possible in part because location information is included and also because of the equipment and staffing implications, which need to be resolved. However it is intended that an image database will be available to the public eventually, possibly with the aid of a bid to the Heritage Lottery Fund.

Evaluation

This case study has a positive message for situations in which different working methods have to be supported across a range of different disciplines: provided common standards and objectives are agreed and maintained, a variety of ways of working can be accommodated within one institution.

Callendar House, Falkirk

The Falkirk Museums, and the History Research Centre which forms part of them, merit a case study both as a local authority institution which has developed greatly in the past few years, and for the unusual range of collections which are managed in a unified way.

Background

The present Falkirk Museums originated in the 1920s as a burgh museum, which continued on a modest scale, for a time without a curator, and never having more than a single curator until 1973 when the present museum manager was appointed. Since then, there has been considerable development. By 1975, the service had four properties, and by 1991 it had a staff of eight. Most of the development has taken place since then; Callendar House (where the History Research Centre is located) is now the museum headquarters, there are two branch museums and a large central stores and workshop facility, where most of the object collections management is done, and there are over 40 staff.

The collections cover objects, archives, photographs, a library, and sites and monuments records. A recent important addition, brought about by the Local Government etc. (Scotland) Act of 1994, is local authority archives for the area. The object collections include archaeology, natural history, costume, social history, industry, and decorative art. The material held at Callendar House (originally a mediæval fortified house, which was added to over the centuries until it reached its present French-château style in the nineteenth century) includes:

- Archives of local businesses, local people, societies and organizations, and some local authority archives
- More than 25 000 photographs
- Maps and plans
- Surveys of local industry, trades and crafts, and of local wildlife
- Films and videos
- Sound archives of local people
- A small reference library
- Microfiche copies of material relevant to Falkirk District
- The collections database for all object and non-object collections of the Falkirk Museums.

Objectives and performance criteria

The changes in local government have brought rapid developments in the management of museums over recent years; performance targets have changed, and there is a requirement to provide evidence of achievement (responsibility for establishing critical success factors and performance criteria rests with museum staff).

The Museum Services Development Plan for 1996–1999 sets out its mission as: 'To serve as a bridge between residents and their heritage', and defines its aims for the next three years in these terms:

- To preserve for posterity evidence of the culture and heritage of the Falkirk area
- To interpret for local residents and visitors the culture and heritage of the Falkirk area
- To encourage learning, both formal and informal
- To play our part in contributing to the quality of life of local residents
- To play our part in the economic development of the Falkirk area
- To achieve, through enjoyment of the museum experience, customer satisfaction
- To play a key role in the development of tourism in the Falkirk area.

Many of the objectives associated with these aims are information related. They include not only development of documentation and resolution of the documentation backlog, but also extending educational activities of various kinds, research and analysis on customer needs and response of visitors to the museums, spreading information about the museums in a range of target markets by a variety of means, and training in interpretive methodology and for raising staff awareness of the collections.

Critical success factors are related to the aims and objectives, and the performance indicators are selected to be appropriate criteria for establishing whether they have been achieved. Some are qualitative (e.g. attaining full registration with the Museums and Galleries Commission), some depend on a simple yes/no answer (e.g. has an annual review of collections policy been carried out), and others are quantitative (e.g. percentage of public research enquiries answered in three days).

Information management

Collections information
MDA cards were used from 1977 to 1987 and they provided the basis for the record structure; a partial card index to them has been transferred to the present computer system. A computer database, for museum objects, photograph and archives, was established in 1984 with Revelation G software, which was upgraded in 1991 to Advanced Revelation. In 1994 a move was made to Vernon Systems Ltd Standard COLLECTION; the system, while described as com-

plicated and time-consuming to learn, is appreciated for its comprehensiveness, its capacity to handle records for a great variety of materials, and its retrieval capabilities. Interestingly, the museum does not at present have the actual collection management module of Standard COLLECTION, but it has in effect established a collections management database through effective use of the various standard record formats available in the software (see Figure 3.1 on p154 for an example of a record). For an account of another use of Standard COLLECTION, see the case study of St Albans Museum, p249.

Everything, from museum objects to archives, sites and monuments records and reference works from the library, goes into the same collections database, which can be partitioned by department. An example of the use of appropriate record formats for specialist purposes comes from Archaeology and History, where the Curator uses the Site Authority format (which includes a separate screen for Site management and use) to record Sites and Monuments information. Standard fields of the software are also used to cover such special library requirements as periodical circulation and class marks. While the detailed conservation recording screen is part of the collections management module, the museum uses a basic, mainly free-text, screen available in its system to record condition at acquisition, completeness and treatment. Standard COLLECTION allows movement from records to images, but as yet the development resources needed are not available.

A very wide range of retrieval capabilities is available, and though this in itself creates problems of finding time to learn to use them fully, the museum is able to make effective use of a number of them. At the simplest level, it is possible to enter an accession number, simple name, classification term, or person name at the first field on the first screen, and the system will find all records with any relationship to the search term entered. The next level of search uses the Index Retrieval Window to search on the contents of one or more of about 50 fields; here search criteria can be combined using Boolean AND. The most complicated searches use Retrieval Tools to search across the whole database.

'Authorities' and terminology control

Standard COLLECTION takes a very distinctive approach, which differs from other systems encountered in the case-study museums (and one which the present author finds it quite difficult to conceptualize!). One area where this quality manifests itself is that of 'authorities'. The 'typical' approach is usually something along the lines of associating with specific fields in a record an 'authority list' of the standard forms of such things as personal or geographical names which the museum has decided to use in that field. Sometimes these authority lists form part of a thesaurus, sometimes they are separate, and the thesaurus consists just of the terms which the institution has decided to use for objects, processes, materials, etc, together with their related 'Non-preferred' 'Broader', 'Narrower', and 'Related' terms. Standard COLLECTION extends the concept of authorities in an interesting way; it provides for a total of no

Standard COLLECTION system. Record for standard form of a personal name

Figure 3.1

```
========================= < Object Acquisition & Provenance > =========================
========================= < Person Authority Maintenance > =========================

System Id        8897                    Record Type     Person
Person Type      Individual              Gender          Male


Name Type   Title      Firstnames        Known As     Lastname            Init
Preferred   Mr         John              John         Crompton            W J


Postnominals
Address Type     Postal
   Line 1        59 Main St          ┌─────────────────────────────────────────┐
   Line 2        Brightons           │ │         More Person Information        │
   Line 3                            │ ├─────────────────────────────────────── │
   Place                             │ │   1> Life Details                  │   │
   Postcode/Zip                      │ │   2 |  Work Details                │   │
Telecom Type                         │ │   3 |  Relations/Contacts          │   │
   Number                            │ │   4 |  Roles                       │ * │
                                     │ │   5 |  Photography & Documentation  │   │
Notes                                │ │   6 |  Action Diary                │ ? │
                                     │ │   7 |  Authority Management         │ ? │
                                     └ └───────────────────────────────────────┘

Pop Up │ Single  │ Select row by pressing (Return) or enter row number [Esc] – Exit

Ed Off │         │         │ Elspeth                              │ Level      7
```

less than 177 supporting databases called 'authorities', which are used for recording a range of information about people, places, etc. which goes far beyond being a mere 'vocabulary' of the preferred form of the personal or place name. The person authority, for example, can be used to record life details (relationships to other people, contacts and events); work details; roles, etc.. More than that, there are four different types of authority – as the manual explains it:

'simple, thesaural, hierarchical, and complex. *Simple* authorities simply provide lists of alternative terms. *Thesaural* Authorities additionally allow Thesaural Relationships to be made between terms. *Hierarchical* Authorities support Thesaural Relationships and additionally allow Terms to be *organised* at different levels of a hierarchical classificatory scheme. *Complex* Authorities are specially designed to store auxiliary data.' Vernon Systems Limited, 1995.

Translating that into terms more generally used in talking about these matters, a simple authority seems to equate to a Roget-type thesaurus, a thesaural one corresponds to the alphabetically arranged listing of a thesaurus, and a hierarchical one to the classified listing which in most thesauri complements the alpha one. (The complex authority has so far defeated me.) In practice, as applied in Falkirk Museums, several thesaural authorities are used, which means that the data entered into fields controlled by these authorities are linked using thesaural relations.

The terminology in use in the museums is described as loosely based on that of the Museum of English Rural Life (MERL) – SHIC (Social History and Industrial Classification) was not found to be detailed enough for the museum's requirements in industrial history. A subject index based on the classification originally used in the museum has been developed, and the aim is to apply subject terms in the same way across all items that are subject indexed, whether museum objects or archival items (see below for the limits to subject indexing of archival material).

Archives and records management

Archives connected with objects were the first to be collected; from 1973 onwards, the scope was extended to trade catalogues and business records (until the arrival of an archivist on the museum staff, these were, of necessity, treated as museum objects rather than as archives). Before the changes brought about by the Local Government etc. (Scotland) Act of 1994 local authority records were handled in Stirling, at the administrative centre for the authority. Sections 53 and 54 of that Act imposed new responsibilities on councils for managing and preserving their records, and those of their predecessor authorities. Falkirk Council is further ahead in implementing these responsibilities than any other new Scottish local authority. Its records management policy gives management of current and semi-current records to the Council's Law and Administration Services, while archival records are managed by the museum's archivist, at the History Research Centre in Callendar House, where they are freely accessible to the public for research and education purposes.

There are limits to the extent to which archival materials can be subject indexed; so, while historic photographs are indexed by their content, it is not possible to index volumes of minutes except at the most general level – for example, company minutes are indexed only with the nature of the company's business.

Integrated information management

The database would form an excellent resource for creating information products, as there is an export facility for downloading to ASCII and Word for Windows, which would permit taking material over to desktop publishing software for exhibition catalogues and special-interest publications; this could draw on the skills of the museum's existing design team. The Standard COLLECTION system does not handle visitor and booking information, so the Museum Service is looking at purchasing another visitor information programme.

Evaluation

The many positive features that emerge from this case study include:

- The decision to develop a unified database covering the whole range of the collections, with management by qualified specialists in each domain
- The benefits which museum staff have gained from using the Standard COLLECTION database, which, in spite of its complexity, has, by their own account, made them much more aware of underlying structures in terminology – as they put it, 'accurate terminology control has taken on a much greater importance and this goes for all the fields – not just the usual classification terms'. It has also provided proof of 'the value of putting good, accurate data into the system ... now that we can see the practical advantages it gives in data association and retrieval; the database also has so many possibilities we want to explore that it's helping to clarify the way we manage our collections information.' This is certainly the kind of testimonial that the IT infrastructure should aim to merit
- The initiatives which the local authority responsible for the museum has taken in records management, and the important responsibility for local authority archival records given to the museum's archivist
- The bringing together of museum and archive professionals to work on an integrated collection. This has led to a mutual understanding of the essential similarities and the critical differences between the approaches of the two (for example in their definitions of terms which both use, such as 'provenance'), and to constructive attempts towards accommodating both within the same system for managing information
- The public access provided by the History Research Centre which is freely open to those who wish to pursue their enquiries there

- The fact that the museum is able to establish its own performance criteria within the framework of local government requirements, and that the criteria are qualitative as well as quantitative.

The problematic areas are fewer; they relate to human resources. The key one is whether the museum will be able to employ the growing number of qualified people who will be essential to get the maximum value out of its developing information resources. Sophisticated IT is no substitute for people; its greatest value is the support it gives in asking new questions and making creative use of the answers, and that demands human minds. A related problem is the complexity of the Standard COLLECTION system; it is admirably powerful and flexible, but it needs more time than is currently available to master and take advantage of its full potential.

Reference

Vernon Systems Limited (1995), *Collection Authority Tool User Guide*

Ceredigion Museum, Aberystwyth

Introduction

Ceredigion Museum, in the Welsh seaside resort of Aberystwyth, and the Museum Service based on it, serve a geographical area recognized since the fifth century AD. Bounded by the sea, rivers and mountains, the region has a comparatively small resident population (65 000), added to in summer by holiday visitors, and in term-time by 4000 university students. The area is one with a high proportion (about 60 per cent) of people whose first language is Welsh.

The museum was set up in 1972 by the Cardiganshire Antiquarian Society, and run by a committee with representation from the local authorities of what was then Cardiganshire. In the 1974 reorganization of local government which followed on the 1972 Local Government Act, the new Ceredigion District Council took responsibility for the museum, and appointed a Museum Officer to run it. More staff were added in the next few years, and, as the collections grew, a move from its original home in a Georgian house in the town became necessary. In 1977 the lease of the Coliseum Cinema in the town centre expired, and after careful restoration which retained the essential features of the original building – constructed in 1904–5 as a theatre and converted to a cinema in 1932 – the museum moved its collections in 1981 and opened to the public in 1982.

More recent local government changes have made the Museum Service a responsibility of the Ceredigion County Council, and it now reports to the Council's Language and Culture Committee. Since the early increase in staffing, there has not been much further growth in the human resources, although the collections have gone on increasing and the work undertaken, particularly in information management and outreach education, has developed greatly. Services offered include support for educational visits and projects and staff visits to schools. Currently there are five full-time and one part-time staff members – two of whom are curatorial. Volunteers (museum studies students, young people on school work-experience placements, and local supporters) make a significant contribution in the form of researching groups of museum items, such as cameras, and producing fact sheets on them.

The collections

The main collections of the museum (about 30,000 items) consist of objects made or used in the Ceredigion district in the period 1850–1950, and representing domestic, working and cultural life in such domains as agriculture, seafaring, lead mining, crafts and trades, education, and eisteddfods. The museum also holds significant collections of local archaeological finds, costumes, printed materials, MSS, pictures, photographs, natural history specimens, and geological specimens.

Collections information management

An excellent foundation was laid by the museum's first curator, who was meticulous in accessioning everything in the collections; each item was given the essentials of an accession number, a catalogue number, and a basic record in a card index. Thus, when the present curator took over in 1984, the foundations for a sound collections information system had been laid. This was the period when Manpower Services Commission schemes provided many museums with teams of people who received payment and training to equip them for their future careers, and who were mainly put to work on inputting museum records to various computer systems which were then being introduced into museums. The quality and value of the outcomes, both to the museums and the MSC-sponsored participants, varied a good deal, depending mainly on the attention that was given to managing the teams. In the case of Ceredigion, the process was efficiently managed, and almost all the existing documentary information about the collections was successfully input (and the card indexes have been retained to this day). The software used was MODES version 1, which has been upgraded as each new version became available.

The present system: MODES Plus

Procedures for entry and accessioning items are straightforward. A bi-lingual entry form is completed by museum staff and the person leaving any item in the museum. All items which are taken into the collections are entered into the accessions register, and an acknowledgement letter, with a list of the relevant items, their catalogue number and a brief description, is sent to all donors and lenders.

MODES Plus has been used since 1987 for creating catalogue records and finding information. The aim is to get all basic information about items in the collections – their history before entering the museum, how they came in, what has happened to them since – into a single file, rather than separate databases for different areas of the collections. The database currently consists of 35,000 records. See Figure 4.1 on p160 for an example.

Hard-copy indexes can be produced by:
- Donor/vendor/lender name
- Classified name (the classification group recorded for each item is derived from the system developed at St Fagan's Museum of Welsh folk life)
- Accession/catalogue number
- Personal/corporate body name
- Place name.

Additional indexes are available on-line: by date, by event and activity (a combined index of specific events and general activities), full name (i.e. the

```
***record ***
*RECORD NUMBER 1978.14.3A
*DOCUMENTATION GROUP 117
*CAPTION BATHING MACHINE COMIC CARD
*IDENTIFICATION
*SIMPLE NAME PICTURE
*FULL NAME PRINT & POSTCARD (COMIC)
*CLASSIFIED NAME AIE & C3E
*FIELD COLLECTION
*PLACE GORSGOCH
*DESCRIPTION
*PART:ASPECT:DESC : material : CARD
*PART:DIMEN:READING : : 11.3 X 7.4 CMS
*CONTENT
*BRIEF SUMMARY BATHING MACHINE COMIC CARD SENT TO MARGARET DAVIES, DOLAI
VILLA, LLANYBYTHER FROM A FRIEND (SALLY)
*SIMPLE CATEGORY DOCUMENT & HUMOUR
*CONTENT
*PERSON : DAVIES, MARGARET
*ADDRESS DOLAU VILLA, LLANYBYTHER
*PERSON : SALLY
*OBJECT BATHING MACHINE
*ACTIVITY LEISURE : SWIMMING
*PLACE LLANYBYTHER
*ACQUISITION
*METHOD DONATION
*DATE 28.1.78
*PERSON From : Owen, J.D., Dr
*NOTE PURCHASED AT SALE AT AROSFA, GORSGOCH
#
```

most precise name for the item sought – 'postcard (comic)' in the example), simple name (i.e. the general group to which an item belongs – 'picture' in the example), person (people by name in any context, referred to in any part of the record), role (people referred to in the record as filling specific roles, e.g. as maker, person depicted), and by storage location. These indexes give direct access to the records. On-line information retrieval allows a wide range of searches, including Boolean; it is possible to find records of items which refer to or depict specific objects in particular places and/or at given dates, records which relate to named people in particular roles, etc.

Apart from the main database, the curator maintains an aptly named 'magpie file' on MODES Plus, which acts as a one-stop 'way in' to a range of hard-copy documentation, including local history materials and sources, bibliographies, details of archaeological sites and finds, illustrations of objects in the museum, biographies. This useful quarry also holds a file of all the museum's labels, and lists of its collection of modern photographs. The records are indexed and retrieved in a similar way to those in the museum object file; for example, an enquirer seeking information about a particular artist will find a record containing the museum labels for his/her works in the museum, a biography, published accounts including catalogues (whether in the museum or not), any obituary from the local paper, modern museum photographs of the artist's works in the collection and elsewhere, and the museum file on the artist.

Terminology control

Work has started on building up a bi-lingual terminology list, based on the terms which have already been used in the records, and including regional terms and standard forms of geographical and personal names. The aim is both to help users find all records relevant to what they are seeking, and to enable them to move from one topic to another as they wish and travel through the database by the paths they wish to follow. Software is being developed at Glamorgan University, Pontypool, which is intended to help in using the terminology lists as a kind of thesaurus.

Plans for future work

The next developments planned include:

- Adding to the records information about the current location of items, and developing a system for keeping it up to date – at present, time pressure means that changes of location are recorded on paper, and that means time lost when staff need to find the items in question
- Bringing the paper-based condition report and conservation records into electronic form, and adding details of condition and conservation treatment to the records in the main database
- As decisions on preferred terms etc. are taken in the course of work on terminology control, using MODES Plus to validate them in the database, and to add Welsh terms to records.

The museum and its public

Who they are
The museum welcomes about 35,000 visitors a year. A survey in 1994 (by questionnaire available in the museum for people to fill in if they wished) showed that three-quarters of the respondents were from outside the Ceredigion area; the remainder were made up of residents in Aberystwyth and elsewhere in Ceredigion, together with students. Nearly a third of them were making a return visit. Ten per cent of the respondents were fluent Welsh speakers. Nearly 20 per cent had an interest in local history. The general response to the atmosphere of the museum was very positive; nearly 70 per cent found it interesting, educational and stimulating, and only 2.4 per cent were bored or intimidated or found it unfriendly.

Information interactions
More information searches originate at present from within the museum than from outside, and the museum staff see helping the outside world to learn what is on offer as a major task. For this reason, there is a plan to make accessible software (In Touch) available in the galleries to stimulate interest and encourage visitors to pursue their own lines of enquiry by straightforward interaction with the collections database.

Most enquiries which the museum handles from its public at present are thematic, often relating to a particular geographical area, village or family. Enquirers often seek the history and associations of objects, but in many cases this kind of information is not available – partly because the cards originally used allowed little scope for recording unstructured information (a deficiency of MDA cards overcome by MODES Plus with its capacity for recording and indexing free text), partly because it can be difficult to decide what to select from the account given by donors, and sometimes because, in the words of the museum's curator 'most donors don't think what they know about objects is important; they assume that the curators know everything'. This undue modesty accounts for the lack of in-depth information about many Welsh domestic and folk items.

The museum also seeks to tap the knowledge of its visitors through small theme exhibitions – for example a small exhibition of knitting sheaths, and an exhibition of items from the collections chosen by friends of the museum and by its staff, with their own comments on the reasons for their choice.

The local-history interest which was a strong feature in the visitor survey is promoted by curatorial involvement in evening classes for researching local topics, for which the students set their own agenda. The Curator is currently working with a number of local groups which aim to set up small branch museums (an interesting observation is that most of the research interest comes from members of the English-speaking population, while most of the knowledge of local things lies among the Welsh speakers).

A different kind of information interaction – between the museum and libraries in Ceredigion – has recently been provided for; resources have been made available to develop access from the libraries to museum and archive databases in the area. There are already co-operative links between the museum and local libraries and archives, including public libraries, the National Library and the Royal Commission on the Ancient and Historic Monuments of Wales.

Evaluation

This case study reflects a museum which has from the start managed information on a sound basis, and has made good, progressive use of limited resources. As with Hampshire and Norfolk Museum Services MODES Plus has been well used and repays the effort put into its use for recording the collections. See p164 and p214. The aim of getting everything into a single database is sensible and feasible for a museum whose collections are not over-large, and which is run by a small team who exchange information informally all the time. The only downside to the situation is that management of the information system has to depend mainly on one person – the Curator, who so far is the only member of staff with thorough knowledge of MODES Plus.

The museum's staff make valiant efforts to let the local public know what they have to offer, to involve them in the museum's use of information about the collections, and to encourage them to contribute from their own knowledge. Raising the visibility of museums in the community is a long-term task, but an essential part of managing information in the museum context. It is encouraging to see the actions which some of the smaller museums described in this book are taking in this direction. For example, see the North Somerset Museum Service, p223, and Callendar House, Falkirk, p151. In the case of Ceredigion, it would be a very satisfactory outcome if the work being done resulted in bringing together the knowledge and interest of both the Welsh- and English-speaking public.

Hampshire Museums Service

Background

Hampshire County Council Museums Service, based in Winchester, provides headquarters administration, documentation services, a departmental library, and design and conservation workshops and stores for a group of local and specialized museums throughout the county. As an intellectual resource for member museums, it holds collections in archaeology, natural science, decorative art and local history; its library covers museology, Hampshire history and other subjects relevant to the collections.

The purpose of the Museums Service is to: 'inspire and satisfy a deeper level of interest, enjoyment and understanding of Hampshire's heritage and environment, by developing the full potential of the museum collections in its care, and assisting other organizations with similar aims'.

In pursuing these aims, it follows a policy of collecting 'material that provides evidence of human activity in the county of Hampshire, and of the natural environment of the county, in all periods'. As well as objects, including photographs, printed ephemera, paintings, prints and drawings, it collects documents which directly support an object or collection of objects, particularly archaeological site archives; books and journals are collected as part of the museum library, or as objects in collections.

Steps towards automation

From their foundation in the nineteenth century until the 1970s, traditional methods of recording information about the collections prevailed in the museums of Hampshire. Acquisition registers of various kinds were the main source of information, supplemented by a few card indexes derived from them.

In the 1970s a decision was taken to set up a computerized system for the museums covered by the service. Typically for the period, it was regarded as something that could properly be dealt with by the staff responsible for the local authority's computing. Equally typically, there was no shared ground of understanding between the IT specialists and the curators; the one knew nothing about computers, and the other was equally unaware of what went on in museums. Because neither side knew enough, the software selected was not appropriate to the tasks it was meant to support, the data structure was weak, terminology was not controlled and curators used words according to their fancy, and editing of records was described as 'anarchic'. The contribution of the computer, as is usual in these circumstances, seems to have been to make things go wrong much faster than unaided human beings could have done.

This situation continued until the late 1980s, when, on the basis of a consultant's analysis, the Museums Service decided to seek a better solution. A Keeper of Documentation was appointed with the remit to carry out this work; his first decisions were to use the Object format developed as a national standard for data structure, and to introduce a considerable degree of terminology control, using the Object Format Rules. After experimentation with the MODES software from the MDA, and with Oracle, MODES was decided on as the most suitable database package.

Modes Plus in use today

Varied and ingenious use is being made of MODES Plus in the Museums Service.

Databases in current use

The main database consists of 82 000 object records; a further 10,000 remain to be integrated into the main database – this will still not cover all the objects. The object record format follows the MDA standard (see Figure 5.1 on p166).

The old acquisitions registers of the museums for which the service is responsible, from the mid-19th century onwards, have been documented as objects in their own right. The records make some analysis of their content and structure, and analyse the formation of the identity numbers used in the various registers, so it is possible to relate records of objects in the object database to the register in which their acquisition is likely to have been recorded. Links between the registers database and the object database are in the process of being created. No attempt has been made, however, to do anything with the card indexes derived from the registers, as they are deemed to be not sufficiently reliable.

The other major database which is in current use consists of Person records (5000–10 000 records). These can be extremely detailed, citing sources of evidence in the collections for the person concerned (for example census returns, bill heads, advertisements, objects made by or related to the person).

Work in progress

The potential of MODES Plus is being further exploited in a variety of ways. The object and person databases are being combined into a single database for purposes of access (the master files will remain separate), using InTouch/Run Touch software developed by MDA. A Place format is under development. Records of Hampshire museums already exist in the MUSREC format developed for the Museums Service.

Also under development is a database for conservation using the CONS-REC format, which is being versioned for release in CATLIST software.

More experimental work in progress includes the use of MODES Plus to put together pre-packaged 'off-the-shelf' loan exhibitions for museums supported by the service. A pilot example is based on a collection of jigsaw maps.

RECORD NUMBER	HMCMS:D1995.25
PREVIOUS NUMBER	HMCMS:D1984.16
IDENTIFICATION	
CLASSIFIED NAME	recreation & toys & puzzles
CLASSIFIED NAME	society & religion
CLASSIFIED NAME	transport & rail
SIMPLE NAME	jigsaw puzzle
OTHER NAME	map & railway map
TITLE	Cathedral
BRIEF DESCRIPTION	jigsaw puzzle, wood, The Cathedral, Exeter Cathedral on one side, railway map on the other, published by the Great Western Railway, GWR, made by Chad Valley Co, Harborne, West Midlands, 1920s–30s?
BRIEF DESCRIPTION	The map scale is about 1:350000, say 36 miles to 1 inch; it shows the rail network, but no other topography
BRIEF DESCRIPTION	The building of Exeter Cathedral started with the transepts about 1112–33 and towers about 1133, and continued through the 12th to 14th centuries and later; major restoration was made in the 19th century; the see of Exeter was removed from Crediton in 1049, and the early foundation was probably one of Benedictine monks
BRIEF DESCRIPTION	The very similar piece shapes make this interesting to do, many of the pieces have three lugs and one hole, the 'side' lugs fitting a hole made by the conjunction of two adjacent pieces not a hole in an adjacent piece; the cathedral picture is uninspiring, the map is much more fun: JMN: 1995
DESCRIPTION	
PART:ASPECT:DESC	: jigsaw feature: two sided & card box & colour printed & fully interlocking & (many) similar shape piece, 3 and 1 & curvaceous pieces & hand cut & 150 piece & small piece & key picture (on box)
INSCRIPTION	: printed: box:: GWR / JIG-SAW PUZZLE / ABOUT 150 PIECES ... / Manufactured by The Chad Valley Co., Harborne, Birmingham ... Published by The Great Western Railway Company.
PRODUCTION	
PERSON	railway: Great Western Railway
PERSON	toy mfr: Chad Valley Co
PLACE	Harborne & West Midlands
DATE	1920=1939(?)
CONTENT	
PERSON	railway: Great Western Railway & GWR
DATE	1920=1939(?)
OBJECT	map & railway map
CONTENT	
PLACE	Exeter & Devon
SITE NAME	Exeter Cathedral
ASSOCIATION	
OBJECT — Totext	

The package consists of a set of records covering:
- Publicity material
- A set of jigsaw maps drawn from the collections of the Hampshire Museums Service
- Captions for items in the exhibition
- Worksheets
- Activities for visitors
- Display equipment required
- A computer display, with instructions for installing an application prepared by the Museums Service. Figure 5.2 on p168 shows an exhibition record.

If a museum books the exhibition, everything necessary can be quickly assembled, and accompanying text material printed out.

Work on images includes trials on digitization and the use of Kodak Photo CD. Images and texts can be supported from MODES Plus, while hypertext software (Hypershell) is also being used for an experimental text and pictures database. The JPEG image file format is being used for everyday access to images.

InTouch is being used to create subsets from the main MODES Plus database which can be distributed to remote users by disk. An upgrade of InTouch /RunTouch will support the same images as are used in the master database.
See also the Norfolk Museums Service case study, p216.

Help for the users

Throughout all the databases, the aim is to retain a common format as far as possible, so as to give maximum help both to those who create records and to those who seek information from them; divergence is limited to those areas where it cannot be avoided, as in the case of records of people and of conservation treatment.

Users can move from database to database within MODES Plus, and can access 'Help' messages in windows on screen for each field label in records (the messages make use of the MODES facility for defining one's own help messages).

The Object Format Rules (OFR) are the main source of terminology control and advice on recording. These are ASCII text files for ease of distribution, and are available free. The suite of 300–400 files can be accessed through a hypertext front-end which uses the Object format to lead the user to the advice needed.

At the practical reference end of the scale, there are explanations in the database of all the codes used in the records, and statements of collecting policies for the areas covered by the service.

The Object Format Rules are designed to be wholly general in application, rather than tied to this particular situation or even to MODES Plus; they provide examples of completed records, notes about mandatory fields, and 'essays'.

RECORD NUMBER	HMCMS:EXH1
IDENTIFICATION	
CLASSIFIED NAME	museum & display
CLASSIFIED NAME	recreation & toys & puzzles
CLASSIFIED NAME	environment & maps
SIMPLE NAME	exhibition
OTHER NAME	jigsaw puzzle & map
TITLE	Cutting Borders
TITLE	Jigsaw Maps
BRIEF DESCRIPTION	exhibition, Cutting Borders, Jigsaw Maps, illustrating maps in early and modern jigsaw puzzles, arranged by Hampshire CC Museum Service, Winchester, Hampshire, 1996
CAPTION	Maps and jigsaw puzzles go together.
CAPTION	The first jigsaws were teaching toys, dissected maps. John Locke, writing in the 17th century, had 'always had a fancy that learning might be a play and recreation to children'
CAPTION	Maps still appear on jigsaws today.
CAPTION	(comment) If you would like to write any comments about a jigsaw please do this on the pad provided; be careful to say which jigsaw you are describing.
PRODUCTION	
PERSON	curator: Norgate, Martin
PERSON	museum: Hampshire CC Museums Service
ADDRESS	Chilcomb House, Chilcomb Lane, Winchester, Hampshire SO23 8RD
PHONE	01962 846304
PLACE	Winchester & Hampshire
DATE	1996
DESCRIPTION	
PART:ASPECT:DESC	: display equipment: clip board, pen, and comment forms
PART:ASPECT:DESC	: display equipment: (other equipment is listed module by module)
NOTE	The exhibition is made up of a number of independent modules; see records subnumbered from this record
DISPOSAL	
METHOD	dummy record
RECORDER	MN: 12.4.1996

OBJECT — Totext

The essays offer straightforward and often very entertaining advice, based on long experience, for people who have to create records – they embody examples of good and bad practice, instructions for labour-saving use of the facilities of MODES, explanations of the use of controlled terms, arguments for and against documentation, and a range of helpful hints supported by apt quotations:

'Do not fill up the Brief description with waffle intended to make the entry look important, or you – the recorder – look clever; if there is little to say, say little. If there is nothing to say, ask why did you collect the object! Goethe put it neatly: "… some books seem to have been written, not to teach us anything, but to let us know the author has once known something"… Don't do the same in a Brief description.'

Classification and terminology control

Classified structure and controlled index terms are fundamental and complementary approaches to finding information; both are available to users of this system. Every record is allocated a classified name, drawn from a straightforward in-house classification which is closely related to what is actually in the collections.

For terminology control, the system uses over 90 term lists, associated with different fields, which together make up a complete thesaurus. The sources of terms are various; in many cases existing term lists have been edited to bring them into line with the thesaural standards adopted. The standards are those of BS 5723, with some useful and ingenious refinements. These include 'General Term' and 'Specific Term' (which allow for 'extended families' that provide for other up and down relations than those of the strict parent/child hierarchy, and so help to avoid using BS 'Related Term' for non-cousins), and various expansions of the Scope Note, which allow for separate identification of, for example, rules and definitions, and for the very important instruction 'DO NOT USE'.

Controlled terms from appropriate term lists are recommended for use for features of objects in the Description (as distinct from the free-text Brief Description) held of records.

Evaluation

This case study shows an ingenious and constructive use of the full potential of a sound and modestly priced system originally designed primarily for data entry. The development work that has extended its range has been possible because the Keeper of Documentation responsible has a particular interest in the problems involved, and a high level of programming skills. While there are problems of human resources for documentation in the Museums Service, there are lessons that could benefit other museums. The access to experience which is built into Hampshire's databases would be a valuable support for museums which are either starting to use MODES Plus, or already using it but at a fairly limited level.

The LASSI (Larger Scale Systems Initiative) project[1]

Origins

To those involved, it has probably sometimes seemed that LASSI (the Larger Scale Systems Initiative) had no beginning but had existed from the start of time. In fact, it began in around 1990, with informal feasibility studies undertaken by a group of large UK museums with the aim of finding out how much ground they shared in the matter of managing their collections and information about them. The results indicated that there was a good deal of common territory.

Formal consultancy commissioned in 1992 looked at the participating museums' existing systems, the requirements they identified for new systems, the business case for developing or purchasing a system that could be used by large museums, and the benefits that might be expected from such a system. The findings suggested that the solution would probably lie in enhancing an existing package, rather than developing one from scratch.

'Analysis paralysis'

The group of museums decided to carry out a detailed analysis, with the advice of consultants, following the government-sponsored SSADM (Structured Systems Analysis and Design Methodology) process.

As the work proceeded, what Grant (1996) has called 'analysis paralysis' set in. The project marked time on the spot, as many people worked on similar analytical tasks, but without producing noticeable forward movement. It became evident that there was a need for integration between, on the one hand, analysis dealing with logical attributes and, on the other, conceptual understanding of information content and what people need to do with it. On one side there were those who wanted an all-inclusive system plan before leaving the analysis stage; on the other, those with perhaps more experience of the world who wanted

[1] Various museums have been associated with the project at different times, though not all stayed with it to the end; some decided that their circumstances made it more appropriate to go ahead with acquiring a system on their own. The final membership of the consortium at the time of the signing of the agreements described in this case study consisted of:
Horniman Museum and Gardens, London
Imperial War Museum, London
Hull City Museums and Art Gallery
Leicestershire Museums, Arts and Records

National Maritime Museum, London
National Museum of Science and Industry, London, York and Bradford
National Museums and Galleries on Merseyside, Liverpool
Nottingham Museums
The parties to the agreements were the consortium of museums, the vendor, and the Museums and Galleries Commission (the MGC's role is to advise the British government on the development of museums; it is also responsible for the museum Registration Scheme).

something less finished which would, by that very fact, be more manageable and more malleable. The argument for 'try it and see' was also driven by constraints on time and resources, especially in those museums which had deadlines by which existing systems had to be replaced.

From specification to procurement

Re-consideration of the business case at the end of 1994 confirmed the decision to seek an existing package rather than develop a whole new system, and to limit the scope.

Once it had been realized that is impossible to anticipate all the potential that a good system will suggest once it is in use (it is, after all, part of the essence of information technology that it is only when you start interacting with it that you get revelations of new things you can ask it to do for you), it became possible to move forward to the operational requirement. Even given this understanding, the document that emerged was enough, as Grant reports, to cause most potential suppliers to be 'taken aback at the level of detail and specificity'.

Transition from the SSADM analysis to the procurement process proved difficult, because there was, as Grant (1996) reports, little guidance available for this stage. Procurement, however, was greatly helped by the CCTA (the UK government's Central Computing and Telecommunications Agency), which is responsible for providing analysis, procurement and contractual guidance to government departments and agencies. When the LASSI group embarked on procurement of a system, it used the CCTA 'Total Acquisition Procedure' (TAP).

- Advertisement in the *European Journal*
- Statement of requirements to shortlisted respondents
- Evaluation of responses
- Issue of operational requirement to a further shortlist
- Evaluation of responses
- Demonstrations
- Contractual negotiations with 1–3 suppliers
- Award of contract
- Signing of contract.

The final decision was to go ahead on a contract with Willoughby Associates (based in the USA) for the supply of a package called Multi MIMSY (the origin of the name has not been explained, but some of the anecdotes have a distinct *Through the Looking Glass* flavour, and there may well have been a few borogoves and mome raths outgrabing in the wabe of the LASSI project).[2]

[2] '*Twas brillig, and the slithy toves*
Did gyre and gimble in the wabe:
All mimsy were the borogoves,
And the mome raths outgrabe.'
As Humpty Dumpty explained it to Alice, '"*mimsy*" is "flimsy and miserable". And a "*borogove*" is a thin shabby-looking bird with its feathers sticking out all round – something like a live mop'.

The progress of LASSI suggests another mythical beast, the hydra – for as one problem was struck off more grew in its place. Work on the procurement plan made it clear there were complex contractual problems to be solved, for which there was little precedent. There were some who wanted LASSI, once the system was commissioned, to become a company; others, more aware of the risks and the resources involved, said 'not on your Nelly', or words to that effect.

The solution: a trinity of agreements

The ultimate contractual arrangement, worked out among the parties with the assistance of a battery of legal experts, consists of three mutually supporting elements:
1. A Framework Enabling Agreement between the Museums and Galleries Commission and Willoughby Associates – an 'umbrella' contract which guarantees terms and conditions for the supply of Willoughby's products in the UK over a five-year term.
2. An Administration Agreement between the MGC and any UK museum wishing to become an 'authorized demander' for Willoughby's software or services. This one sets out the rights and obligations of the two parties.
3. A Supply/Services Ordering Agreement, between Willoughby and individual authorized demanders. Each such agreement sets out the precise details of what the individual museum requires. It represents an independent one-to-one relationship between purchaser and supplier, and covers prices for licences, etc. and details the services to be provided, such as help desk, training and installation.[3]

The advantage of this arrangement is that museums know what they are getting, and are protected by the framework of agreements in which their own contracts are set. All contracts have been professionally drawn up on the basis of experience going far beyond what individual museums could provide. The MGC is not an agent, but its agreement with the supplier on one side and with museums on the other provides protection, not only for actual purchasers, but also for would-be purchasers for whom the software would not be appropriate before they go too far on a costly road.

'But who has won?'... 'Everybody has won, and all must have prizes'[4]

The end of this long march seems to have brought benefits all round. Individual UK museums retain their freedom to choose what system they think

---

[3] High-quality support in the UK was insisted on in the negotiations; an agreement has been made for this with Lusis Heritage, which can provide a wide range of appropriate experience and expertise.

[4] The Dodo's pronouncement at the end of the caucus race in *Alice in Wonderland*. What *is* it about LASSI?

best meets their requirements; if they do choose Multi MIMSY, they know what they are getting, and are protected by solid agreements. Those museums which contract into the system will benefit collectively from enhancements made to meet the detailed requirements of a wide range of museums (all such enhancements are 'ploughed back'). The supplier benefits, in that rights to the enhanced version rest with Willoughby – as Grant (1996) explains, 'the risks inherent in investing time and money in systems development in such a small market mean that any supplier would have been exposed to an unacceptable degree had this not been the case'; the risks might indeed have dissuaded software developers from having anything to do with the LASSI project.

It is also a clear benefit to the museum community that the LASSI project moved forward in parallel with the development of the UK Museum Documentation Standard (SPECTRUM). See p184. The supplier has made a firm and on-going commitment to continue to support SPECTRUM.

Present and future

The National Museum of Science and Industry is the consortium member furthest advanced in implementing Multi MIMSY; the system was installed there at the end of March 1996. Two others have installed it; other members are waiting for the enhanced version; and it seems likely that the rate of acceptance and development of the system will intensify in the near future. Meantime, work is in progress on an enhancement specification for the package, for the LASSI consortium as a whole.

It is encouraging to note that the system is designed, in Keene's (1996) words to be 'future proof', in terms of compatiblity, not just with the Internet, but also with other museum information handling applications, such as finance and booking systems. In that respect, it should help to encourage integrated management of museums' total information resources.

Evaluation

There seems to be general agreement in the museum community that the LASSI project has succeeded, unlike many comparable projects in the cultural and business fields. How did it succeed? What lessons can museums learn from it? What are the benefits? First, the views of the people most closely involved.

Grant (1996), who was one a of small team responsible for the final stages, identifies some key factors:
- Clarity in the relationship between the museums and the supplier
- Advice and co-operation from a range of people with experience in different relevant fields (including the tendering suppliers) – which helped the development of a 'virtuous ascending spiral' of interaction
- 'Perseverance, pragmatic decision-making and good humour'

- Increased willingness on the part of museums in recent years to co-operate and share endeavours – and the participation in this of 'arm's-length' governmental organizations, such as the MDA and MGC, rather than of central government departments
- Simplification of the project management structure just before the procurement stage, so that a team of three project managers was able to concentrate on it in the final stages (while one of them was seconded by her authority for six months to work full time on the project, the two others had to combine it with their other commitments).

Another member of the team emphasizes, additionally, the effort devoted to communication and interaction. 'Nobody's doubts went unexplored', particularly in the early stages. While this took up a lot of time, once people had become convinced that they would be listened to, they were prepared to accept recommendations much more readily at the contract stage. With so many institutions and individuals from different backgrounds involved, it was essential to find ways of presenting information (especially technical information) which matched the existing knowledge and experience of those on the receiving end. Fortunately it was realized that the lack of a common language between the technical participants and those with less IT background could make it impossible to arrive at a common understanding of what was in question, let alone reasonable decisions. On the advice of a consultant, the technical people were asked to present recommendations, and the decision makers to refer them back if they were not happy with them, rather than just rejecting them. This allowed the different disciplines to explain themselves to one another. Similarly, the problem of different interpretations of a given form of words was tackled by asking people to provide examples of what particular phrases mean to them.

The project has been described as a learning process, which starts from those most closely involved in planning, and cascades outwards to bring in everyone with a stake, to contribute their own knowledge. In this learning, being able to try out the system at different stages, question, and negotiate changes has been of the greatest value.

Advice to museums

Asked to sum up the key points which museums should understand about the LASSI project, one of the team provided this list:

- LASSI is there to be drawn on both as a system, and as a repository of experience of the process of analysing needs, specifying requirements and negotiating agreements
- Remember that projects involving IT and information always cost more in time and money than you expect
- Even something that looks very small, if it's right for what you need to do, will take you further along the way than you ever thought possible.

The view of the present author is that the LASSI project reinforces, from practical experience, the message which runs through much of this book: it is the quality of human thought, and the interactions between people, which condition the success of IT projects. Even in a project so specifically technology oriented, the secret of success in getting a product that does the job lies in interactions between human beings with various kinds of skills and knowledge, and in helping them to explain themselves to one another. The group who co-managed the final stages of the project combined a high degree of task orientation with understanding of the people involved in the task, their roles, and their difficulties. Individually and collectively, they seem to have been able to put themselves in the place of others and to see what would cause difficulty in understanding, and what would clarify. They also seem to have known when to be forbearing and long suffering, and when to knock heads together and jump on toes.

References

GRANT, A. (1996), 'Perseverance and pragmatism show LASSI the road home', *Spectrum* 23 (4)

KEENE, S. (1996), 'LASSI: the Larger Scale Systems Initiative', *Information Services and Use*, 9, 1–14

The Manchester Museum

Introduction

The Manchester Museum is a large university museum; the buildings and collections are owned, and the staff employed, by the University of Manchester. The collections include archaeology, Egyptology, ethnology, numismatics, archery and all the natural sciences. The total size of the collections is in excess of 6 million items, which is comparable to some national museums (compare with the 7.5 million items held by the National Museum of Wales). The total permanent staff is around 50, with only 11 curatorial staff, 2 of whom are part-time. Thus the number of items per staff member is nearly an order of magnitude greater than at Cardiff, with its 500 staff, graphically illustrating the idiosyncratic funding of UK museums.

Documentation history

Until the late 1970s the documentation at Manchester was much as in most other museums of the time, a mixture of accession registers kept by the different keepers, some history files, and various card indexes, often incomplete. In one department no less than three systems of card indexing had been started, the last being based on edge-punch cards (the cutting edge of technology at the time!), but each system had been abandoned after the staff member who created it left.

In 1977 an 18-month pilot scheme was set up, funded by the Manpower Services Commission (MSC), a government job-creation agency, and this scheme, which only employed two people and addressed one fairly small collection of molluscs, proved to be very successful. This success lead to a much bigger on-going MSC scheme to catalogue large sections of the collections in all disciplines; it was the first years of this scheme which formed the basis of the case study published in the first edition of this book. The scheme ran until 1984, and at its height had 40 employees, two being supervisors and the rest cataloguers, working in the Computer Cataloguing Unit (CCU); one of the permanent keeper staff was seconded to run this unit. All the information was compiled onto data-input sheets, which were then typed into the computer in batches, and print-outs and indexes prepared for quality control by the relevant keepers. The database management system (DBMS) used was FAMULUS, a package originally written by the US Department of Agriculture in 1970 for handling bibliographic records; this proved extremely easy to modify to handle the museum records, and at the time was unparalleled in its ability to do text searches and to produce meaningful indexes.

As the scheme progressed so did technology, so that while at the start all input was via 80-column punch cards, by its end it had passed though the use of 8-hole paper tape and key-tape encoders (key-boarding data directly to half-inch magnetic tape, without the benefit of a monitor screen), to the use of early personal computers (Commodore PET 8032 series) with in-house written data-entry software. All the data processing was done on the university mainframe computer, which also changed model and operating system twice in the life of the scheme. IBM-compatible PCs were just coming on the market at museum-affordable prices as the scheme ended.

With hindsight it is amazing that, given such ante-diluvian and rapidly evolving equipment and software, in the five years the team was in existence it managed to produce almost a quarter of a million database records which covered a total of nearly two million individual items in the collection. A museum-wide data standard was devised in the early years of the scheme, to which all the database records conformed. However, despite the quality control by the keepers, much editing remained, and still remains, to be done to bring the quality of all the data in the various databases up to an acceptable level of accuracy and consistency.

After 1984 the work continued, but just with the permanent staff and volunteers. By 1985 all collection keepers and the conservation department had 'dumb' terminals connected to the mainframe on their desks, supplied by the university. The keeper who had run the CCU was now designated IT supervisor (in addition to his curatorial role), and he spent some 75 per cent of his time over the next few years assisting his colleagues with their work on the databases; he wrote a museum application package (BPMAP) to enable them to access and interrogate their databases, but editing these on the mainframe was not easy. Answers to enquiries could be seen on the screen, but most people generated a print-out to send to the enquirer, and this had to be picked up from the computer centre on the other side of a main road, which was not particularly convenient. Some data entry continued, using both the data preparation section in the university computer centre and the clerical staff in the museum.

Further changes of the mainframe, and of its operating system, necessitated two complete re-writes of BPMAP; this was a program over 13 000 lines long, and these re-writes took up to six months of full-time work each. However, as far as was possible, the interface, that is, the screens that the keepers and visitors saw, remained the same, so as to reduce the learning curve for each upgrade of the system. In 1992, its last full year of operation, BPMAP saw well over 5000 accesses of the databases by museum staff, volunteers and visitors.

Recent developments

In 1986 the museum bought its first XT-PC computer, which was used by the IT supervisor for system development and familiarization. It had no hard disk until one was added a year later. Over the next five years two or three more low-specification XT-PCs were obtained, and used by the more 'computer-interested' members of the staff, mainly to do word-processing and research work. Most people, however, continued to use the dumb terminals to access their databases. In 1991 the museum successfully bid to the university equipment grant for money to purchase five 'state-of-the-art' XT-PCs; grant aid was given by the North West Museums Service. At the same time the university adopted a policy of networking all staff. A high-speed (100 Mbits/sec) campus backbone network was put in place over the next couple of years, and departments were flood wired, that is, nearly every working space in the museum was provided with at least one network connection point. The university departments so treated were largely self-selecting, and as one of the heaviest users of the university computing facilities after the main science departments, the museum, which is treated as a non-teaching department of the university, was one of the first to be wired for an ethernet.

In the years that followed further funding via the university equipment grant allowed more and better computers to be purchased, along with a file-server and laser printers. The museum now has over 50 computers in regular use, and all keepers have at least a PC-486 with a large-screen monitor, running Windows software. Even some of the old XT-PCs are networked and in daily use, and other XT-PCs are used as stand-alone data-entry machines in some departments. Much of the data-entry is now being done by volunteers, although the clerical staff still contribute some time. Key administrative, technical and clerical staff are also provided with a computer connected to the network, and most of the internal, and quite a lot of the external, written communications at the museum are now conducted by electronic mail (email).

In mid-1993 the university disposed of the mainframe computer, and did not replace it, as 'distributed processing' was now the order of the day. This decision meant that all the quarter of a million records then on the mainframe had to be migrated to the individual keeper's PCs, for at that juncture the museum had not yet installed its own file-server. An outside consultancy firm, working with the IT supervisor, did this job in six months from October 1992 to April 1993. The IT supervisor spent most of this time converting the FAMULUS data into comma-delimited ASCII (i.e. plain-text) files, while the consultants wrote special software to convert these to DBF files for importing into DBMS templates, pre-designed by the IT supervisor in consultation with the keepers, on the PCs. The original (1977–82) mainframe computer was a 64-bit machine, and so much of the FAMULUS data were in uppercase only, although the later version of FAMULUS could handle mixed-case data. Therefore as the data were transferred, the opportunity was taken to convert all the data to upper and lower case, using algorithms designed by the IT supervisor.

The DBMS chosen for use on the PCs was PC-File (which has since gone from version 3.0 to version 8.0 for Windows); this was chosen because it required the minimum of customization, and was simple and intuitive to use, greatly reducing the learning times for the long-suffering keepers having to adapt to yet another package. Another factor in its choice was that it could export data in a variety of formats, including DBF files, which had become a *de facto* industry standard transfer format. However, it is not a relational DBMS, and once the number of entries got to over 20 000 in the DOS versions processing time began to become a problem; this latter problem seems to be partially solved by the Windows version, which has improved indexing facilities.

Although PC-File is seen as only an interim solution, its ease of use has enabled keepers to get to grips with improving the quality and consistency of their information; editing is extremely easy. On the downside, control of data standards is now more difficult, and the museum-wide standard introduced in the early 1980s is now honoured more in the breach than in the observance. Each keeper advances reasons why they must have standards that differ from everyone else's, but this is going to prove a time-consuming problem if the museum moves, as hoped, to a large, unified, communal database management system in the future.

The network wiring extends not only to all offices, but also to all stores and to some galleries. However, the only gallery inter-active displays at present are not connected to the network. A museum file-server was installed in January 1994, running Novell Netware 3.11, and most of the databases have now been transferred to the server. Considerable attention has been given to the security of the data, with regular back-ups and automatic virus checking, and the IT supervisor has tried to make the museum system as hacker-proof as possible.

Future plans

The Manchester Museum already has a number of pages on the World Wide Web, and one database, that covering the 13 000 Bryozoa specimens, has been made available on the Web; this database has within six months generated several research enquiries from bryozoologists around the world. It is intended to make several more databases available over the Web. These databases may be inspected by addressing the URL (Unique Resource Locator): http://www.man.ac.uk/museum/

Triggered largely by the Museums and Galleries Commission re-registration procedure, the museum has just completed a major re-examination of its documentation and information needs, and a comprehensive documentation plan has been prepared. A multi-million pound bid has been submitted to the Heritage Lottery Fund, and if successful will allow a major re-development of the Manchester Museum. In that event, the documentation needs will be met by buying in a large-scale package, probably Multi-MIMSY in the light of the decision of the LASSI Committee to choose this package for their purposes.

It is hoped to develop knowledge-based interfaces for the databases on the WWW, to lead all types of enquirer to the information they need. The other great step forward will be the inclusion of images in the databases, although this will only be possible on a large scale if the HLF funding, or equivalent, is obtained.

Evaluation

The Manchester Museum has been involved in large-scale documentation and computerization projects for longer than most other UK museums, and some lessons can be drawn from this nearly two decades of experience.

- Now is always a good time to start. Don't allow the expectation that better, faster, simpler, cheaper hardware or software will be available 'soon', to delay getting to grips with a documentation backlog. At the end of the day people's time is the most important ingredient in documentation, and so the sooner you start the more time will be available
- Time spent on quality control, ensuring the data standards are adhered to, that information entering the system is accurate and complete, and adding value to that information in the form of indexing tags, is never wasted
- Any documentation project must be designed to be flexible so as to be able to take advantage of the inevitable changes in technology, but remember that museums do not need to be at the 'white-hot cutting edge'; concentrate on getting the documentation done and let others prove new technology first. Don't follow fashions; if your present set-up works well, don't waste money and time upgrading for marginal benefits. At Manchester, for example, a decision has been made recently to stick with Windows 3.11 and not to migrate to Windows 95 for at least two years; the cost-benefit analysis of such a move did not justify it for present projects
- It is of primary importance to ensure that data entered into any system can be exported again in ASCII, comma-delimited, or DBF (dBase) formats, which can then be imported into practically any other DBMS
- Avoid like the plague any software that is tied to a single hardware platform; if the hardware supplier goes out of business, a not unknown event in the computing world, then your whole project is at risk.

The Museum Documentation Association[1]

Introduction

The Museum Documentation Association merits inclusion among the museum case studies, as an organization whose role is to stand up for the significance of documentation in its widest sense. While it is well known in the museum community, it is probably much less so to readers from other disciplines, and they will certainly find it worthwhile to get acquainted with it.

Funded by the Museums and Galleries Commission and the comparable bodies in Wales, Scotland and Northern Ireland, the Association helps museums and galleries to develop their documentation to standards that meet the registration requirements of the MGC; advises on appropriate systems and provides information on relevant developments in information technology; runs training courses; acts as a 'clearing house' for information about documentation developments; and seeks to represent the interests of documentation to the decision makers who control the funds for museums.

Historical background

The origins of the MDA go back to a period in the late 1960s when a small number of enthusiasts (some of them from outside the museum community) became fired with the potential of computers to transform the traditional ways in which museums managed their information. They set up the Information Retrieval Group of the Museums Association, which later evolved into the Museum Documentation Advisory Unit, and finally into the MDA. The focus of their interest was primarily on computing, and computing being the esoteric specialism that it then was, they were effectively set apart from most of their colleagues in the museum profession. In their encounters minds were not so much meeting as going straight past each other in opposite directions. The present author's interest in what museums do with information dates back to that period, and it is fair to say that the early publications in which the MDA and its predecessors sought to explain themselves were pretty stern

---

[1] A definition of museum documentation (the Museums Association definition, quoted in the UK Museum Documentation Standard, SPECTRUM (Grant/MDA, 1994):

Gathering, recording and giving access to evidence of:
- Objects
- Their histories and associations (e.g. people, places, events and production, etc.)

- The processes they undergo (e.g. entry, management within the museum, etc.)
In order to:
- Account for them
- Manage them
- Enable their use to achieve the stated aims and objectives of the holding institution.

stuff, greeted in the museum world with a good deal of incomprehension and some hostility.

The most long-standing of the MDA's products are the record cards it still produces for museums in various subject areas; first developed in 1975/76, they continue in use in many small museums (see Figure 8.1 on p183 for an example). With the development of the GOS software package in the late 1970s, some museums took a first step to computer use by sending their completed cards for central processing by the MDA, receiving in return printed out indexes from which they could locate information about their collections. For a description, see the case studies of St Albans Museums, p249 and the Hunterian Museum in Orna & Pettitt (1980).

Other larger museums such as the National Maritime Museum and the Imperial War Museum themselves installed and ran the software. Using GOS was not a job for the faint-hearted, and seen from today's perspective, it looks heavy and clumsy and hard to manage, but it had the merit of being based on meticulous analysis and a sound record structure.

Over time, the Association developed training programmes and an extensive publishing programme; it instituted a series of international conferences on themes related to documentation; and practising curators became increasingly involved in its work.

The MDA today

The MDA today is a small organization (it employs only nine staff) with a large remit. It operates by a combination of 'outreach' activities, publications, conferences, research, awareness raising, project management and consultancy where appropriate. The main issues and activities with which it is involved are outlined below.

Policy and the Department of National Heritage

The Department of National Heritage (the British government department responsible for cultural policies) instituted a review of policy towards museums in 1994. In its response to the Department, the MDA drew attention to some critical issues:

- The desire to increase access
- The 'tension' between the enjoyment and the preservation of collections
- The concern that the emphasis on the visitor experience will cause the neglect of primary curatorial responsibilities
- The desire not to widen the gap between object and interpretation.

Since then, the DNH has made a grant to the MDA to commission a study on information technology and museums: a recognition of the Association's initiatives in briefing the Department on the potential benefits of IT to UK museums. Electronic access to museum collections indeed appears to be onthe heritage agenda of the government elected in May 1997, as it was on that of its predecessor.

Card of	File		Institution : identity number		Part
IDENTIFICA-TION	Simple name	D	Form		Number
	Classified identification or full name				
C	Current Label Other	System	Status	D	Identifier : date	D
COLLECTION	Place names/detail				Locality number

Lat Long NGR	Other co-ordinates	value & units/accuracy	Altitude Depth	Other position	value & units/accuracy
Complex Rock	Zone Age	Stratigraphy keyword/detail			
Complex Rock	Zone Age				
Complex Rock	Zone Age				

Stratigraphy detail	
Locality detail	D

C	Collection method	Collector : date	Collection number	D
STORE	Store : date		Recorder : date	

GEOLOGY © IRGMA 1975 1/12/75

183

Setting standards

The MDA's long-standing commitment to standards for museum documentation came to fruition in 1994 with the publication of its UK Museum Documentation Standard, known as SPECTRUM (Standard ProcEdures for CollecTions Recording Used in Museums). The publication represents three years of work by the MDA in co-operation with over 60 practising museum professionals, many of whom co-operated in the testing of the standards in their own institutions. SPECTRUM aims to provide a framework around-which museums can 'build their own, institution-specific procedures and which they can use to help identify their own information needs', while ensuring 'a reliable and consistent approach which can be built upon in the future'.

The standard covers 20 procedures for documenting museum collections:

1. Object entry.	11. Insurance management.
2. Loans in.	12. Indemnity management.
3. Acquisition.	13. Valuation control.
4. Inventory control.	14. Audit.
5. Location and movement control.	15. Exhibitions and displays.
6. Cataloguing.	16. Despatch.
7. Condition checking.	17. Loans out.
8. Conservation.	18. Loss.
9. Reproduction.	19. Deaccession and disposal.
10. Risk management.	20. Retrospective documentation.

Each procedure contains standard information:

- Definition
- The minimum standard which the procedure should achieve
- A recommended way of achieving it
- Notes – contextual information, including legal and policy issues
- Sources of advice and help – reference works and organizations
- Relevant units of information – the information requirements created or used by the procedure. Figure 8.2 on p186 gives an example.

Printed products that tell people how to do things usually manage to put a number of obstacles in their way. SPECTRUM is happily free of such stumbling blocks. It is notable for a clarity of presentation, both visual and textual, which reflects a sound conceptual structure, based in turn on solid thinking; it is available in two 'orders of magnitude' for different user needs – the detailed standard and *SPECTRUM Essentials*; and an interactive version (a Windows Help application), which museums can use to develop their own procedures manual, is now available.

SPECTRUM is the recommended standard for meeting the Museums and Galleries Commission's requirements for registration as a museum; the MDA provides a checklist of the minimum SPECTRUM-based records that should be maintained for this purpose.

Terminology control

Establishing standards for the words museums use in describing the objects in their collections is a long-standing interest with the MDA. It has now moved to the top of the list; as their World Wide Web pages put it: 'a key priority for the next two years is to agree standards for terminology'. A strategy for future work in this area is currently being developed.

This time around, the MDA proposes a similar process to the one used in developing SPECTRUM, working from terms already in use, bringing together subject groups to agree consensus lists, and finally making the agreed lists available. New subject groups were set up at the end of 1996 for Ethnographic Terminology, Place Names, and Medical Museums Terminology. An *Archaeology Object Name Thesaurus* is due for publication in 1998, from a working party formed in conjunction with the RCHME and English Heritage in 1996. A railway terminology working group was established in 1997, and another group is working on terminology for weapons. The Association does not at this stage intend to combine the lists into a full thesaurus, with built-in thesaural relationships, instructions, classified structure, etc.; while acknowledging that the job certainly needs doing, it lacks the resources.

Meantime, it is continuing its clearing house function by collecting relevant thesauri and term lists, and gathering intelligence about terminology control initiatives, like those described in this book in relation to the RAF Museum and the V&A. See p232 and p259. The MDA carried out a terminology survey in 1996. While the response rate was very low, it showed that the majority of initiatives on terminology were being taken in a comparatively small number of institutions which have large numbers of machine-readable records. This suggests scope for links between the in-house thesauri developed by such institutions, and between all these and large-scale thesauri like the Art and Architecture Thesaurus and the British Standards Institution Root Thesaurus (the archaeology object name thesaurus mentioned above has indeed been constructed with AAT in mind, with clear points of reference between the two thesauri; it is hierarchical and has similar levels of functionality, while providing a level of detail not available in AAT). Ultimately this kind of integration might pay off for smaller museums, which would be able to draw from the results the terms appropriate for their own collections.

The group responsible for the well-established Social History and Industrial Classification (SHIC, MDA 1993), meanwhile, having produced a new edition, has now developed a new index. This might lead in the direction of a combination of classification and thesaurus similar to *Thesaurofacet* (Aitchison *et al.*, 1969). A simplified version, in the form of a simple subject headings list, to help smaller museums with very diverse collections with their indexing is also available.

The technology

Although the MDA has travelled far from the technology-oriented origins described earlier, helping museums to make productive use of appropriate IT remains an important part of its work. Here too it performs a clearing-house function for information about what IT is being used in museums and how.

Example from SPECTRUM of how the procedure works and interacts with other procedures   Figure 8

Adapted, with permission, from the first edition of SPECTRUM

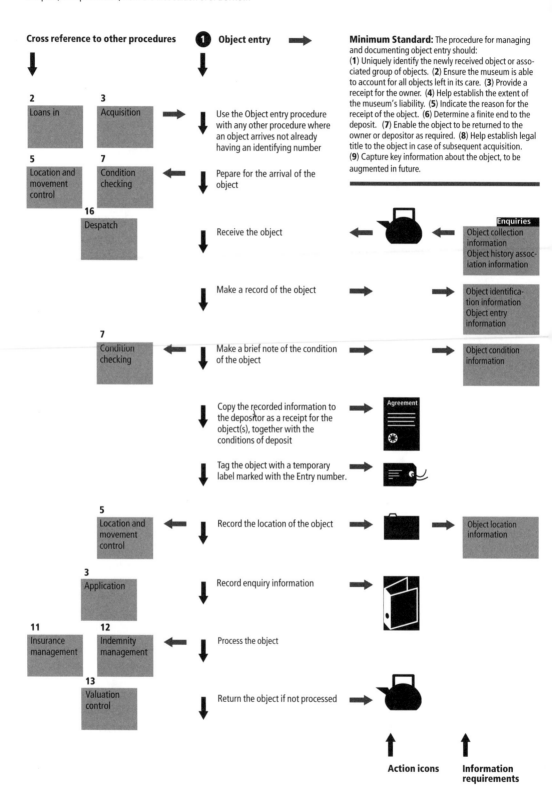

Cross reference to other procedures   **1** Object entry ➡

2 Loans in   **3** Acquisition ➡ Use the Object entry procedure with any other procedure where an object arrives not already having an identifying number

5 Location and movement control   **7** Condition checking ⬅ Pepare for the arrival of the object

16 Despatch   Receive the object

Make a record of the object ➡ ➡ Object identification information / Object entry information

⬅ ⬅ Enquiries / Object collection information / Object history association information

7 Condition checking ⬅ Make a brief note of the condition of the object ➡ ➡ Object condition information

Copy the recorded information to the depositor as a receipt for the object(s), together with the conditions of deposit ➡ Agreement

Tag the object with a temporary label marked with the Entry number.

5 Location and movement control ⬅ Record the location of the object ➡ ➡ Object location information

3 Application   Record enquiry information

11 Insurance management   **12** Indemnity management ⬅ Process the object

13 Valuation control   Return the object if not processed

⬆ Action icons   ⬆ Information requirements

Minimum Standard: The procedure for managing and documenting object entry should: (**1**) Uniquely identify the newly received object or associated group of objects. (**2**) Ensure the museum is able to account for all objects left in its care. (**3**) Provide a receipt for the owner. (**4**) Help establish the extent of the museum's liability. (**5**) Indicate the reason for the receipt of the object. (**6**) Determine a finite end to the deposit. (**7**) Enable the object to be returned to the owner or depositor as required. (**8**) Help establish legal title to the object in case of subsequent acquisition. (**9**) Capture key information about the object, to be augmented in future.

186

Indicates that an object is entering or leaving the museum.

Some procedures require written agreements to be be created and signed to by your museum and other parties.

A decision needs to be made which may require you to check your museum's policy.

At certain times it is necessary to attach information to an object physically, either on a temporary or permanent basis.

You may need to obtain an image of the object being processed.

Information about an object which needs to be quickly & easily accessible may need to be recorded on a paper-based or computer system which enables quick retrieval.

The Accessions Register is a primary piece of documentation which needs to be added to or annotated at specific points in some proedures.

Background information about an object or a procedure (e.g. correspondence) may need to be retained in a related file on a long-term basis.

It will sometimes be necessary to send written information formally to people outside your museum.

Legend

It makes a periodic survey and publishes the findings as part of a guide for museum professionals with special responsibility for IT – particularly the non-specialists doing the job in small museums. Typical content of the surveys includes, besides an alphabetical list of museums with details of their software (and a complementary list of software with details of which museums are using it), straightforward explanatory material about databases, advice on choosing equipment, profiles of software, and a glossary of computing terms. The most recent survey covers 1996–97 (Gill & Dawson, 1997).

The MDA has moved away from supplying comprehensive documentation software; MODES Plus is now the responsibility of a MODES User Association.

Outreach

The MDA uses the term 'outreach' to cover a range of activities and products for, as its Internet pages put it, 'informing people and promoting ideas of best practice, and … equipping people with skills and resources they need to implement those ideas'. The vehicles used to deliver this kind of help include factsheets and guides, training courses and seminars, and one-to-one advice.

Courses are arranged wherever there is reasonable local demand, and are offered free of charge. The outreach programme also offers factsheets covering the most usual inquiries it receives, a pack on *Documentation for Registration,* and a variety of booklets.

The future

A recent series of seminars on 'The Nation's collections' provided opportunities for forward thinking by museum professionals from all over the UK. The question underlying the series was:

'Can we move away from old ideas about a single National Database of museum collections, and think instead of sharing information about the nation's collect-tions?'

As the seminar on technical options made clear, the technology required for a distributed national network of collections databases was already available; the real debate was about steps towards using the potential, and the resources needed. As Gosling (1996) says in his report on the series of seminars, while it was possible to identify some critical milestones in the path, it was impossible to map out the whole journey, and indeed 'there *is* no final destination'. In-stead, perhaps the most pressing priority is to demonstrate the potential of the data and the technology that already exist.

Priorities for action are summarized *(ibid)* as:

- Collate existing research into the users of museum information and their needs, and undertake new marketing research
- Assign to an appropriate body a watching brief for monitoring and dissemi-nating information about current developments, both in the cultural sector and the wider IT community
- Create a single gateway to information in distributed museum databases, offering server space to museums which need it
- Develop the interchange standard necessary to allow searching across a diverse range of distributed databases and other resources
- Link and make use of existing electronic thesauri to improve information retrieval
- Participate in existing pilot projects and initiate others to demonstrate the potential of providing on-line access to information-sharing initiatives
- Continue to support the Museums and Galleries Commission's target of a basic inventory of every museum collection by the year 2000.

Evaluation

In its early years the MDA failed to listen enough to practising museum cura-tors, and it lacked contact with information professionals (which probably accounts for its rather thin ideas at that time about indexing and information retrieval). Over time, there has been a rapprochement between curators and software specialists, and a growth of understanding on both sides. All the As-sociation's present professional staff have up-to-date museum experience, while professionals with an information science and library background have also become involved in its work.

The rigidity of the old-style approach to standards ('all those colons') has given way to the concept of a framework that allows choice, in the light of local knowledge, of how essential things should be done. SPECTRUM is a re-ally useful achievement; museum professionals who contributed to creating it found it a worthwhile experience; and, as mentioned earlier, the presentation makes for easy use.

Terminology control is likely to be a tougher nut to crack; it has to be said that the MDA has often approached the subject in the past without any particular outcome (it formed the subject of the Association's second International Conference in 1988, for example (Roberts, 1990)). Agreeing what to call things is less of a problem than using and managing the agreed terms consistently and productively once you have them. The conceptual difficulty that most people experience in grasping thesaural concepts is recognized, and is said to be successfully addressed in training courses. While thinking is indeed more important than software in this field as everywhere else, if terminology control is to be successfully integrated into museum documentation, there will certainly be a continuing need for good supporting software for the building and maintaining of sophisticated thesauri (see for example, the RAF Museum case study, p232); at the same time those institutions whose terminology control needs are less complex should ultimately be able to benefit from the distribution of thesauri as tagged SGML files which can be converted for use with appropriate collections management software.

On the debit side, the MDA itself acknowledges that, in spite of two decades of work, documentation is still viewed with reserve by many curatorial staff, and not accepted as a legitimate part of their everyday work. While those attitudes are now beginning to change, and many curators have come to see documentation as a continuous process, to which they have an irreplaceable contribution, the most acute problem, as usual, is at the highest level: 'the last people to see the connection between documentation and public access are trustees and directors'. And the slowest progress of all is in getting proper recognition and resources to go with it from government.

References

AITCHISON, J, et al (1969), *Thesaurofacet: a thesaurus and faceted classification for engineering and related subjects,* Whetstone, Leicester: English Electric Company

GILL, T. & DAWSON, D (1997), *The MDA survey of information technology in museums 1996–1997,* Cambridge: Museum Documentation Association

GRANT, A. (ed.)/MDA (1994), *SPECTRUM. The UK Museum Documentation Standard,* Cambridge: Museum Documentation Association[1]

Museum Documentation Association (1993), *Social History and Industrial Classification (SHIC),* Cambridge: Museum Documentation Association

ORNA, E. & PETTITT, C. (1980), *Information handling in museums,* London: K. G. Saur/Clive Bingley

ROBERTS, A. (ed.) (1990), *Terminology for Museums. Proceedings of an International Conference held in Cambridge, England, 21–24 September 1988,* The Second Conference of the Museum Documentation Association, Cambridge. Museum Documentation Association

[1]A second edition was published in 1997: COWTON, J (ed) / MDA (1997), *SPECTRUM. The UK Museum Documentation Standard,* Cambridge: Museum Documentation Association

The National Maritime Museum

Introduction

The National Maritime Museum, founded in 1934, merits consideration for a number of reasons: it holds the world's largest and most important maritime collections; it was one of the pioneering sites for projects on using computers in museum documentation; and it is an institution where it is possible to take a historical view of the development of information management. The museum was the subject of a case study in the first edition of this book, in 1980, when it was at the start of its documentation programme, and the present author has been able to keep in touch with developments ever since.

The case study starts, therefore, with a backward look at the situation as described in 1980 (Orna & Pettitt, 1980: pp170–173).

Historical background

The establishment of the National Maritime Museum in 1934 by Act of Parliament brought together a number of collections, some of which had their own catalogues compiled by the original owners. Initially, a central registry was maintained, but after wartime staff shortage this was superseded, on civil service O&M advice, by departmental recording; each department developed its own systems, and there was no active attempt to preserve common ground between the ways in which different departments managed matters of documentation. Figure 9.1 on p191 shows the early history in the context of developments from the start to the present time.

The reported results were such as might have been expected; one department had 75 000 items, none of them numbered, for which the sole documentation consisted of a typed slip with a description giving location details, but no acquisition data; a variety of numbering systems were in use; and on certain categories of item there were multiple files constructed on different principles and containing different types of information – for example, 43 separate files of records on named ships.

In 1971, more attention began to be paid to documentation with the setting up of a 'general information index' on cards. The index rapidly became the victim of the problems it was intended to solve, because it was derived from files lacking consistency among themselves, and containing incomplete data. By 1975, it had grown to the point where it threatened to become unmanageable, and in 1976, an Information Retrieval Officer (who had previously worked on a project at the Sedgwick Museum in Cambridge for the development of a computer-based system for managing museum documentation) was

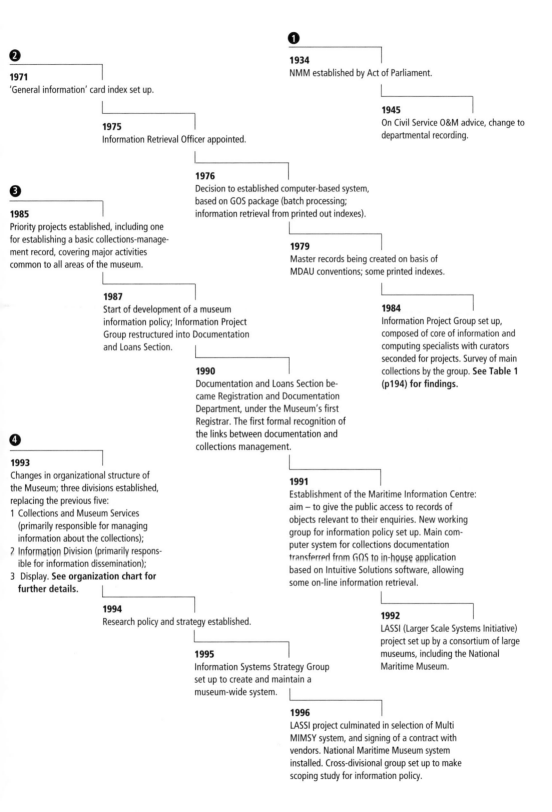

❶

1934
NMM established by Act of Parliament.

1945
On Civil Service O&M advice, change to departmental recording.

❷

1971
'General information' card index set up.

1975
Information Retrieval Officer appointed.

1976
Decision to established computer-based system, based on GOS package (batch processing; information retrieval from printed out indexes).

1979
Master records being created on basis of MDAU conventions; some printed indexes.

❸

1985
Priority projects established, including one for establishing a basic collections-management record, covering major activities common to all areas of the museum.

1987
Start of development of a museum information policy; Information Project Group restructured into Documentation and Loans Section.

1984
Information Project Group set up, composed of core of information and computing specialists with curators seconded for projects. Survey of main collections by the group. **See Table 1 (p194) for findings.**

1990
Documentation and Loans Section became Registration and Documentation Department, under the Museum's first Registrar. The first formal recognition of the links between documentation and collections management.

❹

1993
Changes in organizational structure of the Museum; three divisions established, replacing the previous five:
1 Collections and Museum Services (primarily responsible for managing information about the collections);
2 Information Division (primarily responsible for information dissemination);
3 Display. **See organization chart for further details.**

1991
Establishment of the Maritime Information Centre: aim – to give the public access to records of objects relevant to their enquiries. New working group for information policy set up. Main computer system for collections documentation transferred from GOS to in-house application based on Intuitive Solutions software, allowing some on-line information retrieval.

1994
Research policy and strategy established.

1995
Information Systems Strategy Group set up to create and maintain a museum-wide system.

1992
LASSI (Larger Scale Systems Initiative) project set up by a consortium of large museums, including the National Maritime Museum.

1996
LASSI project culminated in selection of Multi MIMSY system, and signing of a contract with vendors. National Maritime Museum system installed. Cross-divisional group set up to make scoping study for information policy.

appointed, with the remit of examining current documentation problems, and recommending action to solve them.

At the end of 1976, it was decided to move towards integrating the whole of the museum's information processing through a computer-based system. A five-year phased development plan was established in 1975; at the end of that time the system (based on the 'GOS' package developed in the Cambridge project) was to be operational, with all departments participating. In 1977 the Library commenced computerized cataloguing of its whole collection, according to professional standards (AACR2 – Anglo-American Cataloguing Rules). In 1979 master records were being created in each department, based on the Museum Documentation Advisory Unit conventions which had by then been developed. Data were entered by departmental staff on data-capture terminals and then transferred to the museum mainframe. Printed indexes (the standard information-retrieval tool of the GOS package at that stage) had been produced in some departments. The principle adopted was 'that all the elements which need to be manipulated to produce various information outputs should be put on' (op. cit., 172), while other supplementary data could be dealt with by Xerox reproduction, or by putting on to microfiche.

The first benefits observed were 'in consistency of inputs and the development of agreed conventions for recording' (op cit, 172). It was possible to say that: 'applications are ... designed to give optimum service to the needs of curators as defined by themselves – the better the degree of understanding, the better will be the solution' and to predict that: 'Implementation of the system should make it possible for the specialist skills and knowledge of the curators to be used for the maximum amount of time at the highest level. Quick and flexible access to the whole resources of the collections will open up possibilities for full exploitation of research potential. At the same time, it will become possible to exploit information resources to create supporting programmes of publication so that staff time does not have to be spent on repeatedly re-assembling information.' (op. cit., 173). (As time went on, and both curatorial and documentation staff gained experience of the system, and learned more in the process about the collections and the potential for exploiting the information in them, they began to demand more than the existing system could offer, and some conflicts of interest arose between them and those in charge of the system, who did not have such an acute awareness of its shortcomings.)

In 1984 an 'Information Project Group' was set up: the core of its 18 members consisted of six specialists in information science and computing, the rest was made up of a changing population of seconded curators. When the group started work, despite the earlier investigations, it was reported that no-one had any real knowledge of exactly what was in the museum, how big the collections were, or how well they were catalogued; in some cases even the curators responsible did not know the scale of their own collections. One of the group's first actions, over a four-month period in 1984, was a survey, in which 40 main collections covering about 1.4 million objects were surveyed to establish the size and nature of the collections, and their state of documentation. The results are shown in Table 1, on p194.

On the basis of the findings, collections were ranked for priority in project work by 23 criteria, including large size, significance, poor record quality and number of enquiries received. The proportions of various collections catalogued ranged from 0–75 per cent, and the quality of documentation was found to vary, from good to 'extremely sketchy'.

The findings were reported (1985) to have shown:
- Which collections needed most attention
- Shortcomings in administration and collection management
- The need for attention to relations between collection catalogues and other collections of information, e.g. conservation records, acquisition records, slide collection
- The need to decide relations between marketing and curatorial activity
- A range of curatorial attitudes towards documentation, which required individual negotiation.

The group established several priority projects – some were for documenting particular collections, others related to the library catalogue and the museum's acquisition records.

Another major project, the 'activities' project, was devoted to common systems and procedures which cross inter-collection and inter-departmental boundaries; it aimed to start on thinking about the form and content of a basic record for management of the collections. The activities (which foreshadowed the standards embodied in SPECTRUM) were:
- Acquisition
- Loans in
- Object numbering/marking
- Description
- Record photography
- Location recording
- Movement control
- Loans out
- Conservation.
  Key areas where control was needed were identified as:
- Ownership
- Identification
- Location
- State of conservation.

The activities project was complemented by one on standards and conventions, which aimed to develop standards for curatorial description, including object description, to help curators with terminology control, and to provide standards for general conventions like personal names and abbreviations.

The GOS package had been in use since 1976; it had proved very powerful, but was described as needing a great deal of training to use. The group was developing modifications to make data entry easier, and was also looking at

Collection	Number of items (000s)
Ships' plans	750
Historic photographs	300
Oil paintings	4
Printed books	64
Prints and drawings	62
Navigation and charts	52
Weapons and antiquities	19.5
Ship models	2.6
Astronomy and horology	1.3

the MDA's own development of input systems for GOS (what eventually became MODES), although the museum's own version of GOS increasingly diverged from the MDA version. The museum's own input application 'STEER' was written in-house and used from 1985 as a 'front end' to GOS. Fiche had been taken as standard for catalogue and index production, because of the nature of GOS, which was essentially designed to produce indexes ordered by a variety of leading features. Customized off-line products could be negotiated with the (one) person capable of programming in GOS to produce the required manipulations of the data. The anticipated direction of IT development was the production of museum-wide catalogues and indexes, with on-line access to records, as well as fiche-published catalogues, linked to word processing for responding to written enquiries. The possibility of public direct access for simple searches was under consideration, as was increased use of micro-computers for collections management.

The Collections Division at that time produced interim objectives:

• To catalogue, conserve and display the collections
• In particular, to make them accessible to the public and researchers.

In 1986 the Information Project Group reported on progress in documentation. In the years between 1976 and 1983, before the group was established, some 34 000 computer records of the collections, together with 40 000 created by the library, had been created; in the first two years of the group's work, a total of 12 000 had been added; and a further 35 000 were projected for the next year.

By 1987, development of an information policy had begun (an endeavour revived at intervals over the following years), and the need to appoint a head of the documentation section had been realized. Documentation, enquiries and education were at that time all within the same division. In that year, the Information Project Group was restructured into a Documentation and Loans section, and by 1990 this had evolved into a Registration and Documentation department under the museum's first Registrar. This period (1987–1993) was the first time the links between documentation and collections management had been appreciated and recognized structurally.

The Registration and Documentation department built on pre-1987 work on the 'activities' project including:

- A team which provided advice and small-scale systems for different activities such as item numbering, record photography, and location (creating the first documentation manual)
- Identifying current procedures for acquisition, loans, and stock taking.

By 1991, a new development was in progress – a first step towards meeting the objective of improving public access. The Maritime Information Centre was intended to give the public access to collections, and, via keywords, to records of a range of objects from across the collections relevant to their enquiry, and to allow users to define their own ways into the collections. This implied close links with documentation, because the database of collections records would be the quarry from which information for the MIC would come. The centre was seen as having a relationship of mutual support with the documentation programme, acting as an extra focus for the programme, and providing further justification for investment in record structure and terminology control. It envisaged making especial use of the 'Associations Index' produced from the GOS system (the main tool for answering subject or thematic questions) as a means to allow public access to items right across collections. An analysis of visitors' questions by the centre was used by the documentation group as a guide to deciding what part of the collections to tackle next, while planning for the centre was helped by seeing what had already been input to the system by the documentation group. The need to balance the interests of public access with those of collections management, including curatorial research and conservation, etc., and to keep them advancing in step, was recognized.

While those most closely involved with the MIC realized that a large capital investment was required, it was difficult to get commitment from top management either to this scale of investment or to continued revenue expenditure on information management.

During 1991, a new working group for information policy, reporting to board level, was set up, it consisted of the Registrar, the manager of the Maritime Information Centre, and the IT manager. Its aim was to produce a first report, with top-level information policy objectives. Only one member of the group was aware of how long the task would take, and of the need for downstream reporting, and for time for people to absorb ideas, question, and take ownership of problems. There was also a delicate problem of convincing top management that a second string of advice on technology was needed. At that point they were solely reliant on the views of the IT manager, which were limited to small-scale short-term investments, while it was becoming clearer to those most concerned with documentation that more fundamental consideration of future needs was essential, and that the principle of user requirements specification needed to be established.

In recent years, the emphasis in the museum's approach to information management has changed. From the early 1980s, as evidenced above, a great

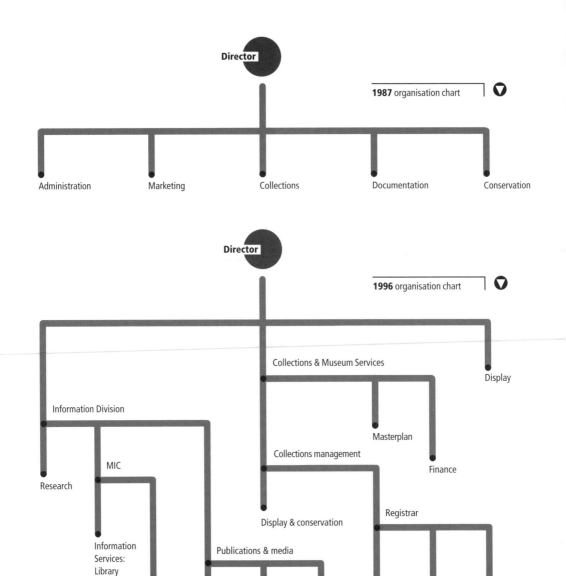

Director

1987 organisation chart

Administration   Marketing   Collections   Documentation   Conservation

Director

1996 organisation chart

Collections & Museum Services

Display

Information Division

Masterplan

Collections management

Finance

MIC

Research

Registrar

Display & conservation

Information
Services:
Library
Enquiries
ORO

Publications & media

Business
development

Collections
development

Visual access

Publications

Storage &
location

Systems &
standards

Systems
development

deal of work was done on documentation; from 1993, with changes in the organizational structure (see below), the resources of permanent staff available for documentation were reduced, and the emphasis shifted to meeting the needs of the museum's users for information.

A major re-structuring took place in 1993, with significant implications for information management. Previously there were five divisions: Administration, Marketing, Collections, Documentation, and Conservation. These were condensed into three in 1993: Collections and Museum Services, Display, and Information, as shown in Figure 9.2 on p196. A key feature of the changes was the functional separation between providing information to the outside world, and managing information about the collections, the one centred in the Information Division, and the other in the Collections section of the Collections and Museum Services Division. The re-organization has been described as 'less 'less drastic than it sounds, because it has led to a harder look at the way information is used within the Museum', and to a process of 'planned and emergent evolution'. There have been conscious efforts to promote understanding and co-operative use of the knowledge resources in the new structure, by means of cross-divisional groups and projects for such matters as information policy, IT strategy, and the development of collections information.

We can now turn to the present situation, in the hope that it will be illuminated by the account of its antecedents.

Mission and objectives

The museum's overall mission is expressed in these terms:

'To promote an understanding of the history and future of Britain and the sea, the story of time and the historic sites at Greenwich'.

Its primary objectives are:
- To maintain and enhance the museum's international profile
- To improve access to the museum and to the collections
- To provide facilities and services attractive to the customer
- To improve the quality of the collections and their interpretation and that of the site
- To maintain and develop the museum's assets including the building and the estate
- To maintain the financial viability of the museum.

'Do-wells' which the museum is seeking to achieve in support of these objectives include:
- Maintaining the pre-eminence of the collections, the research and the expertise base
- Improving the quality and drawing power of displays and information products, and making the collections more available to the public and schools
- Identifying and meeting customer needs on a value-for-money basis

- Refining and developing the collections, and maintaining the highest standards of conservation and curatorship
- Evolving organizational structures to meet the museum's changing needs, and creating a flexible, enterprising and skilled workforce
- Increasing funding through donations and sponsorship, developing the Display and Information businesses, and instilling a more enterprising culture.

The current objectives of the museum reflect the change in orientation in relation to information management, from an inward-directed one, focusing on the problems inherent in the collections, to an outward-directed one, looking towards a wide range of potential users, and towards the concept of the information resources embodied in the collections as a source of information products and services, with potential both for generating revenue and for illuminating new ways of using the collections.

Collections and Museum Services Division

The division brings together the functions of collections management, corporate planning, finance, and personnel. The current objectives (1996–97 Corporate Plan) are:

- To establish a networked system for monitoring admissions and retail income
- To upgrade the system in the Personnel Department to provide further management information
- To begin a functional analysis for a fully integrated business system for the museum
- To meet or exceed all service level agreements, with quarterly monitoring of results
- To install and establish the successful operation of LASSI (Large Scale Systems Initiative) by October 1996.[1]

Information Division

The Division's mission is defined as being:

'To disseminate information of high quality originating in the museum's collections and curatorial expertise through a range of products, services and study programmes.'

Its key objectives under the 1996–97 Corporate Plan are:

- To publish a series of authoritative publications on three major sections of the collections
- To publish at least six new titles by April 1997 and deliver a number of high quality publications and other media products to schedule and budget

[1] The museum was a member of the LASSI consortium, and the Multi MIMSY system procured by the consortium is now installed there. For further details of LASSI see p170.

- To plan a front-of-house facility for the Maritime Information Centre
- To reduce the cost-per-user for accessing the collections by 5 per cent
- To obtain recognition as an NVQ assessment centre
- To present a scoping study on an Information Systems Strategy, and to deliver an Information Systems Strategy to the Trustees
- To develop a strategy for providing information services during the construction period of the new Neptune Hall and surrounding galleries.

Organizational structure

As described earlier, since 1993 there have been three divisions: Collections and Museum Services, Display, and Information.

Information Division comprises the Maritime Information Centre, the museum's Research Department, the Publications and Media Group, Photographic Studio, and the 'Open Museum' – an initiative in continuing and community education. When the division was set up, a number of curatorial staff moved to it, together with an Information Manager with long experience of the work of documentation in the museum.

The collections management group in the Collections and Museum Services Division has two main functional strands: one led by the Registrar, with responsibility for collections management activities, such as storage, acquisition, disposals, loans etc., and the other concerned with those aspects of the collections related to the display and conservation of objects.

The current state of documentation of the collections

By 1995 the efforts put into documentation over the past years had yielded some valuable results, as well as showing that the size of the task was far greater than envisaged in earlier plans.

Documentation of three-dimensional objects was well on the way to completion and that of prints and drawings nearly complete. Fiche and microfilm images of 65 000 items (85 per cent) from this collection had been produced, as a means of protecting the originals, which had hitherto been accessible for browsing, and for staff and public access in addition to print-outs.

A 1992 project to make some 40 000 of the 300 000 items from the historic photographs collection accessible by means of scanning in data from catalogue slips via OCR (optical character recognition) was not wholly successful. Faulty reading of the data required a large amount of editing to clean up the data before it was consistent and complete enough to be usable, and staff were not available for the task. This collection remains accessible only because a curator works with it and maintains a manual index. Technology by itself is seldom the solution; its successful application, as here, usually demands extra human resources.

The ships' plans collection has been documented in part, and the collection is physically in better shape than it was. The collection of manuscripts remains to be tackled, and a plan is currently being worked out for how to do the job; at present access is through curatorial help, a 1970 printed guide, some typed listings and manual card indexes.

Since 1988 three major collections-related publications have been produced on the basis of data largely derived from the collections management system:
Concise List of Oil Paintings (1988)
Historic photographs at the NMM: An illustrated guide (1995)
Ships Models: illustrated from the collections of the National Maritime Museum Greenwich (1995).

Approaches to information management

In effect the process of managing information is shared between the two divisions, and its success depends on interaction, negotiation and co-operation between them. Some 15 areas of common interest have been identified. There is a Collections Management/Information Support Group, which acts as a general management liaison forum for the two divisions; its remit, however, does not specifically cover information management.

There are certain areas where their interaction is essential for achieving the museum's key objectives. The emphasis placed in the objectives on research and publication, and the tight time-scales embodied in the targets, demand that the new collections management system should provide quick access, and ease in manipulating and extracting information for various purposes (a requirement which the Multi MIMSY system resulting from the LASSI project should eventually fulfil). It is essential for the documentation staff to know the requirements of their colleagues on the publications side, and for the latter to be aware of the changes that will be needed in the presentation of existing records to get full value from the new system. Close collaboration is also required in planning for interactive access for researchers to the collections database, so that feedback from their research can be incorporated in the database. Links between collections management and public access are equally significant in the requirements they place on the system.

Collections and Museum Services Division
The Collections Management part of the division is responsible for those areas of information management which are concerned with decisions about acquisition and disposal, policies for development of the collections, storage, conservation, the collections management system, and information retrieval.

A key role is played by the Collections Development section, which has responsibility for overall improvement of the collections. Its remit covers all registration activities, including developing policies and procedures for acquisition, disposal, loans in, storage, and conservation. The approach to acquisition is an integrated one, which considers not only the intrinsic interest of proposed acquisitions, but also their information aspects.

A Collections Development Committee meets fortnightly under the chairmanship of the Collections Development manager; members come both from the Collections and Museum Services Division and from other divisions, and include ex-departmental curators representing the relevant specialisms. The agenda covers acquisitions, disposals, loans in, and policy matters arising from offers of objects, which may lead to the development of a collecting policy in the areas involved. The committee requires a rationale and justification for proposed acquisitions and this provides an opportunity for specialists to educate their colleagues. Collections policy has now advanced beyond the mere filling of gaps; the most recent statement of policy was in 1990 and is now described as being too general. The committee is now looking at specific areas as occasion offers, including boats, modern material, and horological items. It co-operates rather than competes with other maritime museums on acquisitions; they settle beforehand who will seek to acquire particular items. New acquisitions procedures and a manual, integrating acquisitions procedure with inventory creation, were introduced in 1995.

Information Division

While Collections Division is mainly concerned with activities that lead to the input and processing of information, Information Division's responsibilities are primarily for output in the form of information products and services. That being so, it has a key role in decisions about both the form and content of documentation, and priorities. There are three aspects to its work: publications and media, the Maritime Information Centre, and research.

PUBLICATIONS AND MEDIA. This group brings together specialist staff concerned with the planning, marketing,[2] development and publication of both print-on-paper products and those in other media. Its links with the documentation aspect of information management are the responsibility of a systems development manager with previous experience of work in the Collections Management group.

THE MARITIME INFORMATION CENTRE.[3] The centre was set up in 1991. It covers Information Services (including the library, manuscripts, charts, ship

---

[2] The museum lacked relevant expertise in managing marketing information. A report commissioned in 1995 with the aim of guiding the development of a marketing strategy pointed to weaknesses in administration, systems, and management of contacts databases. Little market research to aid the development of a strategy had been done in the industry in which the museum operates, and none among its customers. The report recommended some re-organization of administrative tasks, temporary use of external specialist advice, and training for staff, to overcome the basic problems before starting on any

significant marketing activity. In the long term, a strategy based on direct marketing and using a unified database drawing on recent contacts and prospects information was recommended, together with a communications strategy and a continuing programme of performance evaluation and customer monitoring.

[3] Readers with a particular interest in museum information services and libraries will wish to be aware of a study by Borda (1997) of libraries and information centres in museums in the Greater London area.

models, the Enquiries service and the Old Royal Observatory), and Visual Access (responsible for historic photographs, ships' plans, commercial filming and reproduction rights, picture library and photo sales).

INFORMATION SERVICES. The main areas of work of the Information Services are:

- Providing public services attractive to the customer
- Providing access to and interpretation of the collections
- Making available the work of the documentation teams, currently in print-ed form, but the longer-term aim is an OPAC (on-line public access cata logue)
- Answering specialist enquiries, and providing subject expertise.

The library is the most comprehensive maritime reference library in the world, consisting of over 120 000 volumes. It originated from, among others, the printed books and atlases from the A. G. H. Macpherson collection which were bought by Sir James Caird in 1928 when material was being assembled for the museum; in later years he continued to buy important collections for the Library, and presented items from his own collection. Today its resources include 10 000 pre-1850 printed books, four miles of business records, and the museum's manuscript collection. It has a computer catalogue (available on microfiche from 1978, now superseded by the TinLib library management sys-tem, available on OPAC terminals, which has been in use since 1991). The Re-search Enquiries service handles 600 substantial written questions a month (charging for enquiries started at the beginning of 1995, in order to meet the objective of reducing the number of requests, while generating income); it also advises visitors and provides access to all the paper collections. The Old Royal Observatory provides advice from subject specialists in astronomy, nav-igation, hydrography, horology and instruments. The importance of enquiry analysis and subject indexing in meeting the responsibilities of Information Services is evident, as is their impact on documentation policies.

VISUAL ACCESS. The Visual Access section has specific current responsibility for access to pictorial and paper-based holdings other than navigational and Library materials, in all three-quarters of a million ships' plans, 4000 oil paint-ings, 70 000 watercolours, prints and drawings, and more than 300 000 historic photographs. Historic photographs and ships' plans are among the most fre-quent subjects of enquiries, and the staff concerned with documentation ac-knowledge that for historic photographs a more detailed approach to subject indexing should have been taken into account in designing the computer re-cord. As it is, answering enquiries about historic photographs has to rely on a very successful manual index which has been maintained by a curator. Ter-minology control and subject access to images are a key requirement for the Multi MIMSY system that has been acquired as a result of the LASSI project, and it is likely to be a priority of the UK Multi MIMSY Group to develop sub-ject access to images and image systems. Some work on terminology has been done by a team which includes members from Collections Management and the library, and subject specialists, but the museum is said to be short of resources of staff for this kind of work.

RESEARCH. The museum places renewed emphasis on its support for research and on developing a research strategy. The present research section was established partly in response to a perceived lack of research outputs from within the museum; while some of its staff are world-wide experts in their fields, they have not necessarily had the opportunity to undertake and publish research which contextualizes the collections and explains their significance. Its aim is to provide a basis for the museum's educational function, especially by promoting research partnerships with higher-education institutions, by means of research fellowships offered to scholars in the field of maritime history or related areas. The ultimate goal envisaged is a research centre to support and encourage work based on the collections.

Up to 1994 no research policy existed; there is now a policy and a 'master plan' which sets out a strategy. A Research Advisory Committee has the role of commenting on research proposals and deciding which to recommend for funding. It liaises with an Academic Awards Committee, which gives the museum's research fellowships, and an Assessment Board monitors progress in meeting the research plan. In-house research by museum staff is encouraged by a Research Group, which identifies appropriate areas of research, and suggests ways of improving access to the collections for researchers.

The main problem at present is raising awareness of the museum's resources among those who might undertake research which makes use of the museum's collections in wider contexts.

Systems

From 1991 to 1996, the main computer system used for documenting the collections was an in-house application designed on the platform of Intuitive Solutions software. GOS, the system installed in 1976 (see p192) remained in use for some purposes, but for some years it had not met the requirements evolved from experience by documentation staff. It was based on batched processing, the system was not on-line, and it was not networked. It provided good facilities for entry of structured data, but unstructured text caused problems; for information retrieval, it was primarily dependent on hard-copy indexes arranged according to various key fields. In the final years of the system, a member of the Collections Management group worked with Information Division staff, helping them to use it in their work, and providing tutorials on the system.

Some updating of Intuitive Solutions to provide for on-line information retrieval was carried out in 1993, but the result is described as being too difficult for non-specialists to use. The situation in 1995 was that the content of records held in the collections database was incomplete; an inventory project had produced 200 000 electronic records with sufficient information to account for and manage the collections, and a first level of subject indexing for retrieval, but some associated catalogue information was not in those records, so the combined use of hard-copy and electronic records was still necessary for some purposes. The main problem was the lack of accessibility of this database other than through clumsy print-outs and an inadequate on-line retrieval system. The ultimate aim was defined as a networked computer system that would allow Collections Development staff to enter registration data and curators to input full cataloguing information to same master record.

Only the documentalists had become familiar with the old system, and they were finding difficulty in visualizing what a new one would need to be like. They were certain that it needed to be a total system, centrally managed, but with specific people responsible for particular areas of information; they were convinced from experience that the best results came from having subject specialists join in documenting the collections for which they are responsible. Anxieties were perceived as still existing, so the people with systems responsibilities were spending a lot of time building contacts and helping the ultimate users to develop their ideas about how the new system should assist them. It was seen as particularly important to learn about failures and difficulties encountered with the old system, both to improve it while it was still in use, and to help develop the user specification for what the new one should be able to do. The development of the LASSI consortium project contributed to this process of definition and specification.

IT support

This is described as having been in a vacuum in the two years 1993–95. In 1995 it was still a separate department, but its role was being re-defined. The office systems side went to Property and Technical Services Department in the Collections and Museum Services Division, and the rest of the staff to Information Division.

Information systems strategy and information policy development

An Information Systems Strategy group, reporting to the museum's Executive Team, was set up in 1995, with the remit of:
• Creating and maintaining a museum-wide IS strategy
• Developing an operational plan
• Identifying IS priorities and making recommendations for resource allocation
• Monitoring the implementation of the plan.

The overall aim is: 'To make essential information available (as required by staff and customers in order to carry out their business) within a planned structure (Information Technology)', and to provide information which is accurate, credible, comprehensive, relevant, easy to use, and timely. The benefits to the museum are defined under the heads of:

1. Utility of information
   'Increase intellectual access (both staff and public) to the collections'.

2. Productivity
   'Contribute to improvement in decision making (e.g. in finance), efficiency of operation (e.g. admissions data), working conditions (e.g. statutory personnel data), time saving (e.g. diary scheduling)'.

3. Effectiveness
   In reaching new customers (e.g. customer database), improving customer satisfaction (e.g. bookings unit software).

4. Financial position
   Improvement by contributing to cost reduction (e.g. inventory data and procurement procedures) and increasing profits, to meet the need for increased productivity in the face of a grant for staff costs which may remain level or decrease.

Sub-groups are working on technical and business development, planning and carrying out the installation of the Multi MIMSY collections information system, access development, and information systems support.

Evaluation

The picture of information management in the museum, as it has evolved to the current situation, is one that has many positive features. There are, inevitably, many factors which need attention if the inherent potential is to be fully realized, and they will raise all the familiar problems of resource allocation. And there are – as in all organizations – some contradictions at the level of policy which, if not confronted and resolved, pose a threat to achieving key objectives. The balance between positive and negative features seems, however, to be in favour of the positive, and the National Maritime Museum should be able to look forward with reasonable confidence to the rewards of its long and thoughtful learning process in managing information.

Positive features
Once the Multi MIMSY system is installed, it should be possible for the Collections Management and Information Divisions to co-operate in upgrading the presentation of collections information to support research and publication, and to support access to the collections database across the board, including enquiries, public access, display planning, and conservation. The existing forum for formal collaboration and interchange, and the prevailing informal day-to-day co-operation should provide a sound basis; and the initiatives from the systems side to support users of the previous system should also pay off in the transition to the new one.

The comparatively recent recognition of the need for an information systems strategy, while late in the day, has perhaps come at a time when it has the best chance of succeeding – the breadth of its remit is certainly encouraging. It seems likely that the strategy will recognize the importance of access to independent advice on IT, and of monitoring the development of technologies with potential relevance for achieving the museum's objectives. The lack of such awareness in the past may have held up progress and undermined the high-quality work put into documentation. Areas of current importance include use of the Internet, and imaging technology.

After a period when the museum went through what has been described as a process of thinking it could not afford too many experts, which led to some re-deployment and some losses of staff, it has once again recognized the value of subject expertise, as expressed in its research strategy, the Research Group, and the efforts to draw on relevant outside knowledge available in higher education.

There is also potential for other uses of external expertise through inputs to the collections database from outside researchers working on museum publications. To take advantage of this, the museum will need a standard agreement allowing access for research on condition that relevant findings are made available to it in order to enrich its records.

Areas in need of attention

These are mentioned to draw the attention of readers seeking to learn from this case study to points which need to be considered in managing information in this situation.

SUBJECT ACCESS AND TERMINOLOGY CONTROL. Subject searching, especially of image collections, to meet highly specific user interests, is one of the most difficult requirements that museums have always faced – very often only to turn away again with a shudder once they realized the resources of intellectual effort implicit in meeting it. The essence of the problem is the consistent use of words, and it is less easily solved in real life than in Wonderland, where Humpty Dumpty had them thoroughly disciplined to mean what he chose them to mean.

Terminology control has not been neglected in the museum's thinking about information management, but the current view is that it should not be over-emphasized – which presumably means that it comes fairly low in the queue for resources. Against that, it has to be recognized that the museum cannot achieve the 'do-wells' and change objectives concerned with improved access to the collections without devoting more resources to it in the course of exploiting the new system. The need to rely on a manual subject index for answering enquiries on historic photographs has been noted above. Readers may like to consider the central place which thesaurus development has occupied in the planning of a new system for the RAF Museum (see p232), and the strong interest which the MDA now takes in the subject after some years of what might be described as vacillation. See p181.

RE-STRUCTURING COLLECTIONS RECORDS. It has been pointed out by staff concerned with documentation that once the collections records are readily accessible via the new system, it will for the first time become possible to see the real problems they pose for research and publication, and other forms of staff and public access, especially those relating to the way in which the information is actually recorded. This may in the short to medium term cause difficulties in meeting existing time targets for research and publications, so it would be prudent to examine the implications before the problems become acute and to make any necessary adjustments.

ACCESS TO IMAGES TO SUPPORT INFORMATION RETRIEVAL. One of the most powerful of present-day supports for finding information in museums lies in the potential to link images of items (both two- and three-dimensional) with records, so that users are presented with sets of miniature images matching their search requests, and can select from them before moving to the actual objects. Building up this form of access is a key task in developing the new system.

LINKS BETWEEN COLLECTIONS AND LIBRARY SYSTEMS. At present, the only substantial electronic system in Information Division is the TinLib library management software used in the library. The potential for linking the collections and library systems needs to be investigated, because of the importance of being able to find everything relevant to an enquiry – whatever its physical form – in a single search operation. (The potential of an appropriate module of the Multi MIMSY system is currently being investigated for this purpose.)

INFORMATION PRODUCTS. The information products by which organizations tell their outside world, and their own staff, the things they need to know about the organization are a subject of long standing interest to the present author. It is therefore gratifying to find among the 'do-wells' to support the primary objectives: 'To improve the quality and drawing power of ... information products'. On the evidence of some of the current products, there is a need for an integrated look at the whole process by which information products of all kinds are decided upon, planned, written, edited, designed and produced, with participation by representatives of all the stakeholders.

Unresolved contradictions and possible dangers

The contradictions and threats are related to questions of high-level policy. It is characteristic of many institutions, and not just of museums, that such contradictions become apparent when there is a commitment to developing an information policy. As noted above, this is seen by those with responsibility for it as a very large task, and the road as beset with many obstacles.

One chief need is for policy principles which can aid decisions on conflicting information-management aims. Some demand the reconciling of long- and short-term aims: for instance, the objective of making images available for sale demands investment; how is that to be ranked alongside investment in the 30 per cent of images which are not yet catalogued, and therefore not available to be offered for sale? Others relate to where financial responsibility for investment should rest, for example, for a proposed CD library of oil paintings.

Some of the short-term vs long-term contradictions relate to how different organizational 'cultures' interpret the museum's primary objectives. This can lead to a noticeable distance between the objectives as formally expressed on paper and what is seen as of over-riding importance in practice. The museum's primary objectives seem to imply balance and integration among the concepts of reputation, access, service to users, collections quality, asset management, and financial management – the pursuit of each giving essential support to the others. In practice, there is a danger of conflict between commercially oriented and public service aims, of the long-term 'service' aims and behind-the-scenes work to support them being regarded as secondary to anything which generates revenue. This leads to difficulty in making cases for investment in activities which are necessary but not directly resource- raising.[4] In this connection it is important to recall the findings of the report on marketing strategy development (see p201), which made it clear that the museum had a lot of leeway to make up before it could claim to be managing essential marketing information in a professional way, let alone to have a fully operational marketing strategy.

The information policy initiative emphasizes the need for a high-level forum in which all stakeholders in the museum's use of information can look at the information implications of the museum's objectives. The outcome should be an agreed interpretation of the primary objectives and priorities among them and a generally accepted definition of what information means in the museum's terms. This would form a sound foundation for defining what the museum needs to do with information in order to achieve key objectives, and for principles of guidance on reconciling immediate and long-term returns where these are seen to be in conflict. This would seem to be a realistic way of helping to overcome the problems experienced by information managers in convincing top decision makers of the importance of integrated information management, and in making them as enthusiastic about investing in resources for managing information, as they are about putting on exciting exhibitions.

[4] The argument of the 'bottom line' raises questions of how institutions and businesses of all kinds value their 'intangible' resources, which are currently the focus of considerable interest in the information community. The overall message is that a) they tend to be seriously undervalued, and b) methodologies are becoming available for proper evaluation of them.

References

ORNA, E. & PETTITT, C. W. (1980),
Information handling in museums, London:
K G Saur. Clive Bingley

BORDA, A. E. (1997),*The Museum Library:
A Survey of Libraries and Information Centres in the
Museums and Related Institutions of the Greater
London Area,* PhD thesis, University of London

The National Museum of Wales

Introduction

The National Museum of Wales (NMW), in Cardiff, houses collections totalling some 7.5 million groups. The main museum holds archaeology, numismatics, fine art and natural sciences. Out stations include the Welsh Folk Museum, the Caerleon Museum (roman legionary museum) and the Welsh Industrial and Maritime Museum. In all there are ten branches, although planned cutbacks will close some of these. The staff totals over 500, with a hundred curatorial staff, although these numbers too are set to shrink. Until recently documentation had been the responsibility of individual departments in the museums. In the seven years leading up to 1990 various consultants were employed to advise on a central documentation policy.

Documentation: the current picture

The present senior documentation officer joined in 1990, and in 1992 the documentation policy was accepted by the Trustees; this was a 'roll-out plan' plus a strategy document. The plan is still on course and being funded; although each year the resources get tighter, this project currently receives ring-fenced money from the Welsh Office.

The strategic points considered in arriving at the policy were that it should be PC based, use a package that required minimum bespoke programming and used the minimum in-house staff for software development. Audit was to be the basis of the initial documentation rather than full cataloguing. If possible one multi-disciplinary system was desired, with good import/export facilities to a GIS (geographic information system), and with good report-writing facilities so that it could be userdriven to an extent.

In the event the package Micro-musee was chosen, a system derived from the Clipper database management package. This has been tweaked inside to map the Micro-musee fields to the SPECTRUM data standards; there are some 200 fields available, so it is relatively easy to expand, in a way transparent to users, from an audit-oriented system to a full catalogue system. Each department has its own procedures and extensions of the core, but now the National Museum has an institution wide policy on accessions and de-accessions; this was led to an extent by the requirements of MGC Registration.

It was, however, found that two databases were necessary, one for the humanities departments and one for the natural science departments. Each of these requires a separate Micro-musee licence. The way forward at the Caerleon museum is presently under debate, whether to link it to the central database or to set up its own in-house database. Both options have substantial financial implications as an in-house database would require another separate Micro-musee licence.

The staffing for the documentation work consists centrally of two computer IT officers, who look after the hardware and software, and three central documentation officers, who look after data standards and the maintenance of the databases. In addition there are ten data-entry staff, seconded to departments as required, and seven designated departmental liaison officers. The data entry staff are constrained to do only inputting of data, although this can at times be stretched to include a store audit; they are not permitted to be used for any other tasks within the department. The liaison officers are curators who are responsible part time for departmental information services; they can access the databases and do input or editing if necessary. They are self-selecting by showing an interest and/or knowledge of information technology and systems. There are seven other curatorial staff inputting information as well, and there is a 'roll-out' training programme to allow other curators to take part in the data entry and editing.

The PCs are networked using Novell Netware within the main building and the network includes the Welsh Folk Museum. Dial-up facilities are provided to other sites, but are not often used except for fault diagnosis on the databases being created at those sites.

The databases include information from the conservation department and the library, but not yet from the personnel department.

Performance indicators, checks and priorities

This idea originated in work done at the Smithsonian Institution in Washington. The primary performance indicator (PI) in the system is the number of records input within set periods. Conservation, accession and catalogue records are all counted together in an index of performance, with a six-monthly report to the Museum Council. The report of the number of records 'achieved' is accompanied by a 'health warning' pointing out that different departments have different types of records and that like-for-like comparisons are not simple.

The basic audit information as input has to be monitored for quality. This includes the 'audit core' fields together with six extra fields at discipline level that make the object identifiable as an individual object. The quality control markers are checked at input time or else automatically flagged as unverified. There is a two-level check, first physical (does the object exist, has it been seen?) and second at the terminology level (have the data standards been adhered to?).

Each department has to deal with its A class priority material, that is, all material on display, all material received since 1990, and all loans in and out. This A class group has to be completed within two years of starting, and progress is monitored monthly. Then the department has to define its priority col-

lections, and this work has to be project led, e.g. a proposed published catalogue, an exhibition or a move to a new store.

The user perspective

The first question that the NMW staff ask of the documentation effort is: 'will
it allow us to look at our collections in a different way, that is serendipity with
object level information which may show unexpected connections and new
thought processes?' But as yet this question is still unproven.

Some expert systems are being considered, for example one to allow the
identification of painters. It is felt imperative to have discipline-relevant fields
in addition to the audit core, and it must be possible to link the initial text records to images, archives and geographical information systems, to extend
their usefulness.

Initially the primary users were seen as the hundred or so curatorial staff
themselves. Now, however, there is a groundswell of opinion that use should
be extended to the general public; this opinion is especially strongly expressed
by the marketing department. The National Audit Office has recently been conducting a survey to see how to justify a return on capital and revenue invested
in documentation in terms of public access, but this has not concluded yet.

Senior management do not see themselves as direct users of the databases,
but recently have become more interested, particularly as they are more
aware of the popularity of the Internet.

The documentation department was originally driven by the auditors, but
is now much more interested in portability between systems, in increasing efficiency (making routine life easier for curatorial staff, for example by automating loans-out documentation, so as to release time for what they are
professionally trained for and good at), and in increasing public access in the
widest sense. They consider the client groups should include senior management, curators, researchers, other museum departments (such as marketing),
the general public (especially teachers in schools, with emphasis on helping
with the national curriculum). For the latter group, all the boxes in the schools
loan service are already on the system.

Other ideas under consideration at present are producing a CD- from the
Micro-musee records in the art department, supplemented by scanned-in
transparencies. No imaging projects are being considered for at least five years
because of the uncertainty of how technology will develop in the near future;
staff do not feel it has yet reached a sufficient level of maturity to provide a
stable medium. Public access via the Internet is on the cards, as are gallery
inter-active displays, but the resources to develop and maintain these have yet
to be identified.

One of the questions most exercising the documentation staff at the moment is how to use the system to increase curator productivity, for example by
automating the servicing of loans out using the catalogue.

Evaluation

This case study highlights the training and performance issues that must be considered when a new, centralized documentation strategy is being developed: training of curators and other relevant staff in the documentation system is vital if the full benefits are to be achieved. The use of performance indicators (PIs) to monitor progress of the documentation plan can be useful, but PIs must be interpreted with care to ensure that like is compared with like.

Norfolk Museums Service

Introduction

The Museums Service of Norfolk County Council is an example of the unwisdom of prophecy; a case study in the original edition of this book (Orna & Pettitt, 1980, p143), described it as having a manual system which was likely to stay that way. This return to the scene will show how wrong the prediction was.

The development of electronic information management

One of the main reasons for the conviction of museum staff in the early 1980s that their systems would remain manual was the fact that the then director 'didn't like computers'. The first examples of the despised breed (seven Amstrads) got in under the budget heading of 'typewriters' in 1988. They were distributed among the county's museums, and the curator of Cromer Museum, who was already taking an interest in their potential for information management, started using the early version of the MDA's MODES on his Amstrad. In the course of time he became the person with most experience of the use of software for museum records. As part of a management studies course, he carried out a project on documentation policy, on the basis of the MDA's 1989 targets for what later became SPECTRUM. See p184. Norfolk's museums at that point had no documentation for the entry of items; the project rectified the lack, and also led to a redesign of the documentation for accessions and exit procedures. This work formed the basis for continuing development of a documentation manual, which has been written in parallel with work on actual documentation of the collections, issued in stages, and revised and updated in the light of the lessons of experience.

The curator responsible for these initiatives took the decision to concentrate the limited resources in museums where the benefits were likely to be immediately appreciated; only now is he working with more sceptical colleagues, who in the past three years have had a chance to see in operation some of the practical benefits a computerized system can bring.

Human resources in applying the technology

In deciding who should use the technology to help museums to improve their existing records, the argument was that it would not be economic to put poor-quality and unintelligible records outside for data capture. Retrospective conversion was seen as needing in-house effort by people with some understanding, who could use their knowledge to disentangle the puzzles and, often,

enhance the quality of the records. Working with volunteers who had relevant subject knowledge revealed that there was good sense in matching data-
capture operators to collections; one such volunteer in due course came to be
employed as a member of the documentation team. The use of two part-time
data-input members of staff, rather than one full-timer, is considered beneficial, because the work demands not only meticulous copying but also interpretation and concentrated intellectual work in collation. Quality control is
provided by the curator responsible for documentation.

Database development

MODES, in the latest MODES Plus version, is still in use. At present there are
many different databases for individual museums; the curator responsible for
the work does an annual back-up for all the county's museums. He also holds
nearly 100 000 records in a central database on his own machine, which he uses
for experimental work directed to the ultimate aim of managing all the county's museum records as a total database – something which he describes as a
'craft activity' rather than a simply technical one.

From the beginning of 1993, all new material in most of the county's museums has been catalogued according to Norfolk Museums Service's manual,
using MODES Plus. The finds data held by the Norfolk Archaeological Unit
(see p218) in its own database is also transferred into MODES Plus. Meantime,
the retrospective conversion of records is proceeding at Cromer Museum on a
10-year programme, at a rate of 20 000–30 000 a year.

Standards and documentation

Standards – for example authority lists for such fields as storage location – are
being developed as the work progresses. The 'simple name' and 'full name'
fields of the MDA record structure continue to create problems, because of
varying conventions in their interpretation in different collections and departments. Terminology is controlled in some fields, using various authority lists
specific to the fields; these include lists for people, Norfolk place names, locali-
ty type, archaeology artifacts, archaeological periods, storage locations, condition, and acquisition method (see also p217 for terminology control in the
Norfolk Sites and Monuments Record). SHIC is the preferred classification for
appropriate material, but where museums have their own entrenched classifications for manual systems, MODES Plus is perfectly able to accommodate
these as well. A truly county-wide classification has yet to be developed, but is
seen as necessary before databases of individual collections can be merged into
a single one. It is, however, appreciated that classification becomes conceptu-
ally less important once records can be searched electronically.

The documentation continues to develop organically by means of 'suc-
cessive approximations' in the light of learning from experience. Entry documentation has been completed, with line-by-line instructions, a policy on
unclaimed enquiries has been established, as has a collecting policy, proce-

dures have been developed for acquisition and transfer of ownership, and the historic thickets of accession numbers are gradually being tidied.

Towards public access

Some experiments are being made with InTouch software. See also the Hampshire Museums Service case study, p167. This gives access via a touch screen; buttons give access to MODES Plus secondary indexes of Subject, Date, Name and Place keywords. Clicking the command Search leads to presentation of an edited minimal description from the record, with a thumb-nail image, which can be enlarged to whole-screen by touching a button. Boolean searches are possible; in response to them the system presents a list of records meeting the required criteria. The first project was the Cromer Print and Photograph collections. Some 6000 pictures are being scanned in as part of the record, and the records have been enhanced as part of the process.

The InTouch software has been demonstrated at the Norfolk Show and Norfolk History Fair, where it met an enthusiastic response from the public. It was placed in the Gallery at Cromer for public use on Museums Day, 18 May 1996, and sponsorship is to be sought from local businesses to enable it to be installed in more of the county's museums.

Recent developments

At Cromer, MODES Plus is now being exploited in other useful ways, on the basis of copying entry forms to a file (as they were based on the MDA data standard, conversion of boxes to MODES Plus fields is straightforward). This allows various interesting developments:

- Ability to search on donor, address, date, field collection place, etc., which was not possible before
- A database of enquiries, etc., which can be used to answer questions from management, and others
- Ability to output letters of thanks for groups of items offered for gift to the museum (based on a display specification)
- Production of answers to enquiries, using the word-processing and paste facilities of MODES Plus, into which standard informative paragraphs on such subjects as the Cromer Forest-bed fossils, can be inserted.

The possibility of converting the entry record to the beginnings of an item record for the catalogue is also under investigation; so too is the possibility of using MODES Plus to assist the Archaeology Department and the staff responsible for the Sites and Monuments Record (see p217).

Field archaeology

Norfolk Museums service has a rather unusual responsibility for field archaeology in the county (since 1989 all counties have had to maintain a Sites and Monuments Record; this usually falls to the lot of their Planning departments, rather than the Museums Service). The Field Archaeology Division of the Museums Service consists of two sections: Norfolk Landscape Archaeology and the Norfolk Archaeological Unit.

Norfolk Landscape Archaeology
This section, based at Gressenhall Museum of Rural Life, is responsible for recording and safeguarding the county's archaeological heritage. Its remit covers:
- Managing the County Sites and Monuments Record
- Identifying and recording archaeological discoveries
- Recording historic landscapes by air photography and maintaining an air photographs library
- Advising planning authorities, conservation bodies and the public on archaeological matters
- Recording historic buildings
- Advising on monument conservation and display
- Promotion of conservation and research on the historic landscape
- Monitoring the work of archaeological contractors.

The users are primarily the staff of the division, who make searches in connection with planning applications and for their own research, planning consultants, outside researchers, and educational institutions.

THE SITES AND MONUMENTS RECORD. The Record now contains details of 36 000 casual finds, sites and buildings of archaeological and historic importance in Norfolk, ranging from the Palaeolithic to the 1960s. Its origins go back to a card index established by R. Rainbird Clarke in the 1930s when he was asked to collect information on Roman Norfolk for the Ordnance Survey Map of Roman Britain. The index was extended to include records from other periods, and came to Norwich Castle Museum when Clarke joined the staff there in the 1940s; when the original Norfolk Archaeological Unit was set up in 1973, the index formed the basis for the records it established.

TECHNOLOGY APPLICATIONS. Since 1984 the SMR has been held in a computer database, using a succession of packages originating from the Royal Commission on Historic Monuments; the current one is ORACLE based (ORACLE VIIADAPT), though it is understood that the Commission is considering an adaptation of Windows. (The Commission's own MONARCH national monuments and archaeological sites database (see p244) appears to have proved unsuitable for county SMR.) Records are created first on hard-copy forms, resembling an accession register entry; they are entered weekly into the database.

The record structure is essentially oriented towards sites, and is said not to provide enough space for object records. A thesaurus, also originating from the Commission, is available on-line, but provides rather minimal help; it does not, for example, allow the creation of links between preferred and non-preferred terms, and if users input a non-preferred term in either inputting or searching, the only response they get is the distinctly discouraging one of 'Term not in thesaurus'.

Information retrieval can be by Boolean search on combined features, which yields the description field of relevant records, or by SQL, which presents a list of numbers. It is not possible to search on the free-text fields.

Compatibility with the records of the county's museums is seen as highly unlikely because of the necessity of using the Royal Commission's software, so there seems no immediate prospect for users of being able to search in one operation for museum records and SMR records of comparable items. The Norfolk Archaeological Unit, however, constitutes a kind of a bridge between the two, in that it feeds data to the SMR, as well as to the MODES Plus database (see p215).

The Landscape Archaeology section suffers from a lack of technical support – no other institution in the county uses the same software, the human resources available (in effect one specialist) are too thinly spread as between the two sections of the Field Archaeology Division, and the 20 miles or so between the two compound the difficulties.

Norfolk Archaeological Unit

The unit offers a range of services to a variety of bodies besides its parent organization, including:

- Archaeological consultancy
- Preliminary site assessments
- Site evaluations
- Watching briefs on construction sites
- Rescue excavations
- Site interpretation schemes
- Surveys for farmers, landowners and developers.

It operates as a self-financing business unit, and has a pro-active policy of IT development built into its annual business plans. Information technology is used for a variety of purposes, such as word processing (currently being standardized on MS WORD), project management, financial controls, database work, graphics, and conservation management. DTP applications are currently being developed, and a Geographical Information System (GIS)[1] is in use for a major project within Norwich. The unit's training programme includes computer training for staff; software support is provided in-house, and hardware support through an outside contract.

ACTIVITIES. Probably the most widely known of the unit's operations in recent years was the large-scale excavation in the area of Norwich Castle in the course of the construction of a shopping mall, which added considerably

[1] Readers interested in geographical systems are referred to an issue of *MDA information* devoted to the subject (2 (3), 1997).

to knowledge of a very important area of the city. It also provided a first opportunity for computerization of a large-scale archaeological project.

The scope of the Unit's survey work includes earth works, monuments and buildings. It is increasingly involved in management exercises, such as commissions from English Heritage to review churches and church sites, and the different strategies employed in managing them. The unit is also contributing data about Norwich to another national initiative for English Heritage: the creation of urban archaeology databases covering 30 major urban sites where the traditional methods of Sites and Monuments Records are not applicable. These 'referential databases' cover a whole range of urban activities and locations, and all kinds of records of them; the information for Norwich is entered into the database and managed and accessed on a Geographical Information System.

Another major piece of fieldwork – the excavation of the skeleton of an early pleistocene elephant (some 600 000 years old) on the North Norfolk coast in the winter of 1995 – involved archaeologists from the unit and from UK museums and universities, together with colleagues from Sweden, the USA and Canada, under the direction of the Head of Palaeontology at Norwich Castle Museum. The Swedish archaeological consultancy, Arkeologikonsult, sponsored the project with electronic surveying and computing. Detailed recording of the elephant was carried out using digital cameras to make plans, sections and drawings direct in the MicroStation CAD system, which was used to create animations and three-dimensional models of the skeleton. Sponsorship from the Swedish state telecom company Telia also provided the means for an on-site connection to the Internet, so that the site team could consult with specialists all over the world direct from the excavation – the first interactive use of the Internet in an ongoing excavation project (see Figure 11.1 on p220).

HUMAN RESOURCES AND TECHNOLOGY APPLICATIONS. The 25 staff members of the unit are described as being 'nearly all computer literate' and all have access to PCs. This reflects the significant changes in recording methods over recent years, which have led to intensive use of information technology in all aspects of archaeology. In field work, AutoCAD is used for digitized site plans; it has been used mainly for plan outlines to date, but three-dimensional models have been built up for some jobs – as in the case of the Norwich Castle excavation, where the ditch was so deep that each level had to be stepped, so that the bottom vertical plane was 10m out of alignment with the top and thus could not be recorded in the normal vertical section. The 3D model showed the correct location of the finds. A model that could be rotated on screen was also produced for the Castle Bridge, in the course of the same excavation. Auto CAD is also used to provide drawings for artists to work from. The unit is now exploring the possibility of linking a text database with AutoCAD, for quick retrieval of such information as the distribution of specific kinds of artifacts.

The first interactive use of the Internet on an on-going excavation project
(From the Norfolk Museums Service World Wide Web site)

Figure 1

The West Runton Elephant Project

In 1990, around 600,000 years after it died, the remains of the West Runton Elephant was discovered after winter seas had eroded the cliffs at West Runton, near Cromer, Norfolk, U.K. The huge pelvis was the first bone to be revealed in the base of the cliff, and a year later many more bones were found. By 1992, some 25 % of the skeleton had been recovered and plans were made to recover the remainder, still buried beneath 20 metres of cliff, and to obtain evidence of the elephant's ancient environment from the abundant associated plant and animal fossils. The excavation (Phase I of the project) was made possible in 1995 by a grant from the National Heritage Lottery Fund, and by commercial sponsorship. The excavation of the elephant was carried out under controlled archaeological conditions by the Norfolk Archaeological Unit and specialist surveying and computing services from the Swedish consultancy Arkeologikonsult. This work resulted in the recovery of almost the entire skeleton. Some 10 tonnes of sediment samples were taken to be processed for small fossils, ranging from pollen and seeds to beetles, snails, fishes and small mammals.

The elephant, a male, has been identified as an early form of mammoth Mammuthus trogontherii. It stood about 4 metres at the shoulder, and at ten tonnes would have been nearly twice the weight of a modern African elephant. It had died in its 40's, long before old age, in a shallow, swampy river channel. Hyaenas had scavenged the carcass, leaving tooth marks on some of the bones and their characteristic fossil droppings (coprolites). Other elephants appear to have scattered the bones and trampled one of the tusks. Similar behaviour has been observed with modern elephants who seem curiously drawn towards the remains of their own species. The river mud and silt which buried the skeleton comprises the fossil horizon known as the West Runton Freshwater Bed, now exposed in the cliff face. West Runton is the international type-site for the Cromerian Temperate or Interglacial stage, currently dated to about 600,000 years ago. At this time, Britain was connected to continental Europe across what is now the southern North Sea and the climate was similar to that of today.

West Runton is a Geological Site of Special Scientific Interest (S.S.S.I.) and is of great significance in our understanding of the complex changes in climate, flora, and fauna of the Quaternary period, or 'Ice Age'. For more than 170 years fossil remains of elephants, rhinos, deer and many other animals have been collected from what is known as the Cromer Forest Bed Formation, which includes the West Runton Freshwater Bed, exposed along the coasts of Norfolk and Suffolk. However, never before has an entire skeleton been reported from these well-searched deposits.

A second grant from the Heritage Lottery Fund has substantially aided the current phase of the project (Phase 2) – conservation of the elephant bones and research on the elephant and its ancient environment. More than fifteen specialist researchers are gathered together as the West Runton Elephant Project Team, led by Dr Tony Stuart, drawn from the Natural History Museum, Cambridge University, University of East Anglia, University College London, Royal Holloway College London, University of Nevada, Coventry University, Michigan State University, and University of Hull. Preliminary results will be discussed at a two-day workshop in December 1996.

The conservation of the elephant bones, and the research programme is scheduled to take two years. The final

Integration of text and graphics is also being explored; line drawings are being scanned in. In survey work, theodolite readings can be converted to an AutoCAD-readable format. A GIS-type application developed within the unit uses the 'AutoCAD SQL Extensions' supplied with release 12 to link drawn entities with rows in a 'flat' database containing basic information about each context. The application allows entities in the AutoCAD-drawn site plan to be selected on the basis of information in the text database – e.g. 'Highlight all the features assigned to Phase 5 of the site'. The links also allow the text information to be accessed graphically: i.e. by selecting an entity on the site plan it is possible to view the Phase Assignments, a summary of the finds, etc. This application currently exists in a very cheap and cheerful format, using the standard AutoCAD dialogues rather than any specially designed user interface.

Most large excavations are input to a database designed in-house, based on Fox-Pro, which is used for data entry and reports. Word processing is used for writing evaluation reports, excavation reports, and academic reports.

IT is also used in unit management; Microsoft Excel is used in preparing costs for projects, for monitoring project expenditure, and for keeping track of staff time and of the rate of budget expenditure. Project management software is used for the more complex projects. There are long-term plans for improving in-house communication, which is complicated by the distribution of the Field Archaeology Division's staff among four locations in Norwich and Gressenhall. Recently the unit adopted a five-year development plan for IT based on a minimum standard which is now being implemented. It includes access to the Internet and email.

Evaluation

Despite severe limitations on resources, there are many positive features in the work of the professionals in the Museums Service. The museums are getting a good deal out of well-used small resources in the development of the MODES Plus database; skills and knowledge are particularly well deployed in the process. Many benefits are coming out of a back room in the converted fishermen's cottages which house Cromer Museum; as the curator there observes: 'There's a mountain of data to climb, but once you're at the top, you can ski down it!'.

There is an interesting contrast in the uses of technology in the two sections of the Field Archaeology Division. The Archaeological Unit enjoys considerable freedom for development, which it uses constructively throughout its work, together with strong systems support; as a result, its work is widely known, and productive collaborations are possible, as in the case of the West Runton elephant. The valuable work of Landscape Archaeology, on the other hand, seems to be hampered by being tied to software which is not entirely appropriate for the materials it has to handle, and by lack of on-site technical support. It would seem that the nature of its work would benefit from something closer to modern museum collections management software (as de-scribed in other case studies in this book), which would allow flexible record structures that would accommodate both object and site records, and would provide upto-date support for terminology control. The lack of compatibility with museum records remarked on earlier also imposes costs and reduces opportunities.

References

ORNA, E. & PETTITT, C. W. (1980), *Information handling in museums,* London: K G Saur/Clive Bingley

North Somerset Museum Service

Background

The North Somerset Museum Service is based on the museum at Weston-super-Mare, a seaside resort on the Bristol Channel. The collections mainly cover the natural and social history and the archaeology of North Somerset, including material relating to the development of Weston itself.

They also reflect changes in local government boundaries and administration. The museum has been a local authority institution since 1901. Up to the re-organization of 1974, following the 1972 Local Government Act, the Borough of Weston administered its own library and museum service. With the re-organization, libraries went to the new authority of Avon, while the museum became the responsibility of the new Woodspring District Council. It was at this point that the museum took over the former premises of the local Gaslight Company. Originally, the collections had focused on Weston-super-Mare and its geographical hinterland; this area, however, did not coincide with the boundaries of the new District Council, so after 1974 the collecting policy changed to reflect the new territory.

In 1996, with further changes in local government legislation, the title changed again, to North Somerset Museum Service, under the new unitary authority of North Somerset Council, which covers a population of about 177 000. Libraries as well as museums are part of the new Council's responsibility, within the Directorate of Economic Development and Community Leisure. The museum now employs a total of about 12 full-time-equivalent staff, of whom 2.5 are managerial and 4.5 are curatorial.

Objectives

The museum's 1996–97 Business Plan defines its objectives as to:
* Encourage the survival and preservation of the North Somerset heritage
* Provide long-term displays on major themes of that heritage to inform, educate and provide enjoyment for residents and visitors
* Interpret it in a variety of ways to make it accessible to everyone in the area
* Find ways of encouraging public participation and contribution to the work of the service
* Maintain high standards and professionalism in dealing with users
* Co-operate with other sections of North Somerset Council and with other organizations.

Performance indicators for assessing how well it is achieving its objectives are in terms of ratio of market-generated to public-sector income; users per employee and per curatorial staff member; number of records from the back-log accessioned; number of visitors to the museum; return visits as percentage of tickets sold (target 65 per cent); average spend/visitor in the museum shop.

The museum defines its main activities in fulfilment of its objectives as shown in Figure 12.1 on p225.

Collections information management

The present Museum Services Manager, on his arrival in 1989, inherited a mix-ture of documentation, of varying quality. A decision had already been taken to transfer to MDA format and to set up more indexes. The manager, with previous experience of setting up a new collections information service which was electronic from the start, decided to move straight to the electronic ver-sion and as a start acquired the MDA's MODES software and one PC, mov-ing to MODES Plus as soon as it became available.

Today, all current acquisitions are entered into a manuscript archival re-gister and then input straight into a MODES Plus database. All curators have their own computer for handling records relating to their own parts of the collections, and one curator maintains a 'global file' with the total database. The backlog of unaccessioned and uncatalogued items is being worked through in the same way as current acquisitions, and the earlier material which was accessioned and catalogued with varying degrees of indexing is being upgraded.

The procedure followed with input files is to add data to them from exist-ing manual files; they are kept small, added monthly, or even weekly, to each curator's own database and to the main database, and then wiped. A tape back-up is held elsewhere. The procedures being followed meet the Museums and Galleries Commission registration criteria, and the museum's collections man-agement policy is committed to the SPECTRUM data standard. The use of printed-out indexes has been discontinued except for special research pur-poses; all other searches are now done on-line. Ultimately the intention is to have a cloned database on the Internet.

The museum plans to experiment with using InTouch in the galleries, and to get feedback on it from the visitors, who include many older people; their response to this use of technology will be carefully studied.

Integrated management of information

Visitor surveys have been used to guide decisions on what the museum should offer, and to gather demographic information. One recent use was in trying to find out the frequency of visits by individuals, in order to take a sound decision on how to charge for admission. On the basis of the data gath-ered, the system adopted was for a single payment at a uniform rate, which allows as many visits during the year as the ticket holder wishes to make. This

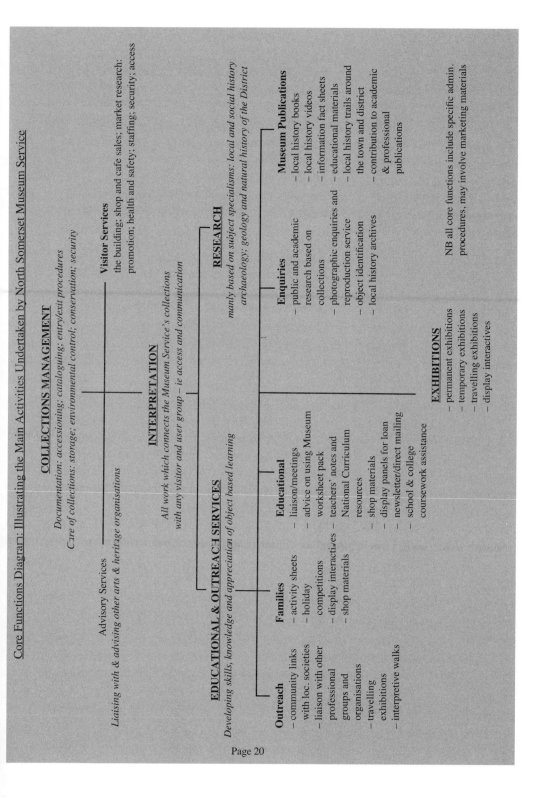

Core Functions Diagram: Illustrating the Main Activities Undertaken by North Somerset Museum Service

COLLECTIONS MANAGEMENT

Documentation: accessioning; cataloguing; entry/exit procedures
Care of collections: storage; environmental control; conservation; security

Visitor Services
the building; shop and cafe sales; market research: promotion; health and safety; staffing; security; access

Advisory Services
Liaising with & advising other arts & heritage organisations

INTERPRETATION
All work which connects the Museum Service's collections with any visitor and user group – ie access and communication

RESEARCH
manly based on subject specialisms: local and social history archaeology; geology and natural history of the District

Enquiries
– public and academic research based on collections
– photographic enquiries and reproduction service
– object identification
– local history archives

Museum Publications
– local history books
– local history videos
– information fact sheets
– educational materials
– local history trails around the town and district
– contribution to academic & professional publications

NB all core functions include specific admin. procedures, may involve marketing materials

EDUCATIONAL & OUTREACH SERVICES
Developing skills, knowledge and appreciation of object based learning

Educational
– liaison/meetings
– advice on using Museum worksheet pack
– teachers' notes and National Curriculum resources
– shop materials
– display panels for loan
– newsletter/direct mailing
– school & college coursework assistance

Families
– activity sheets
– holiday competitions
– display interactives
– shop materials

Outreach
– community links with loc. societies
– liaison with other professional groups and organisations
– travelling exhibitions
– interpretive walks

EXHIBITIONS
– permanent exhibitions
– temporary exhibitions
– travelling exhibitions
– display interactives

Page 20

225

is simple and cheap to administer and, while available to everyone, has a built-in bias to favour local people.

For financial data, the museum has access to the Town Hall's financial management system; while this is primarily an accounting system, at least it allows a way of checking that overall expenditure is running in line with budget provisions.

The museum makes intensive use of its collections and the knowledge of staff about them as a source of information products of various kinds. The large local topographic collection has been the source of several joint publications with publishers who specialize in postcards and old photographs. There has also been a collaboration in the production of a very successful local history video. Information sheets – about 20–30 in all – are produced to answer frequently asked questions.

Other information products are related to the museum's education activities. An information pack on seaside holidays at Weston-super-Mare 1820–1920, for example, is designed to enhance visits to the Museum's Seaside Holiday Gallery; it contains a brief history of seaside holidays, a map of the town in 1903, and notes, illustrated with material from the collections, on entertainment, bathing, transport, and holiday accommodation, as well as teachers' notes, and suggestions about methods and resources.

Careful attention is also given to the presentation of information within the museum, as shown in Figure 12.2 on p227.

The museum also aims to encourage schools and colleges to use its resources more formally. An ambitious recent product is a resource pack for GNVQ Leisure and tourism, and GCSE Travel and tourism (1996). Created by the Museum's Educational Assistant with feedback from teachers, its content includes information on the Museum Service and its place in the local government structure, its objectives and services, staff and career profiles, funding and budgets, flowcharts of museum processes, and examples of collections documentation, and of museum publicity materials.

The museum has also given advice and help for a group of local primary schools to develop their own Historical Artefacts Scheme, which comprises a series of boxes (one for each school) of historical objects with supporting information. The boxes circulate among the schools in the group on a half-term rota.

Outreach activities

In 1995, the Museum Service started a programme of mini-exhibitions (moved around weekly) of secondary material, based on the collections, in supermarkets, pubs and hospitals in the district. The themes are mainly local history and archaeology and the aim is to make information about a limited theme accessible to wide audiences, many of whom may never have been to the museum. In the first phase in 1995, over 100 000 people had access to the material on show; in comparison, the museum itself has 35 000 visitors each year. The pro-

COMMUNICATION, INFORMATION & CUSTOMER CARE
The Structure of Textual Information in Exhibitions

GALLERY NAME
* physical orientation and location within building (eg museum gallery plan)
* intellectual orientation – identifies general content/subject areas
|
INTRODUCTORY TEXT PANEL
* introduces visitor to gallery or exhibition area
|
TITLE OF DISPLAY
* breaks up gallery or exhibition area into smaller displays or exhibits
|
CENTRAL/MAIN TEXT PANELS
introduces and outlines key concepts of display or exhibit
(eg – Seaside Holiday Gallery, Natural History Gallery)
|
SUB HEADÎNGS
*use of questions as headings - key questions are asked and then answered below
* used on main text panels or dispersed throughout display area
* used to break up text into easily comprehensible "chunks"
* orients reader to different areas of text content
|
LABELS
*identifies and provides specific information on individual objects

Other Issues Which Affect the Structure of Textual Information

- "Style" of language - academic/impersonal or conversational - eg use of "we" & "you"
- Reading levels:
    - length and complexity of sentence structure
    - use of difficult, abstract words or unexplained jargon
    - reading level tests – eg Fry or Fog tests

- Size of print - quality of graphic design
- Eye levels
- Relation of text to layout of objects and illustrations
- Scope for two way communication and feedback (see *Two Way Communication* Diagram)
- Other provision or "levels" of information and interpretation:

    - family activity sheets, competitions, local history trails
    - Museum Service publications - fact sheets, booklets, books & videos
    - general enquiry service
    - object identification and enquiry service (see separate diagram)
    - other shop materials – eg background publications suitable to the collections

- **Consistency** of information and labelling strategy. Students should view the above structure as an idealised model. They might investigate how, and if, it is adopted throughout the the **Time Machine.** What are the reasons for this? What issues do they think are the most important in communication and information systems?

gramme will continue because of its value in reaching such a wide potential public.

Also in 1995, the museum and the Library Service staged a joint exhibition – 'North Zomerzet folk' – on family history in the area. Mounted in both the library and the museum, it aimed to help people to set about tracing their own family history. The museum provided three-dimensional material and exhibition production expertise, while documentation came from the libraries and from a local historian who has details on 600 families in the area (his archive has been copied and donated to the Museum Service). The response was excellent.

Evaluation

The North Somerset Museum Service is noteworthy for its lively and creative use of information about the collections, and of the knowledge embodied in its staff; and for its energetic approach to finding out about actual and potential users, and to building up interactions with them. It appears to get the most out of the local authority connection, and in particular uses its links with the library service to good effect. The range of information products drawing on collections and curatorial knowledge is outstanding; the resource pack, from which the illustrations are drawn, is an unusual and particularly valuable product.

References

North Somerset Museum Service (1996), *Resource Pack for GNVQ Leisure and Tourism and CSE Travel and Tourism*, Weston-super-Mare: North Somerset Museum Service

Woodspring Museum Service (1995), *Seaside Holidays at Weston-super-Mare 1820–1920*, Weston-super-Mare: Woodspring Museum Service

Portsmouth City Museum and Records Service

Introduction

Portsmouth Museums consist of the main City Museum and Art Gallery together with a number of branch museums, including the D-Day Museum, Charles Dickens Birthplace Museum and Eastney Engine House. Total staff size is about 40 including seasonal staff. The collections, of over 250 000 objects, cover archaeology, art, local and social history, military history and natural sciences. In the mid-1980s a 'Report on Museum Documentation and Information Technology' was commissioned, but not implemented when presented. Entry documentation was by daybook, and accessioning was done in a central accession register; only the natural science department had a computerized catalogue system covering part of its holdings. Thus documentation at Portsmouth was then in a similar state to many other museums in the UK at that time.

More recently the need for improved documentation and information services has become apparent, and the necessary resources have begun to be provided.

Existing databases

A stores location database, written in dBaseIII because the storeman had expertise in that package, was created because of a serious need for such a facility; by the end of 1995 some 20 per cent of the stored objects had been included. A Manpower Services Commission team catalogued some 12 000 items of social history using MODES, but this database is presently unused and awaiting conversion. The City Records Service, with whom the museums were amalgamated in 1994, had a database called ARCHWAY run by a firm which has now ceased trading, and negotiations concerning the future of the database are in progress. ARCHWAY entries are composed of a reference to the first part of the archive, coupled to an idea of the 'way in' in a form comprehensible to archivists.

Current state of documentation policy

In 1995 a concerted 'bottom-up' approach to documentation policy was begun by the collection managing staff. The objective was ' To agree on a coherent approach to the computerization of the collections that would yield the earliest benefits and make the best use of staff time.'

The following points have been agreed:

- Computerization was the best tool to allow greater access to the collections for the public and to increase the efficiency of the staff in dealing with all aspects of their work
- The collections should be broken down into manageable projects with definite start and finish dates and with obvious visible benefits at the conclusion
- Deadlines should be set for each stage of the process and the correct level of resources set for each project
- 'Exciting' projects should be mixed in with the normal business of computerization to provide focus points for councillors and community alike
- The system is to be compliant with SPECTRUM. The preliminary timetable covers a range of collections and extends to the end of 1998.

Some collections gained their place in the timetable because they were also scheduled to be moved to new storage, and this was by far the most sensible time for the cataloguing to be done. Work capturing information from parish records, and gathering oral history recordings, is to be done with the aid of 'outworkers'. In the museum one technician spends 25 per cent of time on data input, and the aim is to have all keepers devoting 20 per cent of time to documentation – upgrading information for inclusion in the database, but not actually doing the input. Some input is done by volunteers.

Implementation of the documentation policy

An internal network has been established and a system for data input and back-up is now in place. Daily back-ups are made to an optical disk on a rotational basis with one disk always remaining in the photographic store. Permanent back-ups of all image files are made to CD-ROM and duplicates stored in the photographic store, where a fireproof safe is to be installed. The Council's CIA unit (Corporate Information Advisors) has approved the system and have undertaken to provide emergency recovery services provided full documentation of the system is maintained.

The computer system hardware and software is being standardized as far as possible, and compatibility on a long term basis will always be the main criterion when considering future changes to the system. The aim is to have only one machine on a persons desk that delivers all the available internal and external information services.

MOIRA

Various database packages such as MODES Plus and dBaseIII were considered, and opinion was divided. However it was decided to go forward with an in-house Windows-based visual database called MOIRA – Museum Object, Image and Record Application. The information in MOIRA will be divided into 'object information' available on all screens connected to the network, 'stores information' available on a more limited number of screens within the museum, and 'private information' only accessible by a very limited number of screens. All the collection databases are being registered under the Data Protection Act.

Images
Many of the databases within MOIRA will include small images of the objects. Also, mainly for internal use, ultraviolet or infra-red images of paintings will be provided to show restoration and conservation work.

SLAC
The School Loan Allocations and Catalogue (SLAC) database replaced the previous manual system in 1996; it contains some 850 items used by Portsmouth schools.

Developing the use of the information

The recent developments at Portsmouth have been public access led, in line with the current political emphasis on 'customer care'. Such 'care' requires intellectual access to allow curators to answer enquiries faster and more fully. The local colleges and universities are now being targeted; for example, it was found that art students at Portsmouth University were travelling to London to see works by artists present in the Portsmouth collections. Another aim is to provide intellectual added value, for example by allowing a lecture on pottery and ceramics to be illustrated by objects in the collection and expanding horizons by providing pointers to similar objects in other institutions.

Public demand has led to the extensive postcard collection being placed on a visual database, with plans to site terminals in six local libraries. The opportunity will be taken to use accesses to popular collections such as this to draw attention to other sites and resources within the group.

Evaluation

The lessons which emerge from this case study apply to any organization considering new software and systems:
- Avoid getting involved with any software that only runs on one maker's hardware
- Long-term compatibility of equipment is an important planning criterion
- Setting and keeping to targets are important if the work is to be done within a sensible time-scale.

The RAF Museum

Introduction

The RAF Museum is a worthwhile subject for a case study, because, in 1993, some 20 years after it opened its doors to the public, it embarked on a significant project for documentation and information management. The early years were devoted to intensive collection development – ranging from historic aircraft to uniforms and weapons and including major collections of aviation art and documentary archives together with a library – and to a large building programme. Procedures for recording its collections and making information about them accessible for purposes of inventory, management or research received comparatively low priority and limited resources. Museum staff devoted a good deal of attention to answering enquiries, often undertaking detailed research – but their efforts were on a basis of severely restricted knowledge of what was actually in the collections.[1]

The steps by which the museum has moved from this situation towards a comprehensive modern system for managing the resources of information embodied in its collections form the subject of this case study. The fact that it is undertaking this development within strict constraints of financial and human resources gives an extra interest to the process.

The RAF Museum was founded by a Deed of Trust in 1964, with the purpose of recording, caring for and displaying exhibits which embodied the history and traditions of the Royal Air Force, its predecessors, associated air forces, and aviation generally. This responsibility includes British Airways and its predecessors. It opened to the public, on the historic site of the former Hendon Aerodrome, in 1972, and within its first ten years two new buildings to house the rapidly growing collections had been erected: the Battle of Britain Hall and the Bomber Command Hall. The rate of expansion soon outstripped the resources for even the most basic processing, but it was only in the mid-

[1] A survey made in 1993 (see p234) estimated these numbers and percentages for the items in the six main collections:

Collection	Number of items accessioned (K) estimated	Percentage of total items accessioned to date
Documentary archives	91	15
Library	45	40
Photographic	123	37
Fine art	6	84
Film and video	1	21
Aircraft and exhibits	38	78

1980s that recognition was given to the backlogs that had built up. The situation was not just a matter of restricted resources; the 'culture' of the institution set a higher value on acquiring objects of historic importance, which in many cases were fragile and all too likely to disappear from view, than it did on the 'paperwork' that would enable it to account for its holdings and give access to information about them.

The initial approach to collections information

The history of the original exhibits catalogue illustrates the approach that prevailed up to the mid-1980s. It was the work of one member of staff, who, after studying current best practice in several museums, did his best over a period of 20 years, without any formal terms of reference, to provide the basis for an accounting inventory. He worked under some difficulties; in some instances he had to catalogue objects without even seeing them, because they went straight from acquisition to being displayed; and his workplace was remote from the library and he had little reference material to hand. The card catalogue was complemented by a hand-written acquisitions / accessions register, a stock register and a donor register.

Meantime, the museum's library and archives were engaged in quite separate operations.[2] The library developed an extensive subject index to its book collection, based on a 'subject headings list' in the honourable tradition of the library of Congress, and using the old-established library technique of 'chaining' sub-terms. The archives which were deposited in increasing numbers with the museum were listed in traditional style, but insufficient resources were available to provide a subject index. A change of policy in 1980 led to some archive groups being split up, with documents being accessioned individually. Although this change brought the creation of an index, the accessioning and indexing process became more labour intensive and thus the backlogs increased, and the relationships between documents in the archive groups became less clear.

Thoughts of computerizing the cataloguing process began to be entertained in about 1985. As part of a project to make records computer compatible, a basic 'database sheet' was developed; its 27 fields allowed for bringing together details which had previously been distributed between catalogue cards and the registers, and it was intended as a temporary record for completion by curators, from which data would later be input. This was implemented in the Aircraft and Exhibits collection, for Fine Art, and for Photographs, but not elsewhere in the museum. Unfortunately, in moving to this form of recording, without actually implementing a computer system which would have allowed

[2] Readers with a particular interest in museum libraries will wish to be aware of a study by Borda (1997) of libraries and information centres in museums in the Greater London area.

access through multiple points, the museum discontinued the manual indexes by donor which had previously been maintained, and so lost access via this feature. In the museum, the database sheets were filed by accession number; in the storage centre they were filed by the classified arrangement as devised in 1965 (a letter code in the accession number indicated the broad group to which each item belonged, eg. A – Aircraft, E – Engines – within each class the sheets were filed by accession number). No further move was made towards a computerized system until 1993, when the documentation and data management project began.

A survey of collections records

One of the first actions undertaken by the team responsible for the project was a study of collections records, designed to show the nature of the systems currently in use, to identify strengths and weaknesses of the current management of the collections, and to identify major issues for the project.

The survey found 59 different registers in use, together with 61 numbering schemes and 44 indexes to collections, all embodied in three basic systems, overlapping in point of time, and in the collections with which they were associated. The shortage of resources for this aspect of the museum's work, and the priority inevitably given to what the report describes as 'reactive tasks which demand immediate attention' were reflected in such features as insufficient subject indexing, lack of aids to consistent terminology, poor donor records, loss of group integrity in some collections, accessioning backlogs, and overall lack of standardization (though there were some standards within individual systems, they were not documented). This outline of its initial findings serves as an introduction to the Documentation and Data Management project.

The documentation and data management project

The project was set up on the initiative of the present director five years after his appointment, as the next most significant task after a period of essential revenue raising to restore the museum's financial situation, which had become unstable in the mid-1980s. The underlying aim was accountability; since the museum knew only about 27 per cent of what it actually had, the most urgent task was an inventory which could lay the foundations for the development of a collections management system.

Terms of reference

The most significant fact about the project is that it was not simply a computerization initiative; instead, the remit was to:

1. Take stock of current systems and identify needs for improvement.
2. Research best practice and available standards in museum collections management.

3. Devise a project strategy and plans for improving collections management practices, including a computerized collections management system.
4. Ensure that appropriate documentation standards are followed.
5. Procure an appropriate system, install it, devise procedures and documentation, and ensure that staff are trained to use it.
6. Plan and carry through the conversion of existing collections records.
7. Plan and carry through accessioning and recording of presently unaccessioned collections.
8. Provide support for all users.

Outside expertise + inside knowledge

In view of the lack of experience within the museum of managing large-scale projects of this nature, a deliberate decision was made to seek outside help in establishing and running the project, with a strong contribution from museum staff based on their own strengths of knowledge and experience. An equally significant decision was to look for a consultant from outside the museum community, on the argument that it would be more productive in the initial stages to buy project management expertise gained in industry or business and to add museum knowledge to it. Oversight of the project was vested in a Project Board – a senior management forum with responsibility for directing and monitoring progress, and supporting the consultant and the project team, who would manage it on a day-to-day basis. The consultant's role was to start the project on a sound foundation, to integrate museum staff into its work via secondments for specialized tasks for which their experience suited them, to make recommendations on any appointments which might be needed to take the system forward, and to hand it over as a going concern for implementation by the museum's staff. A further key decision was to employ a registrar from the museum world with experience of managing large-scale projects as one of these appointments.

Preliminary research

The first tasks – devising work methods and planning and carrying out the survey quoted earlier (see p234) – were completed in the first three months of the initial two-year project. The in-house survey was complemented by research visits to other relevant institutions at home and abroad. With the Director's full support, museum staff took an active part in these visits, as a means of gaining experience, extending their knowledge and acquiring confidence – particularly in relation to the potentialities of computer-based systems, and the implications for doing things differently.

The main conclusions from the in-house review of existing systems were:
- It would be impracticable and mistaken to replicate the range of existing records and methods in a new computer-based system. Instead, a single common-core record should be developed, hospitable to necessary local variations

- As far as possible, existing accession numbering systems should be left unchanged, to avoid the large effort that would be involved in changing them
- A lot of work would be needed to take existing records into a new system, and it would be complex and demanding to manage
- Records would need cleaning up before data capture
- Few of them were in usable computerized form; most would need conversion either by scanning or by re-keying
- Terminology control by means of a thesaurus or thesauri would be an important element in any new system
- The large scale of the collections demanded careful database design, and a powerful database server computer would be essential for satisfactory performance
- Once a new collections system was installed, a major accessioning effort would be needed to catch up
- If the new system was to succeed, greater management attention and more resources than before would have to be devoted to records and collections management, both during and after implementation of the system.

The strategy

By May 1994, proposals for a consolidated 'system procurement and implementation strategy' had been prepared. Among the major elements in the proposed strategy were:

Standards
- For data and documentation: common standards, using the UK Museums Documentation Standard as a basis
- For the technology used: an appropriate mix of *de jure* and *de facto* industry standards; and a system architecture with a certain future, which should be scalable and expandable.

Terminology
- Terminology control was essential from the outset, not only for ultimate information retrieval but to establish control of terms before starting to build the database
- Establishment of a terminology working group.

Key system functions
- A schedule of functional requirements, as part of the operational requirements for the system (this schedule was presented with the strategy document; it was drawn up by the project team and two Senior Keepers).

The emphasis of the strategy
- Building a sound collections information database in which the information-related activities of acquiring, accessioning, cataloguing, and informa-

tion storage and retrieval, rather than automating museum functions, predominate, because the process is large scale and lengthy; the limited resources need to be managed to provide a well-ordered project; the museum and its staff are at a relatively early stage in using information systems of any kind. The capacity to absorb change at all levels 'must not be exceeded or control will be lost', so concentrating on the recommended database will be 'quite enough to begin with'.

The basis of the collections system

- Package software is feasible, and a package solution should be implemented with little amendment, to minimize cost, complexity and risk
- One system for all collections, including the library
- Imaging capability is essential
- Networked PCs should form the platform, on grounds of lower initial cost, price in relation to performance, common standards, availability of software for all purposes, low-cost graphical user interfaces, and modularity.

Procurement steps

- Specification of requirements
- Request for proposals
- Evaluation plan
- Formal evaluation.

Record conversion

- Since the aim is to produce a database of basic accession and catalogue information for as many items as possible as quickly as possible, rather than comprehensive catalogue records, a limited number of fields is recommended initially, with progressive upgrade over time
- Capture of over 300,000 manual records in machine readable form, modification to meet terminology guidelines, and transposition to appropriate formats, to be spread over several years, starting with a pilot collection
- Database creation to be handled and managed in the museum, using permanent and temporary staff in a Data Conversion Unit
- Recommended stages: define data structures by collection, develop terminology controls by collection and overall for the museum as a whole, develop tactics and procedures for data capture.

Steps towards implementation

- Training before implementation, with emphasis on training trainers on the museum's staff by a cascade process; training not only on system functions but also on how 'people can use the system most effectively in doing their jobs'
- Reviewing experiences with users soon after implementation, identifying problems encountered, and finding solutions
- Pilot running in a selected department, with full staff training and support

- Using the system for a wide range of functions in the pilot operation over three months, monitoring progress, evaluating results
- Phased implementation, department by department, after the pilot results have been absorbed, with check points and deliverables for each phase
- Constant review and revision of the strategy in operation
- Total time to complete implementation – probably 12 years before all the collections (including those presently unaccessioned) are fully catalogued in the computerized system.

Staffing needs

- A registrar, to lead the development of policies and procedures for all movements of objects, inventory, and audit, and their documentation
- A Terminology Working Group leader, to manage terminology development
- Terminology analysts, to compile thesauri
- A data manager, data editors and data recorders
- An IT manager.

Applying the strategy

At the time of writing the period of the consultancy is nearing its end, and the strategy is in the process of implementation.

Collections management policies

Policies for acquisition and disposal have been implemented; those for loans in and out, entry and exit, are at an advanced stage, including a review mechanism. Others are under development. A standard record format has been established.

The data manager is creating a data dictionary and cataloguing rules, and developing a strategy for capturing data from the original systems and for the un-accessioned backlog. This is the point at which detailed decisions have to be taken on some fundamental questions, such as:

- Tackle one backlog collection at a time, or start on them all at once?
- If something from each collection, how much? What criteria for making the decision?
- Basic inventory-level recording first, and add more detail later? Or are there cases (e.g. Fine Art) where it is feasible to do the complete record at one go?
- What level of inventory check? Complete or sample?
- What is the best use of resources of time and people?
- How should short-term and long-term developments be reconciled? (While a 12-year term has been assumed for completion of the project, the computer system could well change in five years, and the implications of that need careful consideration).

Another problem that has to be taken into account in looking to the future is the learning effect curators will experience from entering data during pilot testing. As they become acquainted with the system and that knowledge interacts with their knowledge of the collections, their view of what they can do and the questions they can answer is likely to be enlarged, and that is likely to influence how the strategy develops.

Human resources

The data manager and registrar posts recommended in the strategy were filled in time for there to be an overlap period between the registrar and the consultant, allowing for a proper hand over of management responsibility for the new system. The IT manager took up her post early in 1997. The involvement of existing museum staff in the project has gone as planned, though it has sometimes been difficult to manage because of competing pressures for time and restricted finance. One staff member worked with the consultant on the initial survey, and went on to develop the new record format; two curators began work on thesaurus control as terminology analysts during 1994, and the Terminology Control Group has been active; staff have taken part in the initial external research, strategy formulation and review.

From the start, the museum director has been committed to drawing every professional person in the museum into the project (in fact, some technicians and craftsmen have also become involved, for example in conducting an inventory of large items in store), and to using it as a means of staff and career development – three members of staff have actually used the project for postgraduate dissertations, etc. Matrix management is applied to seconded staff working on the project; they continue to report to their own line managers, while being supervised by the project team on a day-to-day basis. Secondments last about a year, including training, and the museum's existing development appraisals have been modified to take account of this experience.

Terminology control

The project has paid an unusual degree of attention to terminology control; though this has been a subject much discussed in the museum community, it is rare to find a museum which considers itself justified in devoting large resources to creating thesauri or authority lists (for a view at the other end of the spectrum, see McCorry, 1993). In this instance, the consultant's experience from other fields of the dangers of uncontrolled terminology was reinforced by external research in comparable institutions which considered that lack of control could lead to databases being 'corrupt at every level'; it also received support from existing curatorial staff on the basis of their own experience.

External research confirmed that no single thesaurus covering all areas of relevance to the museum was yet in existence. As a result of consultations with the MDA and with various information consultants, the construction of such a thesaurus from scratch was ruled out on grounds of time and cost. It was decided instead to make best use of the museum library's Subject Headings List mentioned on p233. This 40 000-term list was re-organized with a view to using it for subject-indexing not only the content of the library but also all other collections. The list was initially subdivided into about thirty subject 'segments', named to help users decide 'intuitively' which 'segment' a given subject would belong to.

The other area needing attention was object names; here it was felt that sufficient resources were available for the construction from scratch of an 'Object-Naming Thesaurus' following MDA guidelines, and with the normal ISO thesaural relations.

The two projects were carried out by two curators with relevant experience in the museum; for the Object-Naming Thesaurus, thesaurus construction software was successfully used, while the capture, manipulation and adaptation of the Subject Headings List made extensive use of OCR and word processing.

As work on the thesauri and consultation with their eventual users developed, it became clear that difficulties would arise from trying to run two separate banks of terminology to index the same collections. It was also realized that the Subject Headings List vocabulary too would benefit from a hierarchical structure, because that would contribute to the objective of making collections information accessible to as wide a range of users as possible. These views were reinforced by the new registrar, who also proposed breaking up the complex pre-coordinated terms in the Subject Headings List, and merging object and subject terminology into a single thesaurus. He recommended assigning each simple term to an 'entity', for example Events, People, Places, Organizations, Objects, Structures, etc. (readers interested in the history of library classification will recognize the similarity to Raganathan's fundamental divisions of Personality, Matter, Energy, Space and Time, and to the later developments of faceted classification and its application in such thesauri as Thesaurofacet – Ingwersen & Wormell, 1992). The computerized collections management system will permit co-ordination of terms from different 'entities', in order to permit highly specific indexing and retrieval. As far as possible, international standards for thesaurus construction are being followed in building the thesauri (BSI/ISO, 1987).

The ultimate thesaurus will be used to index all the museum's collections. It will be held on-line and will be accessible on screen for use while creating records. An advantage of doing so much work in advance on terminology is that it will increase accuracy and save time during object data capture.

The approach to terminology control that the museum has now developed is a logical one; it is in line with modern thinking on the subject, and in advance of probably the majority of museums.

The museum's commitment to terminology control is demonstrated by another aspect of its approach. From the outset a Terminology Working Group, chaired by a deputy keeper and with membership drawn from key curators and documentation and data management professionals has guided the developments. The group meets about once a month and has been instrumental in deciding the museum's overall strategy and operational approach to the control of terminology in the new system.

Choice of system

In response to the operational and functional requirements specification for the system, a small number of proposals were received from suppliers. These were evaluated by an evaluation team, and three suppliers were shortlisted. Demonstrations of the systems and further research showed that two of the three systems were to be redeveloped by their vendors to work in new software environments. This introduced a serious element of uncertainty into the procurement; the museum's users could not see what they would be using as the user interfaces were to be redesigned, and there was no proof that the systems would work satisfactorily in their new form. As a result, in Autumn 1995, the Project Board decided to defer the procurement of the system. It was expected that the system would be chosen in the middle of 1997 and installed by the end of the year.

In the light of this change the project was replanned to bring forward work on policy and procedure development. The work on planning and constructing the terminology control instruments described above was well under way, using thesaurus construction software, in the period prior to installation of the final computerized system.

An evaluation

The experiences of the RAF Museum in the course of the project described have much that is potentially useful and instructive for readers who are concerned with similar situations.

Positive features

There are many features in this case study which suggest that the documentation and data management project has a good chance of success. The way in which it was set up and managed is the first of these: seeking outside expertise in large-scale project management to complement the museum's own knowledge resources, establishing a strong group to supervise the project, and making sure that museum staff were fully involved in the work and in interchange of knowledge, all contributed to a sound foundation.

The strategy built on that foundation takes account of the constraints of the museum's situation, and addresses the main needs revealed by the preliminary research. Realistically, it defines the aims in terms of action to strengthen the museum's use of information, rather than in terms of using computerized systems as such; the technology is given its proper role as a support for human beings in carrying out work which they themselves define as essential. At the same time, there is an appreciation of the need to monitor developments in the technology, and to be ready to take advantage of those which can help the museum in fulfilling its strategy.

While the strategy concentrates on getting as quickly as possible to a reliable database of basic information, it does not skip over the meticulous preparation which is essential if that is to succeed – hence the emphasis on a disciplined approach to data structures, terminology control and data capture. Implementation is envisaged in the same thorough way, through a relevant training programme, pilot running, and phased introduction of the new system, with pauses for evaluating what has been learned and making any necessary changes.

Because it concentrates on activities driven by human beings, rather than on the wonders of technology, it is realistic about the requirements for human resources which may arise from the 'more professional management of collections made possible by the proposed comprehensive approach to documentation and the computerized system'.

Possible problems

While there is general agreement about the appropriateness of the strategy for the present situation, there may be some potentially conflicting views in the museum on the future orientation of its information management. The areas of possible disagreement on policy relate to:

- Priority for collections management procedures as against priority for basic records for inventory purposes
- The appropriate point for adding public access facilities to the collections management system – while there is probably general agreement that this is a refinement that can wait for the present without any harm being done, if a point is reached when it becomes feasible, there may be those who resist it on the grounds that it is not appropriate for the museum to offer an 'electronic textbook' to its visitors. If there is disagreement on this matter, it is, however, likely to be resolved on the sound basis of providing the best possible access to the collections
- Emphasis on information retrieval versus emphasis on accountability and registration. The perceived potential conflict here may in time come to be seen as not a conflict at all, when the capabilities of the system are fully understood through use. There may, however, still be arguments to be resolved on curatorial time devoted to research. On one view, it is a great asset of the system that it should allow more interactive use of the collections, permitting an informal but more disciplined methodology for examining the collections. This view implies that curators should be guaranteed some research time, so that they can use the system they have helped to develop in order to support them in developing their knowledge further for the benefit of the museum. As against that, there may be arguments for other more urgent uses of time; the project has already meant reduction of some activities – particularly dealing with public enquiries – and it may be considered essential to redress the balance

- The time-scale for implementation. A 12-year period is an unusually long one, forced on the museum by constraints on its resources. The difficulty in relation to possible changes in the system within a shorter time span has already been mentioned (p238). There are also dangers of sheer weariness at the long slog setting in, with loss of the motivation which so far has been a positive asset. It certainly makes it essential to meet time targets, and to ensure that the implementation process delivers tangible, even if small, benefits at regular and frequent intervals.

References

BORDA, A. E. (1997), *The Museum library: A Survey of Libraries and Information Centres in the Museums and Related Institutions of the Greater London Area,* PhD thesis, University of London

British Standards Institution/International Standards Organization (1987), *Guide to establishment and development of monolingual thesauri,* BS 5723: 1987 (ISO 2788)

INGWERSEN, P. & WORMELL, I. (1992), 'Ranganathan in the perspective of advanced information retrieval', *Libri,* 42 (3) 184–201

McCORRY, H. (1993), 'Thesauri and terminology control', *MDA Information* 1 (1) 12–14

The Royal Commission for Historic Monuments of England (RCHME)

Introduction

The RCHME is a museum, but an unusual one, based in a custom-designed building in Swindon. Most of its primary objects are extremely big, and are scattered across the face of England. It has information problems which, while they can be found in other more 'mainstream' institutions, are here writ large. The authors therefore thought that the approach used to information handling at the RCHME, which regards itself as an information-based institution, would form a useful case study.

There are some 250 permanent staff employed at the Commission, and a variable number of temporary staff are recruited on a project basis. The culture is somewhat different from a 'normal' museum (if there is such a beast) and most of the permanent staff are working managers rather than academic curators, though there are some academics whose input to the documentation work is very important.

Information Systems Strategy

The information systems strategy was developed between 1990 and April 1993. The objective was to produce a unified database from various text databases which had been formed during the previous decade, and the result was MONARCH – the national monuments and archaeological sites database. The work was spurred on by some international initiatives from the Council of Europe, primarily the core data index for architecture, a planned data standard for archaeology and a multi-lingual thesaurus of architecture and archaeological terms. Therefore part of the information strategy at RCHME included national initiatives on the two latter projects.

The MONARCH database is designed to include event records with links to the museums's holdings (see Figure 15.1 on p245). Before the Commission moved from London a collection management database had been created with approximately two million basic accession records, which included some location information. During 1994–95 ways of integrating this with MONARCH were explored, so that it became usable by internal managers, but this part of the work is also seen as the key to providing links to the images that it is planned to scan in future.

RCHME is collaborating with the Department of National Heritage and with English Heritage to create a computer listing of all buildings in England of architectural interest. This is expected to contain some 450 000 records when completed; text input was started in October 1994 and was planned to

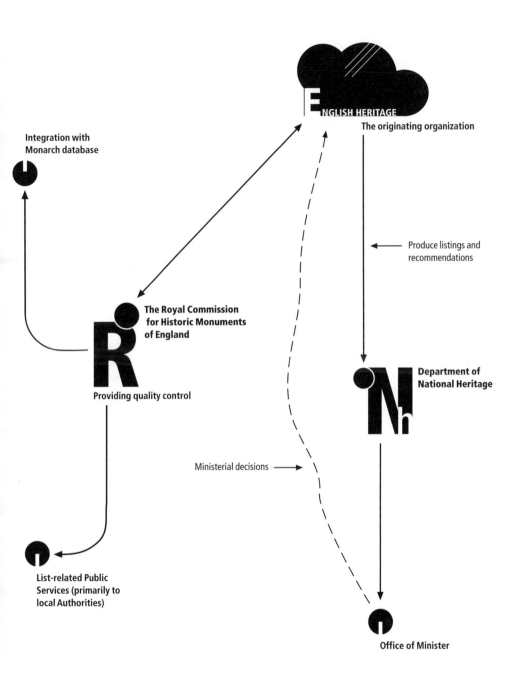

Integration with
Monarch database

ENGLISH HERITAGE
The originating organization

Produce listings and
recommendations

The Royal Commission
for Historic Monuments
of England

Department of
National Heritage

Providing quality control

Ministerial decisions

List-related Public
Services (primarily to
local Authorities)

Office of Minister

finish in March 1996. As a separate but related project 40 people are indexing and quality assuring all the source documents, for example updating administrative boundaries. Referential integrity needs to be ensured between subunits such as house, garden, stables and so on; all must be correctly linked. A commercial firm was employed to scan in the documents, but many had to be re-done because the quality on the first run was not acceptable. These scanned images need to be linked to the catalogue entries and eventually to images of the properties (the 'objects' of the museum collection). As might be expected, with three organizations involved, some logistical problems have had to be overcome (see Figure 15.2 on p247). One of the benefits seen from having this database is in facilitating responses to requests for listed building consent (that is, permission to alter a listed building); up to 50 000 such requests are received by local authorities every year. Eventually it is hoped that the information will be provided on-line to the users.

The RCHME holds some five million photographs, and a decision still has to be taken whether to catalogue these fully. Another option under consideration is to create a series of CD-ROMs from them.

The documentation system

Some 60 of the permanent staff are directly concerned with documentation; the high number reflecting the importance placed on information in this institution. Also most of the temporary staff, who can number up to 50 at any one time, tend to be employed on the various documentation projects feeding into the information databases.

The aims for the system were that it should be a stable, modular open system of the client-server database type. For the file-server the Unix-based Solaris operating system running an ORACLE 6.0 relational database management system (DBMS) on a Sparc platform was chosen. The client systems use ORACLE Forms, Word Perfect and Lotus 1-2-3 under SCO Unix on 486 or Pentium machines.

The strategic aims for the communication network were high-performance connectivity, structured cabling, dynamic routing, with strong network security measures including IP addressing; ISDN is provided to permit dial-up connection to smaller servers on the network. The network is based mainly on a UTP (unshielded twisted pair) Ethernet with stackable hubs and TCP/IP.

The user requirements for the design of MONARCH were determined by interviewing people, auditing the existing systems, and agreeing the principal requirements. In the design work ORACLE CASE methodology was used to create the data model, with entity and function descriptions. To develop the specification, 'story boards' were used to design the screens and establish how the various parts of the system would work together. Migration documents were written for each old system, showing what had to be done, and the mapping of the old data into the new data standard. The system was then built using SQL and Forms within ORACLE version 6; menus were created to pro-

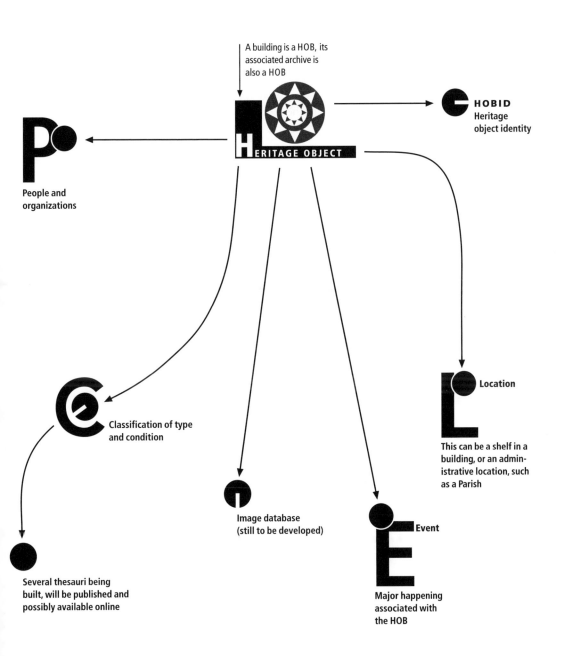

A building is a HOB, its associated archive is also a HOB

HOBID
Heritage object identity

People and organizations

Classification of type and condition

Several thesauri being built, will be published and possibly available online

Image database (still to be developed)

Event

Major happening associated with the HOB

Location

This can be a shelf in a building, or an administrative location, such as a Parish vide the user interface, and the structured query report-writer (SQR) used to provide the tools for generating reports, doing data audits and for the data-migration projects. Overlaying this is a general enquiry mechanism, not using SQL.

Data integrity is addressed using role-defined access control, with record stamping: every access and change, such as a deletion or an update, is logged securely. Referential integrity of the records is also checked within the system.

Dissemination of the information

The RCHME has a general commitment to making its information available, and already many visitors make use of the large archive of documents and photographs. The Commission has a site on the World Wide Web, and sees the Internet as the main means of electronic dissemination in future. It is not currently looking at a knowledge-based interface for the Internet, as staff feel they know too little about the potential users as opposed to current users, of whom they have a fairly clear profile. What questions people will ask once they know they can ask them is unknown, and it is hoped to use the WWW to monitor this to inform the service development.

Once someone finds a document of interest then copies can be requested via email, for a fee. The usage will also be monitored, as will the yield, or 'hit rate', as this is important in judging the utility of the service in delivering what the client wants. Image copyright will be protected in that those made available over the Internet will be usable but not of reproducible quality.

Evaluation

The experience of the RCHME highlights some important information-handling and management lessons for museums:
- Contracts with outside data-processing firms must specify clearly the quality of results expected
- The design stage of a custom system must not be skimped
- Time spent establishing firm objectives for the system is never wasted.

St Albans Museums

Introduction

The first public museum in St Albans, the City Museum, opened in 1898. It did not have a formal catalogue, and an accessions register was begun only in the 1950s. The Verulamium Museum was opened in 1939, essentially as a museum on the site of the Roman town, to house the finds from the excavations by Sir Mortimer Wheeler and Kathleen Kenyon, to which were added finds from Professor Frere's excavation of 1955–61. The two museums are administered by St Albans District Council.

Originally the only documentation for the Verulamium Museum was a rough card index, with one or more cards being prepared for each object as it came into the museum. There was no accessions procedure, and the cards were of limited use, even when taken in conjunction with the relevant excavation notebooks.

Today St Albans Museums consists of three sites, the St Albans museum itself, Kyngston House, and the Verulamium Museum. There are some 25 (full time equivalent) staff, with six curators, one of whom concentrates on documentation; the curators spend some 30 per cent of their time on various aspects of documentation. The Keeper of Documentation obtains help and advice from the IT section of St Albans Council.

The first documentation project

The early stages of the first attempt to improve the documentation was described in detail in the first edition of this book (Orna and Pettitt, 1980, p160). In 1977 a start was made on tackling the documentation problems, with an examination of the feasibility of using the MDA system. The permanent appointment of a Keeper of Documentation in 1979 allowed a consistent programme of work to start. A decision was made to use MDA cards, and for these to form the master record; no accessions register was kept. The cards are in a single sequence in accession number order; the numbers used are sequential but include an element indicating the date of registration. The degree of detail to which the MDA cards were filled in was deliberately kept to a non-intensive level, so as not to overtax staff resources.

This system has been continued until 1993, with all the cards being kept up to date. In the mid-1980s a project was set up with the MDA to input the data from the cards and to provide computer-produced indexes from the information using the GOS package. This project continued until about 1988, when the last of the GOS indexes were delivered. The indexes consist of ten sequences, each arranged according to a different element of information, and within that element by a hierarchy of other elements; this was the typical format for GOS indexes. At present most 'access' to the information is done via the MDA card file, which on the whole is found more useful than the GOS lists.

Current developments

In 1993 the present Assistant Keeper of Archaeology was appointed. He also acts as a Documentation Officer, and soon after his arrival began an overhaul of the system. It was decided to install a new in-house controlled database management system, and the package COLLECTION from Vernon Systems was chosen. This initially was the DOS version, but may be changed over to the Windows version when that becomes available. There was a need for customized screens, and these have been developed.

St Albans was the first UK museum to adopt COLLECTION, although there is now a user group including Falkirk Museum and the Wedgwood Museum. All the '1978 system' records held in the GOS system are being transferred to COLLECTION, but some difficulty is being experienced. Considerable 'tweaking' of the records is required. The older system placed most of the information in the note field for about a fifth of the records, and also the 'mapping' of the sometimes less comprehensive information from GOS to the COLLECTION field structure has proved complex. Although aware of SPECTRUM the museum has a large backlog of original MDA cards to convert, including information on social history and natural sciences where local extensions to the MDA system have been developed over the last two decades. At present there is an intention to remain with the COLLECTION package.

Both the natural science and social history collections are in a fragmented state of data capture. The natural sciences information was input some years ago to an arcane system that is now defunct, and the information is inaccessible. The plan now is for the curatorial staff to spend a couple of days each week preparing fresh input sheets which will then be input by volunteer staff.

The length of the new documentation project is still uncertain. The archaeology and social history collections consist of 35 000 recorded objects, a backlog of fresh material, and new material is still being excavated. The archaeology centre is the fieldwork base, and holds the material awaiting processing before it is accessioned. A new card has been designed to replace the MDA card for primary recording, and this will form an input document for COLLECTION.

The social history collections are smaller, but are being actively added to, and the natural science collections are also growing slowly. Audits of the two latter collections are in progress to establish the exact number of objects waiting to be accessioned into the new system. At present there is a network with a server and two client PCs; expansion plans are dependent on future resource allocations from the council. There are several stand-alone PCs, but these are presently only used for word processing.

The future

The users of the information being put into the new system will initially be the local staff, to help with collection management tasks, to facilitate the answering of enquiries and, in the future, to assist visiting researchers. At present there are no plans to include loans out in the computerized system. Increased public access to the information is the medium term goal, with particular emphasis being placed on improving access for educational establishments in the area. Development of a knowledge-based interface is not planned.

Imaging is seen as a major need, particularly as a means of making the information content more accessible to the public. Both the DOS and Windows versions of the COLLECTION package can handle images as part of the object record. However, it is possible that the image database may be formed as a stand-alone system, linked to the text databases by individual codes. St Albans has a considerable photographic archive, which it is hoped to input and distribute in the form of a CD-ROM disk.

Evaluation

One of the most important lessons to be learned from this case study is that, as the loss of the natural history data in an 'arcane' (and now defunct) system demonstrates, transferability of data is a prime criterion in specifying a system.

Scienceworks[1] (Museum of Victoria, Melbourne, Australia)

Background to the museum's development of information strategy

The Museum of Victoria (MoV), in Melbourne, began in the nineteenth century as two separate museums, one of natural history and the other of science and technology. The two continued separately until, in 1983, they amalgamated to form the present museum. This history accounts for differences in the ways in which the divisions of the museum (Science and Technology on the one hand, and Natural History and Human Studies on the other) approached the management and documentation of their collections. To quote from a case study of the museum published in 1990 (Orna, 1990):

'The Division of Science and Technology made a start in the late 1970s on a computer-based system. Though based on very modest technology and a low budget, the system was well thought out, and provided a range of files of records, with a strong subject orientation which, as well as meeting collection management requirements, permitted information retrieval from a variety of viewpoints – though the retrieval had to be from hard-copy rather than by interaction with the computer. The Division of Natural History and the Division of Human Studies embarked later on the process of collections management, and from different starting points.'

During the mid- to late 1980s studies of the future development of the museum and of its information systems were initiated; these led to the development of a corporate strategy plan for the years 1989–1993, and to an information systems strategy plan for the 1990–1995 period.

The Museum of Victoria today

The museum's 'Core Themes' today are the origins, diversity and development of Australian society; the natural environment; and the application of science and technology in society. Its collecting departments – Science and Technology, Social History, Indigenous Studies and Natural Sciences – are part of the Division of Research and Collections. An important development is the setting up of a new museum, to be opened in 2000, which aims to reach out to Australia-wide and international audiences. The new museum will re-

[1] Scienceworks is the Science and Technology Division of the Museum of Victoria; it moved in 1991 to a new building of its own at a historic site on the Yarra River in Melbourne (see p255 for more details).

place the original Museum of Victoria building, in which the former Natural History and Human Studies Divisions are currently located, and will house the staff and collections from those areas; its public programmes will reflect the three core themes, and, like Scienceworks, will use IT intensively to reach its defined public.

Current information management

While strategic planning and resourcing are carried out on a museum-wide basis dating back to developments of the 1980s, there is still little standardization in the matter of collections management, and individual databases proliferate in departments. The management of information has traditionally been done at the departmental level, and one of the main current challenges is to achieve co-ordination in this aspect of the museum's work. Meantime, a Web browser-type front end has been introduced which will at any rate allow staff to access collections databases across the museum.

The other challenge in information management is to enhance the data in the collections databases to the level where it is acceptable for public access. These concerns are among the priorities in IT planning for the museum.

IT planning

Information technology is prominent in the museum's current development of its new strategic plan, under which a Business Process Re-engineering grant has been provided for reviewing IT provision, and for implementing the results of the review. By October 1996, tenders were being evaluated.

Development of the new IT strategy has begun, with consultation with staff via email and meetings; it is hoped that the issue of information policy will be considered in the context of this process. The remit of the IT Committee charged with this work is:

- To develop and oversee IT planning
- To direct resources into development of the plan
- To make decisions on recommendations by working parties
- To integrate the plan into divisional operations
- To champion the re-engineering of all MoV systems
- To report to the Executive Management Committee on progress
- To approve and monitor budgets.

In the meantime, in advance of the long-term plan, the museum is working on a short-term IT plan to modernize and consolidate existing systems and improve corporate communications, which involves a single comprehensive network.

1. Collections management:
- Registration
- Images
- Context (placing collection information into a context appropriate to the end user)
- Research.

2. Public access:
- Exhibition interactives
- Multi-media products
- Internet access
- Electronic publication.

3. Business systems:
- Admission
- Bookings
- Human resources management
- Finance
- Planning
- Productivity tools (the use of IT to provide better and more efficient means of sharing, finding and accessing all kinds of information).

A museum-wide Computer Users Committee serves as a forum for the interchange of information between users and IT specialists.

IT services
An Information Technology Services Department, servicing all museum campuses, was established in the early 1990s under the Strategic Plan. It now has nine staff, with specialisms covering KE TEXPRESS and UNIX:2; PCs, mail and network; Internet and Web sites; and image capture. Almost all sites have been on an ISDN-based wide area network for the past two years. The installation of a Novell network across all the campuses marked a significant advance in information management. Most staff have access to Schedule, Microsoft Mail, email, Netscape, and networked access to computers running on UNIX; and scanners are available. These developments have completely changed ways of working; documents can be circulated to all staff, or placed on public drives, and in consequence communication has improved markedly (there was some room for improvement; the case study quoted above describes a meeting at the museum in 1989 at which some of the participants found themselves together in the same room for the first time, and had their first opportunity to tell each other directly about what they were doing).

Public access
The aim of giving public access to the museum's information resources is one of the main driving forces for a number of IT projects. Some of the most recent developments include:
- A hybrid CD-ROM project which both provides access to collections materials, and allows end users, such as teachers and students, to create their own multi-media products. It offers 'seamless integration' to the World Wide Web, via software that provides an automatic link to it, so that users can extract and combine data from the CD-ROM and the Web to make their own products, which can then be accessed through the CD-ROM
- A partnership agreement between the museum, Telstra (formerly Telecom

Australia) and the Victoria Department of Education to deliver curriculum-related content direct to the classroom via Telstra services. For the future, the museum plans to extend this service to the rest of the Australian education market, and then to South East Asia

- A Web site (MOVinfo) which is accessible to the public, but also includes internal documents for staff only (see Figure 17.1 on p256)
- Agreement in principle to participate in the European RAMA (Remote Access to Museum Archives) project.

Scienceworks

The 1987 decision by the Victorian government that there should be two new buildings to replace the one which the museum had shared with the State Library – one for Science and Technology and the other for Natural History and Human Studies – began to be put into effect in 1990. In that year, the Science and Technology Division acquired a site, based on the heritage building of the old pumping station on the Yarra River in Melbourne. The reason for choosing this out of town site in a run-down industrial area was partly the historic interest of the building itself, with its links to the public health of the city at a period in the 1880s when its sewage caused it to be known as 'Smellbourne', and partly the space which the site offered for activating such exhibits as steam traction engines, cars and solar vehicles in an arena area between the old building and the new. The aim in designing the new accommodation was to get an affordable product for a modest budget, that could quickly be brought into use. A light steel-frame industrial-type building was quickly erected on the site. It provides a large amount of storage space, which allows the majority of the reserve collections to be housed on site, and so permits easy interaction and integrated management of exhibition and storage areas.

Scienceworks aims to inform visitors about the relationship between science and everyday life through a range of visitor programmes; these include exhibitions which always incorporate interactives, educational programmes, 'Science Stage' live science demonstrations, outdoor activities such as steam rallies, and tours of the collection storage area and of the Pumping Station. The development of the new museum referred to on p252 makes it necessary to redefine the role and market niche of Scienceworks, and this is one of the main strategic decisions facing the museum's executive.

Under the present organizational structure of Scienceworks, collections and curatorial staff form part of the parent museum's Research and Collections Division. Services such as IT, conservation, photography, and exhibition construction are provided by the main museum. Finance, marketing and design staff are located at Scienceworks, but report to the centralized departments in the parent museum. Scienceworks itself manages public programmes, education, site development, local promotions, and operations (which includes security, buildings, publicity and administration). Most of the information in these sections is managed independently.

MOVinfo – Museum of Victoria Corporate Information

This information can only be seen by people using computers within the museum.
Follow this link to visit the public web site – Museum of Victoria Welcome Page

Contents

General
Carlton Gardens
Council of Museum of Victoria
Documents and reports
Internal database search engine
Internet starting points
Policy and procedures
Webmaster

General

MOV Library
Stores Catalogue
Victorian Public Service Notices

Carlton Gardens

MOV Relocation Project (update)

Council of Museum of Victoria

Minutes of the 135th Meeting
Minutes of the 136th Meeting
Minutes of the 137th Meeting

Documents and Reports

Many of the tracking reports and other documents in this section were out of date. They
have been moved to an archive. Any documents still required on MOVInfo will be
restored if requested.
Oceans of Life – Tracking Report

The collections and their management

The collections grew from those of the nineteenth-century Institute of Applied Science, and comprise mostly historical material together with some more recent exhibits. Subject areas include transport, engineering, photography, electronics, computing, medicine, rural technology, mining, arms, and domestic technology. There are also extensive collections of photographic archives.

The early start on electronic management of collections information mentioned above means that a very large proportion of Scienceworks' objects – probably around 80 per cent – are catalogued on the main collection database, which holds about 43 000 records. 19 000 of these are linked to videodisc images which can be viewed on a separate monitor, and printed out – a development from a pioneering project for historical photographs in the 1980s which used Cardbox Plus for records. Before the move to the new building the videodisc project had already captured 11 000 images of objects, through the analogue system then in use, which could be linked to the database record using a separate monitor. Cardbox is still in use (in the Cardbox for Windows version) for multi-media projects, and Cardbox Plus with its Term Manager thesaurus is also used for terminology control. The main database software is KE TEXPRESS (developed from a UNIX-based local product, TITAN, which was used in the museum from 1988). This software is used across the museum for collection databases – its advantage is that it allows individual users to design their own databases; the downside is the proliferation of separate, non-standardized databases.

Other databases for which KE TEXPRESS is used in Scienceworks include the multi-media database, the trade literature databases, and the acquisition proposal and loan databases. The multi-media database currently consists of 56 000 collection items and plans are under way to increase the database to 100 000 items of static and dynamic two-dimensional materials, including audio, video and archival/documentary material relating to museum objects. It is available both as a part of the main database, and as a separate database (using Cardbox Plus) with a simple record format, which includes digitized images, for public access. The terminology used in the records is controlled by a thesaurus, constructed and maintained using Cardbox Term Manager, and managed by one member of staff. Two dedicated staff, two project staff, and up to 30 volunteers (retired people with specialist knowledge) work on the database. Integration of the multi-media database with the main object database is planned for 1997, when it should be possible to move from an object record to relevant oral history, video, text documents, and photographs.

Imaging

While most of the collections are stored on site, this is achieved by intensive use of space, so that a lot of material can be got at only with a forklift truck – which does not make for easy browsing. This was an additional stimulus to a new approach to information access; the others were expectation on the part of users of being able to get to the information they wanted, and the need for an efficient delivery system because economically the old curator-intensive approach was no longer feasible. The rapidly developing technology for manipulating images was an evidently appropriate solution, and planning and experiments began within months of the move into the new building.

Eighty thousand images have been captured using videodisc technology. They have been updated from analogue to digital format. The technology has been upgraded from a Sony WORM videodisc recording system to a digital imaging program. The equipment used is a JVC TKF 7200U video still frame camera for 3D objects and Microtek film scanners 45T+. Polaroid Sprintscan scanners are used for photographic material up to 5 x 5 in. The Laurie Richards[1] collection of 85 000 mainly 5 x 4 in black and white negatives has been sampled to select 6000 pictures which have been digitized at 370 dpi, and 6000 images have been linked to database records. They are stored on digital audio tape (DAT), and thumbnail images will be used for collection access. The logbooks were also captured to help interpret the images; over 20 000 records have been entered on to a Cardbox for Windows database.

Evaluation

Scienceworks and its parent museum are undergoing rapid changes in the area of information management. Although considerable progress has been made in using new technology, the staff of the museum acknowledge that there is still a need to improve both the co-ordination of information management and the quality of information content. In seeking to achieve this, they can benefit from a long history of careful thought about managing collections information. One of the encouraging features about Scienceworks is the holistic approach taken to information technology, as a means of supporting all aspects of information use. Another is the way in which those concerned with managing information 'sell' proposed developments in terms of the bottom-line business case, founded on the importance of thoroughly managed core information about the collections. The groundwork which has been laid over more than 20 years, and the developments in strategic planning soon to take place, should ensure that the totality of the rich collection of images and information which Scienceworks holds will become available to the public.

References

Museum of Victoria (1995), *Information Technology Planning Synopsis* (unpublished), Melbourne: Museum of Victoria

NICKSON, M., DIPLOCK, A. & DEMANT, D. (1995), 'New technologies create new opportunities at the Museum of Victoria', *Museum National*, 4 (2) 26–28

ORNA, E. (1990), *Practical Information Policies. How to manage information flow in organizations*, Aldershot: Gower, (209–220)

[1] A Melbourne photographer working from 1950 to the 1990s.

The Victoria and Albert Museum

Introduction

The founding of the Victoria and Albert Museum in 1857 was part of the mid-nineteenth-century movement to spread practical and theoretical knowledge throughout British society, which found its best-known expression in the Great Exhibition of 1851. The circumstances of the museum's foundation led to its being managed within the government service[1] for much of its existence, and the traditions of that service influenced the way in which the museum handled information.

The museum holds the world's largest collection of applied art and design in its main building in South Kensington. It is also responsible for the collections of three other museums: Bethnal Green Museum of Childhood, the Theatre Museum, and the Wellington Museum. The National Art Library, which forms one of its departments, actually pre-dates the museum, having been founded as part of the Schools of Design established in 1837, to provide a library for artists and craftsmen. Together, the collections making up the V&A contain over four million items, which are cared for by over 800 staff. As a national museum, its main funding is by grant in aid from central government, supplemented by income generated from its own commercial enterprises and admission receipts, alongside bequests and sponsorship.

The museum merits a case study not merely because of the size and splendour of its collections, and its long history. From the point of view of information management, it is of particular interest as an institution which held to old traditions for longer than many others. At the time when the first edition of this book was being prepared, it was untouched by the interest in computers which was then stirring in many museums; traditional devices such as card indexes and 'handlists' were still in use, and there was little apparent thought of change. In more recent years, the museum suffered a period of unwelcome public attention, with a good deal of adverse publicity. During that time, however, there was unobtrusive progress in thinking about information and how the museum needed to use it. Today the museum is – with the acquisition of a modern collections information system – on the threshold of being able to reap the rewards of taking thought. And coming late to electronic management of information means that the museum has to a large extent avoided most of the costly blind alleys into which some of the pioneers were led.

[1] In its early days the museum was part of the Board of Trade. The first unit was the department of Practical Art in the Board of Trade; in 1856 it was renamed the department of Science and Art and was placed under the control of the Privy Council committee on education. Much of the early history of the museum is documented by Physick (1982).

Early approaches to managing information

Traditional manual systems held sway until very recently. As explained in the 1994 system requirement for a new collections information system:

'The main record is a register entry (registered description) which is the official catalogue record, arranged in Accession Number order. The entries vary in terms of fullness; sometimes very detailed and extensive, and sometimes very brief ... Indexes to the registers by artist, donor, material, etc., often exist, usually in the form of card indexes ... The registers do not record the location of objects.'

The museum's progress towards automation was a slow one; it seems to have been checked in the early 1980s by the report on its operations prepared as part of the Rayner scrutiny of the Civil Service. Reputedly the work of a civil servant specializing in stocktaking and inventory procedures, it concluded that the museum should not change its present manual system of record keeping to a computerized system for custodial purposes, and that the use of computers for these purposes should be contemplated only if a cost-benefit analysis showed it to be justified – and it made it clear that in the opinion of the writer of the report the cost could never be justified. The conclusions were disputed by a consultant's report in 1985, but it was not until 1988/89 that the first steps in installing information technology were taken – primarily with the aim of providing a complete inventory of the collections. (The NAL, meantime, had joined the OCLC network in 1987, accumulating data until the Dynix system was installed in 1990.)

The Recording Object Locations On-line (ROLO) inventory system was developed in-house in 1988; the record for each object consists of accession number, object type, classification, and location. The system made it possible to search for the location of objects by Accession Number, and to produce lists of objects by various criteria. In order to run the system, personal computers were acquired for each collection.

Other systems grew up in this period in various parts of the museum. The Prints, Drawings and Paintings collection, which had a traditionally high standard of catalogue descriptions, began entering acquisition and cataloguing details of new accessions on to a database (the MDA MODES Plus). Other collections developed their own individual-enterprise databases at this time, using such software as dBase, Cardbox or word-processing packages.

The Conservation department used a system developed in-house in 1986 (the museum's first system for handling corporate data) in order to track objects while in the care of the department. In effect it relied on a combination of paper records and a fairly primitive database system.

The library,[2] after an early attempt in the nineteenth century to create a

---

[2] Readers with a particular interest in museum libraries will wish to be aware of a study by Borda (1997) of libraries and information centres in museums in the Greater London area.

Universal Catalogue of Books on Art, abandoned the idea of a printed catalogue in favour of cards. Up to the mid-1980s it had made little attempt towards automation; its staff at that time were curators rather than qualified librarians, so the contemporary developments in library management software may well have passed unnoticed. British Museum cataloguing standards were in use, with a variety of separate card catalogues which required prior knowledge for their successful use. The year 1987 was a watershed; as already mentioned, the library joined the OCLC network, and moved to using the US version of MARC as the standard for bibliographic records (see Dodds, 1993). Work began on specifying an integrated system for the library as a whole, including the museum's archives. (The museum's own records were not at that time administered by the library, but the Archive of Art and Design was; see also p266). Dynix software was acquired, and developed for the library's specific needs, including multi-level hierarchic records for archives.

The museum's externally generated archives of art and design were initiated in 1977 by the then Director, Roy Strong; previously such archives had been dispersed among relevant departments of the museum. The internal archives were formerly managed by the department of Education and Science and the Public Record Office; periodic weeding was carried out by DES non-specialist staff according to 'guidelines'. What were essentially acquisitions files were weeded so drastically that supporting documents were removed and only forms left; it was in the course of such treatment that treasures like correspondence with William Morris were lost. It was not until the museum became a 'place of deposit' for its own records, that this practice ceased and the post of Museum Archivist was established, in 1992.

The museum's first Documentation Officer was appointed in 1987, and a Data Standard Group was established in 1990. A list of fields required for museum records, and the data types which should go in them, was produced, and the results formed the basis of the Collections Data Manual and also laid the foundation for the MDA's SPECTRUM standard for UK museums. See the case study of The Museum Documentation Association p181 for details of SPECTRUM.

The museum today

Mission and objectives

The museum's mission, derived from the Board of Trustees' functions under the National Heritage Act 1983, is:

'To increase the understanding and enjoyment of art, craft and design through its collections.'

Its current priorities for fulfilling its mission are defined in the Corporate Plan for 1996–2000 as:
- Bringing the museum's buildings up to sound, safe and environmentally acceptable standards for visitors and staff
- Increasing its accessibility and attractiveness to the visiting public

- Maintaining and enhancing its standards of object-based scholarship and research
- Further improving the standards of organizing and recording the objects entrusted to the museum,[3] particularly through investment in the Collections Information System.

Many of the strategic goals for achieving these priorities involve the use of information, in such areas as:

- Information for visitors
- Publishing
- Education
- Standards, systems and procedures for collections management
- Research
- Development of the Collections Information System to support access to information about the collections and the management of information
- Staff training and development
- Information technology to support access and information management
- Financial management and management information.

Organizational structure

The museum's major departments are divided into two main groups, concerned respectively with the collections and with administration. The branch museums, as shown in Figure 18.1 on p263, report to the Head of Projects and Collection Management.

The museum is governed by a Board of Trustees to whom the Director reports; policy decisions are the responsibility of a Central Management Team, and a Director's Council, which consists of heads of department and senior managers, advises on policy issues.

The museum's organizational structure, with its eight collections departments, staffed by curators, is an interesting contrast with that of the National Maritime Museum (see p190), where curators now form part of other departments and there are no curatorial departments as such.

Information resources and their inter-relations

We turn now to the information which is held in various parts of the museum, the ways in which people use it in their work, and the role information plays in their interactions – within the museum and between the museum and its outside world of visitors, researchers, other museums, providers of finance,

---

[3] *Every* object in the museum currently has a registered description, however brief. There is a good deal of variation in the depth of recording, both within and between collections; some records, like those of Prints, Drawings and Paintings (see p266) are very detailed.

V&A Organizational chart

Those departments set in the black typefaces, are mentioned in the case study

Figure 18.1

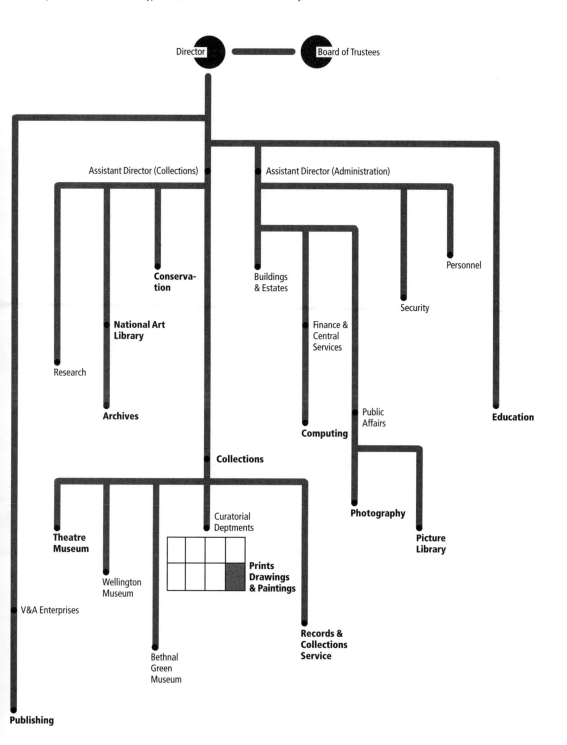

educational institutions, etc. (The systems which have been developed to support the information activities described here are dealt with in the next section, see p270).

The collections

The curatorial departments are responsible for the care, documentation, research, and display of objects. Documentation activities include the registration of acquisitions and the creation of catalogue records. Some collections have historically created records and indexes very similar to library catalogue records; others have used fuller, analytical, free-text descriptions of objects with minimal structured information. The main record is organized chronologically by museum number and there are usually indexes on cards by artist, subject, etc., although these vary again between collections. All collections have maintained accessions registers, location lists (by museum number and store), and daybooks to track the movement of objects. Because these records are all in paper form, there is duplication of data and maintenance of the data is very time consuming. The introduction of a computer database for this information will bring a significant increase in efficiency and provide a much higher level of access.

Museums differ from libraries in that information about the objects in their collections is constantly changing, reflecting new information that arises from research, display and publication activities. Staff are encouraged to develop subject knowledge and to publish widely. Data and procedural standards for the Collections are established by the Records and Collections Services Section (part of the Collections department) which was established in 1990 with the objective of introducing standard documentation practices across the museum, producing a Museum Procedures Manual for collections management activities, and introducing integrated, museum-wide computer systems for objects.

Collections management and documentation

Records and Collections Services provides central support covering documentation, systems, and technical services; it was responsible for procuring the collections information system, installed in 1996 (see p271 for more details).

Within the museum its main interactions are with the curatorial departments, computing services, the National Art Library, conservation, photography, and the branch museums. See p281 for a case study of one of them – the Theatre Museum.

Externally the department is involved in a number of international information projects. They include the CIMI (Computer Interchange of Museum Information) Consortium – a group of 14 institutions in Europe and North America which is working on the issues of access to cultural heritage information over networks, especially the Internet. The Consortium is particularly concerned with standards for structuring information (Standard Generalized Markup Language (SGML)) and for retrieving it (ANSI Z39.50, which allows a searcher to submit queries to databases without regard to the software or hardware they use). A demonstration project – CHIO (Cultural Heritage On-line) – is being used to show the utility of these standards, through an information resource on the theme of folk art. The museum has also participated in the ELISE project (Electronic Library Image Service for Europe), which invest-igated the feasibility of developing a text and image service in Europe by means of a demonstrator system based on images from the V&A and else-where. The original partners in the project (besides the V&A, De Montfort University, IBM Scientific Centre UK, and Tilburg University) have now been joined by others from Ireland and Belgium, in ELISE 2, and are planning pro-gress towards a fully operational service. (It should perhaps be noted here that the view has been expressed that the projects in which the museum has joined 'take an optimistic view of the Internet', in that it is not so easy for most users to download large quantities of information.)

These projects have given rise to some interesting ideas about the possibili-ties for people with expert knowledge who are not on the museum's staff to catalogue and create records at a distance, using the Internet; in turn, this rais-es questions of how participation of this kind could it be managed so as to pro-tect the museum's control of its records, while allowing it to benefit from external expertise.

The National Art Library and Archives
The library is a curatorial department of the museum, and hence interested in books as objects as well as for their information content, so its records of phys-ical characteristics are more detailed than usual, including such features as typefaces and printers. Current work includes the cataloguing of all publica-tions relating to the 1851 Great Exhibition (a project funded by the still-existing Commissioners for the Exhibition), of departmental libraries which are not ad-ministered by the NAL, and of Bethnal Green Museum's collection of 80 000 children's books from the seventeenth century onwards. The library has now put all V&A publications on to the system, a project which included transfer-ring from pre-1890 cataloguing, upgrading standards, and re-cataloguing all V&A publications elsewhere in the museum. It will lead ultimately to pub-lication of the museum's publishing history, and a chronological list of past exhibitions. Electronic publications are being acquired as a matter of policy, envisaging the day when 'they will be like incunabula'.

There are many areas of interaction between information in the library's holdings and collections information.
- The library has taken a lead on terminology control (see Dodds, 1994). Its co-operation with the Art and Architecture Thesaurus (AAT) involves sub-mitting candidate terms, which has produced a fuller representation of British English in the thesaurus, and integrating the library's list of subject terms with the AAT. Staff in the collections departments have also taken part, and the new collections information system will use the AAT
- The library system maintains bibliographic references in the literature to

museum objects, but it cannot replicate the detailed entries for the objects themselves that the CIS will hold. Instead, reciprocally, records in the new collections information system may have a control number to link them with the library system wherever it holds information related to objects
- Codes are used for the conservation status of library items, and it is anticipated that there will be links to detailed conservation information in the ultimate conservation database (see pp269 and 271)
- The library also has responsibility for the museum's historic records. The planned records management system (see p274) will be linked to both the collections and library systems, so that there are links between objects and their associated historic documentation.

While direct physical access to the library for external users has to be controlled, its interactions with the outside world will develop through its World Wide Web site (http://www.vam.ac.uk), through which its catalogue will be accessible on the Internet (the catalogue is also available direct via telnet: nal.vam.ac.uk).

ARCHIVES. Museum Archives is a section of the NAL, consisting of:
1. The Archive of Art and Design for externally generated archives on art and design, initiated in 1977, which contains the archives of individual artists and designers, and of companies involved in any stage of the design process from production to consumption. Prominent archives include those of Heal & Son Ltd, the furniture manufacturer and retailer, and Sir Eduardo Paolozzi's Krazy Kat Arkive of twentieth-century popular culture. The Archive of Art and Design is a curatorial section of the NAL.
2. The museum's own archive, for which it has been solely responsible only since acquiring Trustee status in 1984; this is essentially acquisitions documentation, but, as mentioned above, some of the earlier files suffered drastic weeding which removed some choice flowers.
3. The Registry – not to be confused with a registrar's department in the museum sense. The registry system was set up by the Treasury for management of files and papers in the government service. Updated in the 1950s it remained unchanged for many years thereafter. About 2500 files a year were opened by staff operating within broad guidelines. A Records Management and Archives Policy developed by the present Museum Archivist and implemented from the beginning of 1997 covers all administrative documentation, whether managed centrally by the Registry or locally in the departments, in whatever format.

Prints, Drawings and Paintings
This is a curatorial department, with its own Head of Documentation; the department is responsible for the open-access Print Room, and for cataloguing information from the point of acquisition onwards. With 3000–5000 acquisitions a year, it is essential to provide access as soon as possible after acquisition. Traditionally a great deal of effort has been put into creating detailed records with a high level of description in order to minimize handling of valu-

able originals. Access is by artist name and subject; subject access started with a hand-written subject index, which ultimately became a published subject index to the visual arts (Glass, 1969). The department plans to transfer from its own subject headings to AAT when it is brought into the new collections information system. Curatorial staff share responsibility for cataloguing; their entries are input in the documentation section of the department, printed out, and put into binders in the reading room (see Figure 18.2 on p268); fiche catalogues are provided for frequently used parts of the collection.

At present users who require photographs of items note what they want and send an order identified by accession number to the Picture Library. The new system will allow orders direct on site. Staff responsible for the collection have up to now had no means of knowing which items have been photographed, but this will form part of the record in the new system. Captions in the Picture Library will also gain in accuracy when the new system is in operation; at present they can be garbled by misreading of handwriting – a potentially dangerous situation because of legal liability for attributions. Picture Library users will search the Collections database or the NAL Catalogue.

Photography and the Picture Library

More people are aware of the museum by means of images than through actual visits. The foundations were laid from the earliest days, when it was the policy of the museum to use photography (then a 'leading-edge' technology) to disseminate knowledge. Every object photographed from 1856–1956 has a contemporary print available in the Picture Library; they constitute museum objects in their own right, and provide a record of the evolution of photographic processes and style.

Black and white was used up to the 1950s; the first colour slides date from 1954, and today 75–80 per cent of the museum's photography is in colour. The original reference system for black and white continues; for colour, the system of recording between 1954 and 1974 was not consistent or coherent; an acceptable standard was achieved only in 1974. The department is now going back to ensure that the first 15 000 colour slides are re-done to modern standards, using modern technology which allows cheap and easy copying.

The department has many interactions with other areas of the museum. The photography studio responds to the museum's planning processes; exhibitions and publications set its primary pattern of work. The William Morris exhibition of 1996, for example, required work for the catalogue, for archives, for commercial activity and for product licensing, in that chronological order. The user groups in the museum change over time according to the stage which projects have reached. Research departments and collections also require purely internal images for their own work.

The photographic section is increasingly used by V&A Enterprises; objects have become a trading resource, and images are the essential interface with potential licensees.

Date of receipt   2.3.1994   No. E, 312 – 1994

R. P. 94/335

Source Robert Douwma Ltd
173 New Bond Street

Purchase 548.00 (with E.311)

CONDITION: One vertical and six horizontal creases. Four glue stains and skinning of old
backing sheet on the back.

CATALOGUE ENTRY   Print

WALKER Anthony (1726–65) attributed to

BM: S = <u>British Museum: Catalogue of Political and Personal Satires</u>, London 1870–1954
The Sacred Lion Conquers Every Foe … (BM: S 2789). Caricature of George II backecl by
the British Lion overcoming the Young Pretender, the King of France, the Pope and the
Devil. Contained within a decorative rococo framework made up of three main
compartments. British c. 1976.
Numberd in pencil on the back <u>248</u>. Lettered with fifteen lines of verse extolling
George II. On laid paper with a fleur de lys and shield watermark, also lettered <u>LVG</u>.
Etching and engraving
Cut to 37.7 x 25.1 cm

                                                                       E. 312 – 1994

<u>Literature:</u> R Douwma <u>English Caricature to 1800;</u>
<u>Catalogue 34</u> London, 1993, (Research consultant Rosemary Baker),
p. 31 no. 248 (illus)

The attribution of thls print to Anthony Walker was made by Rosemary Baker
(see Literature) on the basis of comparison with both signed and unsigned material
in the British Museum, Department of Prints and Drawings, including
BM:S 2790, 2880, 3364, 3590. For further details see registered papers
94/335. The watermark is similar to fig.187 in A. H. Shorter <u>Paper Mills and</u>
<u>Paper Makers in England 1495–1800</u>, Hilversum 1957, except that the
letters JW at the top are missing. Shorter lists his fig. 187 as the watermark of
James Whatman, in use 1747–59. James Whatman was active as a papermaker
from at least 1740.

Catalogued Elizabeth Miller
Approved Gill Saunders

The department is preparing for both creating and converting images for electronic format; CD-ROMs are being used for inventory purposes. From the point of view of the end users, electronic handling is seen as most valuable in the search and retrieval stages, rather than for final use. The staff responsible take the view that the determining factors in photography must be the ultimate users and the way in which the images will finally be used, and they go to considerable lengths to establish this. The point is also made that current changes in electronic image technology are not yet proven and that quality standards should not be jeopardized by accepting what is just average use of the technology, without sufficient experience. Nor is there enough research as yet on how people use electronic images. Most users probably still find reproductions of images easier to use if they are in hard-copy form, rather than on-screen. It is suggested that users may take on-screen images as more ephemeral; they 'can't come close and take possession of screen images'.

Conservation

At present, the essential exchanges of information between conservators and curators are laborious and difficult to maintain. Paper-based records are set up; curators fill in object information on conservation requests, and conservators transfer this to a conservation management system (COLA – Conservation Online Administration). It is hoped to combine the conservation database with the object database to eliminate this duplication of recording.

From the point of view of information retrieval, this system has not much to offer. Such reports as are available are described as being what the system permits rather than what is useful to the museum. This is not surprising, given that, as mentioned earlier (see p260) the system was designed for handling transactions rather than information retrieval; it reflected the priority of the period, which was the need to manage the objects in the department. The COLA1 system represented the first phase of a long-term strategy for conservation automation; when it was initially developed, an analysis of information requirements was made, but the results were not included in the specification, and the later version did not take advantage of this work. So the search facilities remain fairly basic; it is not possible to answer questions that require finding items with multiple features in common, such as: 'What lacquer objects have been conserved by a particular treatment in a given period?' And finding paper records also presents problems, as various sequences have been used at different times.

Education

By virtue of its wide outside contacts, the Education department is probably the most knowledgeable about the museum's actual and potential public. It publishes books and packs for teachers, runs courses for teachers and tutors, and for other adults, arranges gallery lectures, and organizes outreach programmes and programmes for museums overseas.

The department takes a holistic rather than a compartmentalized view of knowledge. Its approach is based on an adult-education model and the associated concept of life-long learning, because the formal education sector forms only a small proportion of museum audiences. Alongside it, there is a large 'hidden university' of informal learners, who set their own targets about what they want to know. The museum is now moving towards providing for this kind of informal self-directed learning by establishing study areas in new galleries.

The department draws on internal and external knowledge resources in delivering its programmes and writing its publications; curators, education staff and outside teachers and researchers all contribute. Its staff monitor current trends in education at all levels, social developments, and local and national demographic changes as a necessary basis for knowledge about potential audiences and their needs.

Publishing

The museum's publishing activity forms part of V&A Enterprises. Like Photography, it has a 'bridge' role between the collections and the museum's commercial activities. V&A publications form an important contribution to the museum's information resources. They cover both 'obligatory' publications, such as collections catalogues, and commercially oriented products. In principle, only items that can be sold are handled by V&A Publications; educational material is produced by the Education department. Target audiences cover both specialist and general markets, including non-visitors and international readership.

Publishing policy is the responsibility of the Head of Publications, advised by the museum's Central Management Team and the Director's Council. A publishing plan was produced in 1995, when a decision was made to go ahead with a V&A publishing imprint rather than come to an arrangement with an external commercial publisher.

As publications are normally written in-house, the Publishing Section has many interactions with curatorial staff. It has also built up an informal network of contacts in other areas of the museum; feedback comes from shop staff, who record visitors' comments, and from the bookshop book buyer, who provides information on the competition. Curators are a source of information on the requirements of students, researchers and people in areas from which objects originate, and there is also feedback from the Picture Library.

Information systems

Having looked at what people in different parts of the museum do with information, and how they use it in internal and external interactions, we can now turn to the systems which are intended to support them in the job. Perhaps the most important aspect of the museum's present approach to electronic systems for managing information is that it sees the technology as an enabler of human knowledge, and not as a substitute for it.

The time when this case study was carried out was a period of transition. In the spring of 1996, the museum's major systems were:

- The library Dynix system
- The recently acquired Collections Information System (supplied by ICL Enterprises in co-operation with System Simulation Limited, whose Index + database system forms the basis for the CIS)
- The original conservation database
- The Picture Library administration system
- Education – for handling groups and booking
- Personnel/human resources system
- Finance and accounting system.

Collections and related systems

The museum decided in 1994 to procure its own integrated multi-user collections system independently, rather than as part of the LASSI consortium (with which it had co-operated in the first phase of the project). At that time, apart from the main systems listed above, there were about 32 independent databases in use in the collections departments. The objectives defined in the system requirement were to:

- Bring together the existing inventory (ROLO) databases into an integrated system, with additional inventory-control functions
- Provide for tracking and updating information about loans in and out of the museum
- Support the V&A data structure
- Support re-cataloguing projects, and the conversion of existing documentation by various means
- Provide sophisticated on-line access to help answer curatorial and public enquiries
- Store and display images of objects
- Share information with other systems in the museum (e.g., loans, conservation, Picture Library, NAL)
- Provide mechanisms to supply data and images for multi-media projects.

While the immediate need was to provide improved inventory control and support basic core documentation, primarily for purposes of accountability, the second main aim was to: 'record basic object information in a consistent, integrated manner in such a way that the data is usable in the long term' with the additional benefits of 'greatly improved management information, links to other systems for improved authority control of terminology and exchange of data – links to word processors and DTP (desk top publishing) – and the ability to send and receive object and authority data to and from other institutions'.

The staff responsible for procuring and introducing the system make a clear distinction between the underlying knowledge base, and the 'multi-media manifestations' which will derive from it. There will be direct public access to appropriate parts of the central collections information system through an orientation centre with terminals and study rooms, while in the galleries multimedia stand-alones are planned. For security reasons, the museum will have a cloned database on the Internet, which will not let users into the core system and will omit non-public fields.

Little prospect is seen for immediate convergence between the library and collections systems; it will be very expensive to interconnect Dynix with the CIS system, primarily because as yet there is no overlap of library and museum software vendors – a reflection of cultural differences going back for many decades.[4] It is hoped that over the longer term phased integration may become possible.

The staff of Records and Collections Services have worked with the software vendors to map fields for the new record structure back to existing data structures. The MDA SPECTRUM standard has been used in building a new record structure; its categories for description of works of art have been mapped against the existing V&A structure.

When the purchase decision had been made, the Documentation Manager held discussions with all collections, to establish the screen presentation they needed to match the ways in which they require to manage information about their own collections, and to ensure that interim developments of existing departmental systems did not diverge from the direction of the new system.

The aim was to get every collection using the system live for at least location records by April/May 1996 (the first collection actually went live on 14 May). The next phase of the implementation will include cataloguing functions, and collections will then begin to accession and catalogue new acquisitions on the new system. When collections have transferred to the new system, entry of catalogue records for existing objects will be done through projects in different areas, such as gallery re-displays, publications, research, etc. The projects will include the digitization of the present manual registers – possibly by microfilming them and then digitizing the images for transfer to the new electronic database and linking to the relevant inventory-level records. A pilot exercise has been done on this, but funding will need to be found for the complete project.

Transfer to the new system will actually be based on the progress of networking; departments in the new building will get there first, while those in

[4] At least one user of Multi MIMSY – The Museum of London – is using its bibliographic screen for cataloguing the museum's library; although the package offers no library management facilities, it is described as being quite adequate for cataloguing, and links can be made to object records if required (Roberts, 1996). From the library side, the British Library's Information Systems Strategy (1995) includes long-term plans for a corporate database to support its collections management processes, which will have features comparable to those of museum collection information systems. It will contain information on location, access restrictions, preservation treatment, retention policy and usage statistics, and form the basis for a range of the library's services.

the old building will join in as the network is established there. The decisions about implementing the new system implied a heavy training commitment. Initial training for 20 lead users from all departments was given centrally by the documentation management team and it was then 'cascaded' to more staff and greater depth.

So far as other related systems are concerned, it is hoped to use the main system for conservation, and to use electronic forms for conservation requisitions, etc. The Picture Library acquired a system in 1995 to cover sales and loans; for the future, a single image bank is envisaged, with connections to allow users to complete request forms. The record structure developed by the Documentation Manager provides for a 'subject-depicted' field – something the stock picture libraries have always done, which is, despite its obvious utility, far from common in museums.

The National Art Library and the archives

The library envisages continuing to use the Dynix system as implemented from 1990 onwards (see p261), although it may ultimately become necessary to replace the existing system. The software has a limited lifespan, whereas the data do not. In the next few years the library will continue to undertake the conversion of its older catalogues. Planned developments include a circulation system which allows on-screen requests by users, and a z39.50 interface to the database which allows greater connectivity with other systems within and outside the museum. The library expects to use the Internet and the World Wide Web as the prime method of delivering information to users and potential users.

ARCHIVES AND RECORDS. The Dynix software as used in the library was developed in association with the vendor to meet the need for multi-level hierarchic records for archives. It is presently in use only by the Archive of Art and Design, but is to be extended to the V&A archives in 1997. The library's authority files are used by the archives. Up to the end of 1995, the administrative records and files under the care of the museum Archivist consisted of hard copy files, some stored in the Registry and some held in curatorial departments, together with a vast bank of index cards which forms the 'key' to the files. From the start of 1996, all titles of newly opened files have been recorded electronically, using standalone software (Filemaker Pro), which replaces the card index system. The policy for records management drafted at the end of 1995 and introduced at the start of 1997 proposes links with the main collections information system analogous to those of the conservation system; the CIS database will signpost the existence of administrative files. The policy also provides guidelines for the management of electronic information, whether email, word-processed files, or database. The system is not yet paperless; if records are to be kept, they should also be dumped to paper. For the present, because of the lack of networking, when a new file is opened the creator will have to send a form to the Registry. A Filemaker Pro database of

newly created Registry files has now been established. Data relating to archival files will be transferred to publicly available systems such as Dynix.

Publishing Section

Publishing will be a 'customer' of the CIS, in that it will be able to take inform-
mation from the system into exhibition catalogues and other publications.
Information relating to other aspects of the publishing process, e.g. stock data,
is handled as part of the V&A Enterprise system.

Information technology to support systems

The Computer Section, which is part of Finance and Central Services, is responsible for IT support throughout the museum, although individual departments, for example Collections and the NAL, also have their own specialist IT
staff. As noted on p259 the museum was late in taking to computers; the first
personal computers were acquired in 1985. Between then and 1992, the aim
was to 'get as many boxes as possible on desks'; by the end of that period,
there were more than 300 PCs, together with two mini-computers for the
library and financial services. Since the museum had no history of using central mainframe or mini-computers but went straight to PC technology, there
has always been a lag in the ability of the equipment to run the latest applications and it has been difficult to upgrade machines to deal with the requirements of networks, Windows and imaging. Early automation projects concentrated on museum infrastructure systems such as accounts and personnel
rather than collections documentation. Automation of object information was
initiated locally by the Metalwork department as a method of stocktaking and
controlling the movement of objects. This then developed into ROLO (Recording Object Locations Online) – a system adopted by all the curatorial collections and developed in-house by the museum's Computer Section.

Since the mid-90s, there has been a concerted effort to bring the PCs up to
standard and bring networks up to strategic level. There are now 280 PCs in
use, 250 of them Windows-capable, and Perfect Office has been introduced as
standard. GroupWise email has also been introduced. The aims at the start of
1996 were to increase PC capability, install a comprehensive network, and up-
grade/install seven core systems; it was expected that 90 per cent of this work
would be completed by 1996/97.

While the budget allocation for IT in recent years has been appropriate for
the priority the museum has attached to keeping up to date with the technology, it is fair to say that it may have to struggle in future to maintain that level
of investment in the face of competition for resources with other essential
developments.

When the museum eventually set up an IT Committee with representatives from all areas, the lack of objective criteria for deciding which claims for
development should have priority made it difficult to resolve competition for
resources, and to concentrate on developing strategic goals.

Since then, there has been progress over time in the understanding between the IT specialists and the users. Each section now has its own user representative who can interpret between departmental needs and the computer specialists, and contribute to specifying requirements.

Development of information systems strategy and information policy

The developments outlined above could not have happened without strategic thinking about using information for achieving the museum's objectives. In the V&A, as in many other museums, IT has to some extent been the motive force for thinking about information strategy in relation to the collections (though not in the case of the NAL – a reflection of the difference between the cultures of museums and libraries that prevailed for many decades). This is perhaps understandable – the technology was a novel and conspicuous feature which forced itself on the attention of decision makers by being expensive and capable of causing disasters, in contrast with information itself which could be taken for granted without causing obvious trouble.

A documentation report of 1987 can be considered as the starting point for strategic thinking in the museum; it stated that information held by the museum should be available to staff across departments, and that it should be possible to connect all information resources. From then on, over time, there was a gradual realization that more than just the technology was involved, and that the range of stakeholders went far beyond those responsible for computing. In 1991, the museum's Information Technology Committee set up a sub-group to prepare an information technology policy and strategy. The resulting document was very much oriented to the technology, and the strategies recommended make implicit rather than explicit reference to the museum's objectives.

By 1995, the museum was seeking to revise the 1991 IT strategy, and moving towards a policy and strategy for information and its use, rather than for the technology. The view of automation is said to have changed over time, from being seen as a means of becoming more efficient to being regarded as a means of opening 'markets' and increasing the number of 'consumers' of information. It took still longer to start thinking about the significance of the information that was to be brought to market and consumed, and about the interests of the ultimate consumers. Value criteria moved from looking simply at whether investment costs would be covered, to taking into account the contribution to achievement of the museum's key objectives, in effect from simple cost–benefit to more sophisticated cost-effectiveness.

In 1994, the IT Committee became an Information Policy Committee with an IT sub-group reporting to it. (More recently, this committee itself has been wound up, as part of a policy of reducing the number of committees.)

Rapidly changing circumstances led the committee to develop policy at the level of the museum's Vision, that is, a statement of the principles the museum will follow in its use of information; the strategy through which the principles are realized will change with circumstances. The current thinking also includes the realization that the museum has spent more time deciding what to give people than in trying to learn what information people themselves want to use and the ways in which they want to use it. Information policy and strategy are now seen to depend critically on defining audiences and finding out what they want, and on thinking about how they can be helped to get what they themselves define as important.

An evaluation

What has gone before is an attempt to present the way the museum thinks and acts in respect of information. This case study ends with a summary of positive aspects (some of which, life being what it is, may bring other potential problems in their train), and of areas which look as if they may pose difficulties. The purpose of the evaluation is to draw the attention of those readers who are seeking to learn from the case studies to key aspects of the situation.

Areas which give rise to questions

At the time when this case study began, the provision for training for transition to the new collections information system looked as though it might overstretch resources; the initial critical phase of training, which had to be delivered exactly on time, relied greatly on two key members of documentation management staff who had many other responsibilities. In the event, it was successfully carried through, and other staff have now been brought into delivering training. It is, however, important to emphasize that planning the introduction of any new system should include the provision of adequate resources for training.

The necessity for phasing in the development of networking causes particular problems for many sections, particularly those in off-site locations; where they are in buildings which are low down the priority list for being brought into the network, essential decisions and their implementation are liable to be held up. The stand-alone system now being introduced for the Registry is a real improvement, but networking seems essential for effective co-operation with curatorial departments and efficient working. And so long as a single-copy card index is the sole key to the administrative records, it constitutes a danger point for disastrous information loss.

It is not clear how much feedback there is between those departments which, so to speak, face outwards, as do Education and Publishing, with their wide contacts and environmental monitoring, and those whose orientation is more inward, like the curatorial departments. The new system should offer excellent scope for such interchanges, and it is to be hoped that their value is recognized on both sides, and that the contribution which the education department made to the system requirement will be followed through in the implementation stage. The people concerned with developing the system certainly anticipate that it will encourage and stimulate such interchanges and speed up the integration of separate operational areas.

Positive features

The museum's policy of cautious advance on multi-media, and its realistic view of the Internet, is good news. So too is the fact that it is part of the Computer Section's remit to keep abreast of interesting and relevant developments in technology. There is however a problem, in that the explosion of exciting new technological possibilities may lead to pressure to emulate other institutions and get to the forefront in using them. There are dangers in doing this without a firm foundation in basic technology and training. The growing understanding between technical departments, those concerned with system specification/documentation, and curatorial departments should help to establish such a foundation, but it demands time and resources.

There is some evidence that the museum is moving towards defining information in its own terms (still a rare step for any kind of organization), and that the definition is developing into a comprehensive one, which takes in a whole range from collections information, to environmental and business information, and envisages multiple interactions between them.

The commitment to finding out what users themselves want to do with information, and planning an information strategy that will help them to do it is a welcome feature of policy thinking, even though, as has been pointed out by people interviewed in this case study, it has a downside, in that it will demand intensive efforts on the part of the museum to help users to realize what is available to them.

However, the recognition that, as a senior manager in the museum put it, 'museums should not be the final arbiters' is very cheering to the present author, who wrote a good many years ago:

'The real essential is that museum professionals should try to put themselves in the place of the widest range of potential users when they look at their collections. Then they should think how they can manage the information ... so as to allow users to find their own ways in, even if their ways of looking at the material are very different from the museum's own conception of what it is there for.' Orna, 1990.

The realization that information policy is a matter of top-level principles to guide the use of information, while the strategy for expressing policy will change according to circumstances is a positive gain from experience. It could lead to a policy of using information to promote change and organizational learning, which would put the V&A well at the forefront of thinking in these matters.

References and additional reading

BORDA, A. E. (1997), *The Museum Library: A Survey of Libraries and Information Centres in the Museums and Related Institutions of the Greater London Area*, PhD thesis, University of London

British Library (1995), *Information Systems Strategy*, London: The British Library Board

DODDS, D. (1993), 'Documentation systems in Britain's National Art Library', *Art Libraries Journal*, 18(4) 15–23

DODDS, D. (1994), 'The National Art Library and the Art & Architecture Thesaurus', *Art & Architecture Thesaurus Bulletin*, 22 2–12

GLASS, E. (1969), *A Subject Index for the Visual Arts, Part 1*, London: Victoria and Albert Museum, department of Prints and Drawings and department of Paintings / HMSO

ORNA, E. (1990), 'Helping users to come to terms with the terminology', in D. ANDREW ROBERTS (ed.), *Terminology for Museums, Proceedings of an International Conference*, Cambridge: Museum Documentation Association

PHYSICK, J. (1982), *The Victoria and Albert Museum: The history of its building*, London: Victoria and Albert Museum

ROBERTS, A. (1996), Personal communication

SEAL, A. (1993A), 'Standards and Local Practice: the experience of the Victoria and Albert Museum', *CHArt*, 5(1) 17–24

SEAL, A. (1993B), 'Evolution at the Victoria and Albert Museum', *Computers and the History of Art*, 3(1) 25–32

SEAL, A. (1994A), 'The creation of an electronic imagebank: Photo-CD at the V&A', *Managing Information*, 1(1) 42–44

SEAL, A. (1993B), 'Collections Information at the Victoria & Albert Museum', *MDA Information*, 1(2) 4–6

SEAL, A. (1995), 'Electronic images for libraries and museums: the ELISE project', *Program*, 29(4) 379–395

Victoria and Albert Museum (1996A), *Report of the Board of Trustees 1 April 1992–31 March 1996*, London: Victoria and Albert Museum

Victoria and Albert Museum (1996B), *Records Management and Archive Policy*, London: Victoria and Albert Museum

Victoria and Albert Museum (1996C), *Records Management and Archives: a Guide*, London: Victoria and Albert Museum

The Theatre Museum

The Theatre Museum in Covent Garden – within a stone's throw of the actors' church which forms the site of the opening scene of Shaw's *Pygmalion*, in an area full of historic links with three centuries of British theatre – is worth a case study for a number of reasons.

It is interesting in its own right, as the UK's National Museum of the Performing Arts; as such, it deals with dynamic material (such as audio and video records of performances), static images, and documentary records, as well as the memorabilia of the theatre, including costumes and designs, and fittings rescued from historic theatres. Its focus is on actual productions and on the people who create performances, historic and contemporary.

That focus also makes for an interesting study because of the contrasts in orientation between the Theatre Museum and its parent body, the Victoria and Albert Museum – a large, long-established institution whose collections, 'organizational culture' and information requirements are of a very different kind. These differences make for interesting relations between the two. When this case study started, both museums were approaching critical points in decisions about information management; the Theatre Museum was particularly affected by uncertainties about its future direction. By the time it was being completed, the parent museum had started implementing its new collections information system (see p271), and the Theatre Museum had taken initiatives, in co-operation with V&A colleagues, which look as though they have set it on the road to a positive solution, though there are still many hazards to negotiate.

History

The museum's origins go back to 1924, when Mrs Gabrielle Enthoven donated to the V&A her large collection of documents and memorabilia on the London theatre. The collection formed part of the Department of Prints and Drawings until 1974, when the Theatre Museum was established as a separate department of the V&A in preparation for the opening, in 1987, of a museum devoted to the performing arts. Over the years, other materials were added; the collections grew very rapidly from 1970 on, with significant acquisitions from private donors and from organizations such as the Society for Theatre Research and the London Archives of the Dance.

The collections and their users

The range and scope of the materials held by the museum, as shown by Table 19.1, is extremely varied, and in some areas the rate of growth is very rapid. For example, the museum routinely collects all new programmes from over 200 UK theatres and amasses press cuttings from seven daily newspapers.

The term 'Special collections' in the table conceals a whole extra range of items; these are named collections kept intact because their significance is crucially enhanced by being treated as an integral whole. Normally associated with a particular performer, collector or organization, some of them constitute 'archives' in the strict sense of the term, while others contain mixed media associated with a theme; the special collections also range in size from a few storage boxes full to the 300 boxes of company records which make up the Cambridge Arts Theatre Archive.

As the only institution in the UK offering a museum, library and archive in the performing arts open to the public, the Theatre Museum attracts many researchers and enquirers. Direct public access services account for over a third of curatorial staff time. Access for research is provided through a study room, used annually by nearly 2500 researchers, which runs at full capacity. Were there more reading space, and more staff, the number of users would be greater, as institutions of higher education are developing new courses in the museum's specialist area. A survey in 1994 of a sample of over 80 users showed that the types of material most often used were books, programmes and reviews, biographical files, and photographs. In addition to direct study visits, the museum handles telephone enquiries (about 20 per day), and letters with requests for information (average 85 per month).

The main users are students, private researchers and theatre professionals; the image collections also attract the particular attention of the media and of specialized and academic publishers, and the demand for picture research and reproductions is growing.

The 1994 surveys of the study room and enquiries services showed that three main areas accounted for the majority of research:
• Past theatre productions
• Individual performers and their performances
• Specific subjects – e.g. 'women in theatre', 'stage lighting', 'commedia dell' arte'.

The majority of information searches were for information content – i.e. it was the information rather than the 'container' that was of importance to the user; few enquirers were interested in a specific type of object (in other words, 'feature' rather than 'item' enquiries – to use Jolley's (1968) term – predominate, with all which that implies for the help which users require from information systems).

Object type	Number of items	New items/year
A/V tapes		
National Video Archive of Stage Performance	500	200
commercial	200	50
private	250	12
Architectural salvage	20	–
Autograph letters	8000	100
Costumes and accessories	2500	25
Designs	6000	200
Legal documents and account books	4000	6
MSS and cuttings books	1400	25
Paintings	100	1
Periodicals	2000	10
Photo files	8000	300
Posters	8000	50
Press cuttings		
theatre buildings files	1650	10
company files	1630	50
biographical files	20 000	150
Printed books/pamphlets	100 000	1500
Prints	25 000	25
Promptbooks	1600	10
Puppets	400	–
Song sheets	5000	20
Special collections	270	5
Stage machinery	150	–
Stage models	200	6
Theatre programmes/bills and review files	1 000 000	–
3-D objects/props	500	10
Tickets and tokens	1250	20

Mission and aims

The Theatre Museum's mission and aims are defined in the V&A's corporate plan for the years 1996–2000 as:

'Our purpose is to provide the national record of stage performance in Britain and to increase the public understanding and enjoyment of the performing arts through the expert interpretation of its collections.'

Its aims are:
- To continue to develop the National Video Archive of Stage Performance to create a permanent record of Britain's unrivalled theatrical heritage
- To develop the museum's galleries to create a living experience of the performing arts and a major education resource for visitors of all ages
- To develop the museum's collections and study facilities to create the National Performing Arts Information and Research Centre.

Organizational links with the V&A

The Theatre Museum is one of three branch museums of the V&A (the others are the Bethnal Green Museum of Childhood and Apsley House); it reports to the Assistant Director (Administration). Representation of the Theatre Museum at the top level of decision making in the parent museum is through the Head of the Theatre Museum; specific information-related and funding proposals from the Theatre Museum are taken up to the decision-making level through the line management system.

The museum is dependent on the V&A for many functions, including conservation, loans administration, and object movement.

The physical distance that separates Covent Garden, South Kensington and Olympia (where the Theatre Museum's special collections are stored) presents a challenge for managing information; the Theatre Museum does not yet have a modem link to the V&A finance department, and a date for installing a LAN or for linking the museum to the V&A's network has yet to be decided, while electronic access to the archive records is still a hope for the future.

Information management so far

The ways in which the museum has managed information up to now are influenced partly by its past history, partly by the varied nature of its collections and the ways in which they are used, and partly by the limited resources of time and finance available. Only one half-time curator works wholly on cataloguing, documentation and related activities as a whole account for just under 20 per cent of curatorial time, while public access services take up over a third; and its share of the total V&A IT budget is a very small fraction indeed.

As a recent Theatre Museum document on management of the museum's collections points out, a large percentage of items such as photographs, negatives and press cuttings have not been formally accessioned. The museum acquires a great deal of material for which the full acquisition approval process is not appropriate and also much material that cannot be individually accessioned. Such material is often acquired for its documentary value. The Theatre Museum wishes to integrate these different strands into a single system. Cataloguing records do not exist for large parts of the collections, and 'where manual records do exist they are often variable in their style and level of detail'.

Manual systems

While the museum uses the V&A's daybook and manual accessioning procedures for most of its collections, this approach is not always possible or appropriate with such things as theatre programmes, books, photographs, press cuttings, and other paper ephemera. On the basis of consultation with the V&A Department of Records and Collections Services, collections management procedures appropriate for these categories are being developed.

Book cataloguing follows Anglo-American Cataloguing Rules; for the rest of the collections, a range of different approaches have been followed. Biographical files and similar materials which can be arranged alphabetically are 'self-indexing' and need no further treatment. Manual card indexes have been developed for various media such as costumes, designs, and autograph letters. In addition, the museum maintains a unique index of theatre productions. It includes details of directors, authors, designers etc., and would greatly benefit from automation because of the increased number of points of access it would provide; at present the only access is through title. For the special collections, there are 'survey sheets', prepared in the early 1990s, which describe the content, subject associations, size and conservation needs of each of over 250 special collections, and indicate whether more detailed documentation exists.

Steps towards automation

As the parent museum progressed with its plans for electronic management of information (see p271), the integration of the Theatre Museum into them became a subject of discussion on which there were various views. When the National Art Library acquired its Dynix system, consideration was given to whether it would be appropriate for the Theatre Museum's collection to be handled by it. The museum, however, decided that the system was unsuitable for such objects as costumes, models, pictures, etc. The differences between the collections and cultures of the two museums, and the fact that the Theatre Museum's collections are evidence of the missing central artifact – performance – also meant that the proposed new collections information system would not precisely meet the Theatre Museum's requirement; while any attempt to use both systems would effectively split what had been managed as a single resource. At the same time, it was evident that the Theatre museum was in no position to commission a new system for itself.

In 1993, the Head of the museum's Library and Information Service proposed to the V&A Information Technology Committee that, pending a final decision on large-scale automation at the parent museum and on whether the Theatre Museum would be included in it, an interim electronic system should be introduced to replace the manual medium-based indexes. The justification was that they were not available for public access, and that in answering subject enquiries curators needed to consult multiple indexes. The proposal was supported by the IT Committee, and in 1994 the MDA's MODES Plus system was introduced for cataloguing all new acquisitions which would normally be museum numbered and entered into the V&A's Central Inventory – i.e. all acquisitions except library materials, ephemera and archive collections. A project to recatalogue the poster collection was also carried through in 1995. The data structure for MODES was developed in conjunction with the V&A Department of Records and Collections Services; it is based on the structure established at the V&A for the new Collections Information System which was then being planned, and includes additional fields for subject associations and performance/production information. Although MODES Plus has always been viewed as an interim system, using it has been valuable because it has allowed staff to gain experience of the disciplines of standardized cataloguing, and to test out the special fields for theatrical material. For a case study of very wide-ranging and intensive use of MODES Plus, see p164.

Recent and current developments: towards a solution

More recently, the apparently insoluble contradiction between what the Theatre Museum and the V&A required from automated systems seems to have started to move towards resolution. The head of Library and Information Services at the Theatre Museum and the head of the V&A's Department of Records and Collections Services analysed the operational requirements that had been prepared for the V&A's Library and Collections Information Systems and mapped the Theatre Museum's own requirements on to them. The results suggested that the Collections Information System came closer to meeting the Theatre Museum's needs (it is an advantage that, as mentioned above, the MODES record structure being used in the museum is based on the one developed by the V&A for the CIS).

The Theatre Museum's requirement for subject access (one which it shares with the Department of Prints, Drawings and Paintings at the V&A) has implications for the development of the Art and Architecture Thesaurus in which the V&A Library is participating; an extension to cover the generalized subjects required for image retrieval will be needed.

Discussions have taken place with the vendors of the V&A CIS, who have examined the collections and gained an understanding of the special features which the Theatre Museum requires. The next step is to prepare a formal operational requirement and to decide on the Theatre Museum's proposals for progress towards automation on the basis of the V&A's Collections Information System.

Evaluation

While a 'happy ending' cannot be guaranteed, and there are many obstacles still to be overcome, this is still an instructive and encouraging story. It is instructive, because it is an example of the problems that arise, without deliberate ill-will, between a large parent institution and its offspring, particularly when they are effectively physically separated.

The difficulties which the advance towards automation of information management precipitated probably originate from the inevitable cultural differences in orientation between a fine art institution and one concerned with performing arts, and the very different ways in which the two need to use information. They appear to have been compounded by obstacles in the way of contact (there is still, for example, no computer link between the two institutions), and possibly by the lack of a forum where people from the two institutions with a stake in specific problems can negotiate with one another.

Understanding now seems to be growing through the informed support provided by the V&A's Records and Collections Services. The Theatre Museum has also helped to develop understanding by its initiatives in proposing and implementing an interim automated system, and in setting out issues and proposals for their solution.

While the museum has been 'at the back of the queue' for resources at a time when funding is restricted, this may in fact allow valuable time for the development of an appropriate solution which will eventually lead to advances in the management of information which will be of great benefit to the museum and its users.

Reference

JOLLEY, J. L. (1968), *Data Study*, London: World University Library, Weidenfeld & Nicolson

Index